EVERY MAN A TIGER

Mock-Combat Flying Techniques for Light Aircraft

by Frank J. O'Brien
with Timothy R. V. Foster

Ziff-Davis Publishing Company/New York

Library of Congress Catalogue Number: 80-51120
ISBN 0-87165-076-2
Printed in the United States of America
First printing 1981
Ziff-Davis Publishing Company
One Park Avenue
New York, N.Y. 10016

Design: Falcaro & Tiegreen Ltd.

Illustrations by Helmut Kunst.

DEDICATION
To Marge—A Tiger's Tiger

CONTENTS

Conclusion 220

Appendices

Acknowledgments

A number of people with whom I have been associated over the years have helped in big ways and small to develop the thoughts and ideas collected here. Time dims the names but not the contributions of some, while others are just off the wing tips of memory—still the rock-steady leaders and tucked-in wingmen who made it all worthwhile. A few of those whose kind and generous help made possible a significant portion of this book are Jim Egbert, Col. USAF; Joe Martin, Col. USAF (Ret.); "Digger" Odell, Lt. Col. USAF (Ret.); Joe Olshefski, Col. USAF (Ret.); and John O'Neill, Assistant Chief for Operations, Flight Control Division, Johnson Space Center. Closer to home, the proofreading assistance given by my daughter Mary has been truly appreciated.

I would also like to thank Rudy Frasca, John Kelley, Cole Palen and Leonard Tanner for the invaluable information they gave me in the course of personal interviews.

The corporations and authors listed below have been kind enough to grant me permission to quote from the works indicated:

Norman, Aaron. *The Great Air War.* New York: Macmillan Co., 1968.
Phelan, Joseph A. *Heroes and Aeroplanes of the Great War 1914–1918,* New York: Grosset & Dunlap, 1966.
Oughton, Frederick. *The Aces.* New York: G. P. Putnam's Sons, 1960.
Jablonski, Edward. *Airwar: Wings of Fire.* New York: Doubleday & Co., 1971.
Toliver, Colonel Raymond F., and Constable, Trevor J. *Fighter Aces.* New York: Macmillan Co., 1965.
Gurney, Gene. *Five Down and Glory.* New York: G.P. Putnam's Sons, 1958.
Jabara, Captain James. *We Fly MiG Alley.* Washington, D.C.: *Air Force* Magazine, June 1951.
Frizzell, Colonel Donaldson D., and Bowers, Colonel Ray L., editors. *Air War: Vietnam.* New York: Arno Press, 1978.

—FRANK J. O'BRIEN

Introduction

The basic purpose of this book is to share with you information, ideas, and sensations that will add a new dimension to the enjoyment and challenge of light plane flying.

You may ask, "Why should I make like a fighter pilot?"

Being a fighter pilot is largely a state of mind characterized by an eagerness to learn and a desire to excel. With these traits comes a realization that once you've learned your job, there's nobody better at it than you—and that anyone who doubts this fact will have to prove his point. Lots of people who've never seen the inside of a cockpit fit the fighter-pilot mold, and they include lawyers, housewives, teachers, and others who know that nobody can do their job better than they can. Attitude is the essence of the game. It is what separates fighter pilots from those "who are content with pottage," as the great writer/pilot Gill Robb Wilson once remarked.

This can-do type of thinking is the only prerequisite for becoming a tiger, whether you fly airplanes or not. If you plan to try the various maneuvers I talk about in this book, a tiger's attitude will be a definite asset.

Another question that may crop up is, "What type of training do I need to do these maneuvers safely?" Aside from having a private license, the biggest requirement is the training of one's self—that is, sticking to a commonsense approach to this type of flying, and learning each step thoroughly before proceeding to the next. *If instructors are available, they should be utilized, particularly if a problem arises that fits their area of expertise.*

Fighter pilots must also learn to work as a team, yet have the know-how to go it alone if the situation dictates. Be critical of yourself, and accept the suggestions of others who may see errors in your technique that you are not aware of.

As with nearly all other acquired skills, the most valuable part of your training lies in constant practice. All the hangar flying in the world can never take the place of going out and trying combat maneuvers for yourself. *Keep on* trying it until you can do the required maneuver correctly each time. Even after you've mastered the techniques of a certain maneuver, it's a good idea to repeat it every now and then, just to keep your hand in.

Okay, you're all psyched up, and you've learned all the maneuvers and procedures. Your question now is, "Why? When will I get a chance to use all this good stuff, all these combat flying skills? Is it worth all the time and effort?"

YES! *Anyone* who approaches what is covered in this book with the proper frame of mind cannot help but become a better pilot for his trouble. Acrobatics, formation flying, and basic fighter maneuvers all contribute to the professionalization of a pilot. This, in turn, will advance you beyond the junior birdman stage.

As to *when* you could use something so alien to normal light plane flying as basic fighter maneuvers, the possibilities are numerous. Perhaps the easiest would be to issue a challenge to a neighboring airport. For those with a flair for the dramatic, the challenge could be made by making a low pass over the other field and dropping a glove with a note attached. All but the most timorous would have to accept an invitation like that. If your local field has an acrobatics area, and others in your group are interested in this type of flying, a fair-game area might be the answer. In this situation, it is mutually agreed that during certain hours on certain days, any one of your group in the acrobatics area is considered fair game, and may be bounced. The only ground rules that apply here are that everyone playing the game must be on a predetermined frequency, and that *only* aircraft that are positively identified as one of the group may be bounced.

Probably the best plan is a variant of the first. It is called the Breakfast Patrol and was developed by British flying clubs in the 1930s. The idea is to invite a group from a nearby field to a fly-in breakfast. However, before the guests are due to land, the host group launches all available aircraft to act as defenders of the home drome. Their job is to intercept the incoming group and get close enough to each bird to copy his registration number. Naturally, the guests do all in their power to keep from having their numbers copied, and those guests who make it through the defense and land before their number is taken get a free meal. Those who get tagged have to pay for their breakfasts.

The hazards of flying acrobatics, formation, and basic fighter maneuvers are normally greater than those associated with straight and level operations. Add to this the increased chance for error that is inherent in self-teaching situations, and it becomes apparent that the potential for a mishap increases significantly. Thus, both the author and the publisher must assume that anyone who utilizes this book to learn the maneuvers described here is a licensed pilot of sufficient competence to absorb and apply these techniques in accordance with the directions and limitations given. In addition, it must be assumed that the aircraft used for these maneuvers is certificated for the G loadings and bank angles that will be encountered, and that the maneuvers are permitted by the owner's manual or design specifications. *Acrobatics should never be attempted unless the pilot has been cleared by an instructor to practice these maneuvers solo.* As far as formation and basic fighter maneuvers are concerned, it is strictly the pilot's responsibility to learn the mechanics of each maneuver, and to practice it to the point where he is not a danger to himself or to others.

The descriptions of the various maneuvers covered in this book are generalized guidelines, and are not to be construed as absolutes. There is no way that every possible situation can be taken into consideration, because their numbers are myriad and their variations infinite. The best rule of thumb to follow when working on these parts of the flying game is good common sense. *If you suspect that a certain maneuver is beyond your or the aircraft's capability, don't do it.* Go back to the drawing board, do your homework, go over the problems with your instructor, and work up to it again. As the song says, "You've Gotta Have Heart," and that, plus a little study and practice, is all it takes for anyone to become proficient in any of the maneuvers discussed here. Knowing how to perform the maneuvers and techniques covered in this book will definitely add to your enjoyment of the wild blue, and will increase your proficiency. These are worthwhile ends in themselves.

Before getting into the nuts and bolts of the things that make every man a tiger in the air, I want to set the stage by means of a quick trip through the development of air combat tactics since World War I. In order to get a better feel for how fighter pilots work and what they have had to work with down through the years, we'll take a brief look at the tactics, aircraft, and weaponry that were used during each major era.

PART 1
The Evolution of Air Combat

CHAPTER 1

LAYING THE FOUNDATIONS: WORLD WAR I

During the first few years of World War I, the area of fighter tactics was pretty much *terra incognita* on both sides of the front. Up through 1916, definitive concepts of how to operate aircraft offensively and defensively, as well as how to concentrate efforts—a basic, time-proven principle of war—had not evolved. The decisive role of air supremacy in a campaign and the tactics that could bring it about were only ideas in the minds of such visionaries as the Air Corps' William "Billy" Mitchell, and Major General Sir Hugh "Boom" Trenchard, of the Royal Flying Corps (a precursor of the RAF). The earthbound logic that shaped the strategy of the day relegated the airplane to the same role it assigned to the cavalry—reconnaissance. This myopic viewpoint construed the airplane as merely an extension of the infantry and artillery—a farther-reaching eye to provide information for ground commanders. The primary mission of these early birds was to scout, observe, reconnoiter, photograph, and report. To accomplish this mission, two-seater aircraft were used, manned by an observer and his pilot. Although these airplanes represented the best technology of the day—powered flight was less than 15 years old—they were not quite adequate for the task at hand. In fact, the first airplanes the Allies sent to France were capable of speeds of only about 60 mph at 3,000 feet. This lack of power was principally why these early aircraft were not equipped with machine guns. The only armament they carried was the side arm worn by the observer, who was an officer, and the carbine carried by the pilot, who was enlisted. These weapons were primarily meant for self-defense, in case the airplane was forced down behind enemy lines, but they also provided the opportunity for aircrews to take potshots at the opposition whenever a dull reconnaissance patrol needed livening up.

As the war progressed and more powerful aircraft became available, the machines were equipped with a flexible gun mounted in the rear seat, so that the observer could discourage intruders from interfering with his observing. These weapons, and indeed all fixed and flexible guns used by both sides during the war, were basically .30-caliber Maxim machine guns. Those manufactured in England were known as the Vickers, which was a forward-firing gun, and the Lewis, which was a flexible mounted gun fired by the observer. In Germany, the same types of guns were called the Spandau and the Parabellum, respectively.

The synchronizer was invented by Anthony Fokker, a Dutchman, in 1915; it allowed fixed guns to be fired through the propeller arc without shooting off the blades. Before that, fixed armament was mounted either at an angle sufficient to clear the prop, or on the top wing, to shoot over the prop. You can well imagine the problems that such arrangements caused with aiming, reloading, and clearing jams. The Lewis gun used by the British in this type of installation and the Parabellum used by the Germans were fed by an ammunition drum, rather than a belt. In aerial duels fought with these weapons, the Germans held a decided advantage. The Parabellum utilized a redesigned cartridge drum that held more than twice as many rounds as the drum used on the Lewis. This meant that the German gunner had to reload only half as many times as his British adversary. Things were even better when he was pitted against a Frenchman using a Hotchkiss gun, which had to be loaded four times to the Parabellum's one. Some of Germany's leading aces, among them von Richthofen, Voss, and Immelmann, used the Parabellum in gaining their initial victories.

When the secret of Fokker's synchronizer became known on both sides of the front, the heyday of the single-seat fighter began. Aircraft built strictly as fighters appeared, for the observer and his gun were no longer needed except in those birds meant specifically for reconnaissance. At this time there were no "tactics" that were taught or publicized as such—the game was learned through experience in the air. The early aces were mostly individualists who scored a good number of their victories while flying solo patrols, and whose main purpose was to seek out and engage the enemy. However, a few threads of commonality did link their methods; these would become the basis for the tactical doctrines of a later day.

They would try to climb as high as they could while patrolling, preferably with the sun at their backs, and wait for the enemy to appear beneath them. Once the bad guys were spotted, the attackers dove for the kill, exploiting the double advantage of speed and surprise. The hope was that this first pass would disrupt and confuse the enemy formation to the point that each attacker could utilize his higher speed to maneuver for a second kill, before the enemy pilots got organized to counter the attack. As one might guess, once the initial dive was over, the maneuverings were the typical hard-turning, random gyrations found in any dogfight, with everyone jockeying for position—either to get a shot, or to shake someone off his tail. This type of high-G maneuvering in very close quarters did not lend itself to attacks by small groups of aircraft in formation, because it would have been nearly impossible for the pilots to stay together once they started to mix it up. Richthofen employed this diving technique quite effectively, even after tactics had been developed for the mass employment of aircraft. He would climb above a dog-fight, wait until an opportunity presented itself, and then swoop down for the kill.

Another frequently used technique was stalking. Since the maximum speeds of the aircraft used by both sides were pretty much the same, an enemy spotted some distance away could not be easily caught simply by firewalling the throttle. The case would be nearly hopeless if he saw you approaching and decided to make a run for it. The solution was to stalk him—but only after considering other factors that could make or break the game for the attacker: available cloud cover to mask your approach; whose side of the front you were over; the possibility of antiaircraft fire that would betray your position; and the prevailing wind, which nearly always favored the Germans. The leading aces of that era would work patiently for a con-siderable length of time to arrive at a favorable position from which they could pounce upon an unsuspecting victim. Nearly all of those who had any success in shooting down airplanes held their fire until they were very close to an opponent—often as near as 50 yards. Getting inside the lethal range of your guns before start-ing to shoot is a basic tenet of air-combat tactics that is as valid today as it was in World War I.

In the fall of 1915, the first formalized rules for aerial combat were developed by Oswald Boelcke and Max Immelmann, who saw the benefits of, and established procedures for, two aircraft fighting together as a team. With Boelcke flying lead and Immelmann on his wing, this concept proved devastatingly effective against the Allies. This talented pair refined and expanded the techniques that would con-tinue to shape the conduct of air-to-air engagements 60 years into the future. The lessons learned were written down by Boelcke, whose treatise so impressed his su-periors that "Boelcke's Dicta" became required reading for all German aircrews—to the point where it could be recited verbatim upon request.

Boelcke's theory on the role of the fighter in war went far beyond stick-and-rud-der techniques. He foresaw the fighter as a major factor in the proper employment of air power, and stated its three basic missions: to prevent enemy planes from per-forming *their* mission; to protect friendly aircraft; and to engage in some specialized forms of ground attack, such as strafing. When the Allies saw the obvious advan-tages of these new tactics, they were quick to jump on the bandwagon and adopt the team concept for their own operations.

Up to this time, war in the air was mainly a contest between individuals. For the most part, the man was the thing—individual skill and courage were the hall-marks of success. Chivalry, reminiscent of the days of knighthood, was not uncom-mon, and the use of distinctive insignia and personal color schemes, particularly among the Germans, was a definite throwback to the heraldic traditions. However, by 1916, air-to-air combat had evolved to the point where it was no longer the do-main of the skillful aerial improvisor. Team play came to the fore, and the emphasis was on tactical maneuvers designed specifically for offensive and defensive situa-tions. Superiority in numbers quickly assumed a greater importance than individual ability. Those who still harbored lone-wolf tendencies had to curb their inclinations and learn to fly the more disciplined team approach if they wished to survive. Those who couldn't hack this new regimen and persisted in trying to shine their own tails did not last long against enemy formations.

Following the trend toward massing larger numbers of aircraft over the battle area, the German Air Force developed the renowned Flying Circus. These highly effective units were originally formed and trained by Boelcke, but after his death, caused by a midair collision with a wingman, command was passed to Boelcke's star pupil, Manfred von Richthofen. Under Richthofen's leadership, the various units of the Flying Circus ravaged the Allied squadrons, particularly the British. The Flying Circus units were the first to be used exclusively for air-to-air combat, and were not involved with the lesser chores of observation or escort work.

A significant factor in the success of the Circus was the introduction of the Fokker DR-1. This bird was a triplane, powered by a 110-hp Le Rhône engine, and armed with two Spandau machine guns. It had a very good rate of climb, was sensitive on the controls, and, most important of all, had excellent turning ability with no tendency to lose altitude while being bent around.

The DR-1 had a service ceiling of 20,000 feet, and weighed less than 1,300 pounds fully loaded. Its one serious drawback was its slow speed, especially at altitude. The DR-1's maximum speed just below 14,000 feet was 86 mph, and this

Fokker DR-1——the interplane struts on the DR-1 were not intended to strengthen the wing structure and were not continuous from the top wing to the bottom wing. They served merely to dampen the vibration of the cantilever wings.
(Photo courtesy *Aerophile* Magazine)

improved to only 97 mph at around 9,000 feet. The aircraft also had some problems with structural failure of the wing ribs during high-speed dives, giving it the reputation of a weak airplane. (The cause of this problem eventually proved to be improper gluing procedures.) Despite these shortcomings, and a cramped cockpit, the DR-1 was highly regarded by Richthofen, who, while introducing it to his squadron, described it as maneuverable as the devil, and able to climb like a monkey.

Richthofen was aware that in a dogfight there was a definite tactical advantage to be gained by having the squadron leader's aircraft painted a distinctive color. It enabled his men to pick out their leader quickly in the frantic turning of an engagement, and thus give them a rallying point. Richthofen earned his nickname, the "Red Baron," while flying his completely red Fokker "Tripe," as the DR-1 was also known. Other members of his squadron also employed a red color scheme, but not over the entire airplane—some other color had to be added to the ailerons, tail, or cowl to keep the leader's plane unique.

The DR-1 had few equals in a dogfight until late 1917, and was flown by other notable aces, including Werner Voss and Ernst Udet. Richthofen scored 19 of his 80 victories in the Fokker Tripe and continued flying it until July, 1918, when his unit converted to the Fokker D-VII.

Fokker DR-1——the Fokker "Tripe" did not have an instrument panel. The gauges were hung haphazardly around the cockpit on whatever attaching points were available. The unpadded gun butts were the cause of serious facial injuries in even minor crashes. (Photo courtesy *Aerophile* Magazine)

As the speeds of aerial combat increased with the advent of improved, higher-performance airplanes, acrobatics during a dogfight became less and less important. Many of these maneuvers involved slow speeds near the stalling point, which made the aerobat an easy target. The long, involved aerial duels that ranged from the heights down to the treetops became mostly a thing of the past, and combat became less personal, for now a pilot could not stop to consider the plight of his opponent. (Such a momentary distraction could result in his being shot down.) An interesting side note on combat acrobatics was pointed out in Aaron Norman's *The Great Air War:* "Most German airmen were rather contemptuous of and bewildered by what they regarded as antics on the part of Allied aviators. British and French pilots were taught and encouraged to use acrobatics, but Germans held these to be of no practical value." It should be noted, however, that Lothar Richthofen, the Red Baron's younger brother, was a prominent, and successful, exception.

The Allies were quick to learn, albeit at great expense, the tactical lessons being taught by Richthofen's Flying Circus. The French air force published a formal manual, entitled *The Philosophy of Tactics of Aerial Combat, 1917,* for all pilots training at the fighter school at Pau, France. Recognizing the rapidly changing nature of their topic, the French had this document printed on loose-leaf pages so that changes could be inserted easily. The insight and vision that these tigers of an earlier day had, not only with respect to combat but to flying in general, is shown in one of the opening paragraphs of this manual. This advice given to pilots in 1917 is still fresh and applicable, and will undoubtedly stand the test of time as long as people strap on airplanes and have a go at one another. It cautions the pilot:

Before being able to attack an enemy machine, he must above all be the complete master of his own machine, and know how to profit from the resources it offers him. On this point one is never strong enough; each day, and on each flight, one must perfect one's self. For this one must work without letup in the air. *To steer an aircraft is nothing; to fly it is difficult* [author's emphasis]. A good pilot must be able to do with his machine as he will; even the most difficult of aerobatic maneuvers must be executed with a complete spirit of freedom; flying must be instinctive and in no way mechanical. Such flying is not to be acquired in one day or the next, but by methodical and progressive training to which the greatest importance must be attached.

Along with this gem of flying wisdom, the French manual outlined several other tactics distilled from the experiences and observations of both sides over the front. Some of these were:

"Always fire at close range from a diving attack from out of the sun if possible, never engage in combat unless all the advantages are on your side, don't fly alone, use surprise, and avoid being surprised."

If a pilot forgot this last principle, the following advice was given: "If you are taken by surprise, do not dive, but start a climbing spiral. If you can't climb, keep a turn going."

For those who had run out of airspeed, altitude, and ideas, this rule was established: "Break off combat by executing a spiral, slip, or falling leaf, with the last two being the better options against a skilled opponent."

The final paragraphs of the manual sum it all up by charging that a fighter pilot must be adroit, prudent, and decisive—more good advice that holds true today.

One of the more effective airplanes in which the Allies practiced these principles was the Sopwith Camel. This English design was introduced in 1917, weighed a little over 1,400 pounds fully loaded, and had a top speed of around 120 mph. It was armed with two Vickers machine guns, and could get up to about 20,000 feet. This bird was one of the more notable aircraft in the war. It used a rotary engine. The prop was bolted to the engine case, and the crankshaft was fastened to the airframe. This arrangement, with the mass of the engine spinning with the prop, produced an enormous amount of torque, making it difficult to turn to the left, but the Camel could really swap ends going the other way.

All this made the Camel a very tricky aircraft to fly. It was described by pilots as "answering readily to intelligent handling, but utterly remorseless against brutal or ignorant treatment." Perhaps the most famous Camel pilot was a Canadian, Captain A. R. Brown, who has been credited with shooting down the Red Baron.

Sopwith Camel——the first British aircraft to go into combat with a gun synchronizer. Thirteen hundred victories were scored by Camel pilots during the plane's 16 months of combat service.
(Photo courtesy *Aerophile* Magazine)

Sopwith Camel——large equal-span, equal-chord wings plus a rotary engine gave the Camel exceptional maneuverability. A power loss on takeoff was extremely grave, since the torque from the dead but still turning engine would quickly pull the airplane into a spin.
(Photo courtesy National Air and Space Museum, Smithsonian Institution)

In the early days of the war, a dogfight was usually a contest between two to six aircraft; however, when the opposing sides began to mass their aircraft to achieve supremacy, these engagements often involved 25 or 30 machines. Once a dogfight of any size started, it attracted quite a bit of attention—there were the fiery plumes left by falling aircraft, the smoke from crashes, the puffs of antiaircraft fire. All of this could be seen for quite a few miles, and fighters from both sides would join in the fray, with everyone working for altitude and a position of advantage from which to attack. Since most of these birds were flying at about 100 mph, the entire fight did not occupy much airspace. Today's supersonic fighters cross ten miles of sky just to turn around. That 25 or 30 aircraft could twist and turn in an area one-fourth that size to get in a fast shot and then break away to avoid becoming a target, is awesome to contemplate. The danger of a midair was every bit as great as the risk of being shot down by the enemy.

In 1916, the Allies introduced their big gun, the Spad. This was the best fighter produced by that side during the war. Powered by a 220-hp Hispano engine, and armed with two Vickers guns, the Spad maxed out at about 130 mph. It was very rugged, an airplane that could absorb a lot of punishment, and it had no tendency to shed its wing fabric when pulling out of high-speed dives that would cause other birds to lose their wings entirely. Most pilots considered the Spad a "hot" airplane because of its top speed and because it tended to glide like a brick, which meant a high landing speed.

The Spad required a skillful pilot to realize its full potential, because it lacked the inherent stability found in most aircraft designs. It had to be flown every minute and tolerated no laxity on the part of the pilot. As did most other airplanes of the day, the Spad had problems associated with cold-weather operations. The Spad did not have radiator shutters to regulate the cooling of the engine during the cold months of the year. This degraded its performance to some extent, because the engine could not warm up to optimum internal operating temperatures. The thought of flying a long patrol in an open cockpit during the winter is bad enough, but adding to this a balky engine on which you must stake your life can make one believe that this era, like that of the whaling days, was one of wooden ships and iron men.

Spad VII——this aircraft was the standard French fighter throughout 1918, and although it was less maneuverable than many other fighters of that era, its strength and diving ability made it a formidable opponent.
(Photo courtesy National Air and Space Museum, Smithsonian Institution)

The Spad was flown by the top French and American aces: René Fonck (75 victories), George Guynemer (53 victories), and Eddie Rickenbacker (26 victories.) The two French aces each made an interesting contribution to the tools of the fighter pilot's trade. Guynemer was the first to use a rearview mirror attached to his upper wing so that he could keep an eye peeled for anyone sneaking up on his tail. This device became standard equipment on nearly all fighters in subsequent wars. Fonck introduced the first practical improvement on the sighting system employed by fighter pilots in WW I. The sights used on fighter planes in this war were the ring-and-bead type. Concentric metal rings were mounted on a post in front of the windshield, and in front of this apparatus was a bead mounted atop a post.

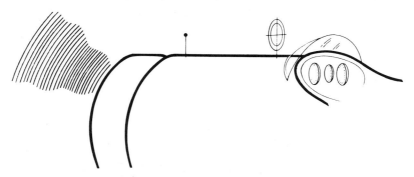

Ring-and-bead sighting system

Straight-on shots were aimed by simply lining up the enemy aircraft with the bead and the center of the ring assembly. Deflection shooting was accomplished by using the proper ring on the rear sight to establish the correct lead. Admittedly, this gave a pretty rough estimate of what the right lead angle was, but then again it was better than using a wad of gum stuck on the windshield. The improvement that Fonck devised was a sighting arrangement that gave the pilot a fairly accurate measurement of the range to his target. Improper estimation of target range had been the bane of fighter pilots since the first time anyone hosed off a burst at the bad guys. A telescopic sight was mounted next to the ring-and-bead setup; on the lens was etched a pair of concentric circles. The diameter of the larger circle covered ten meters at a distance of 100 meters in front of the airplane. Therefore, to accurately estimate correct firing distance, all he needed to know was the wingspan of the bird he was chasing. Assuming the span of the other bird was ten meters, you simply closed on the target until its wings filled with the larger circle in your sight, at which time you were at optimum firing range—100 meters. The diameter of the smaller of the two circles in the sight covered one meter at a distance of 100 meters. If the wingspan of the opponent mentioned above filled the small circle, his range could be estimated fairly accurately at 1,000 meters.

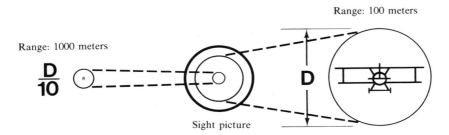

Estimating range with René Fonck's improved sighting system

Since the length of the fuselage of the birds of that era was less than the wing-span, shooting from the beam position required a guesstimate of how much of the larger circle the fuselage should fill at the angle at which you were approaching, at the desired firing range.

Although this sighting system provided only two accurate fixes of range as you approached the target, it was a huge improvement over strictly eyeballing it, especially when dead astern of the target, where depth perception must be used to estimate range. This latter method is unreliable and even to this day is the primary cause of fighter pilots starting to shoot while they are still too far from the target. Fonck's sight at least got you into the ball park, where your primary concern was proper aim, rather than the correct range.

The Spad had one flight characteristic that allowed it to hold more than its own in any engagement with the best Fokker designs of the day. This was a superior rate of climb, which enabled it to attack a large number of the enemy and escape by utilizing the best defensive tactic known at that time—the spiral climb. An experienced fighter pilot flying a Spad and choosing to disregard the philosophy taught at Pau could successfully attack an enemy squadron by diving at his chosen target, firing a quick burst, and then, using the speed gained in his dive, zooming into a climbing spiral to stay out of range of the enemy's guns.

One of the problems that plagued fighter pilots on both sides of the front was frequent gun stoppages. A major cause of this was the canvas ammunition belts used to feed the guns. They were often twisted around by the slipstream, and were adversely affected by damp weather. These problems were eventually solved by installing an enclosed ammunition feed track and utilizing a disintegrating link belt to hold the cartridges. Nevertheless, it was not uncommon for pilots to carry a small hammer in the cockpit to clear jams in the mechanism, because your life often depended on whether you could clear a gun stoppage in a few seconds.

In 1918, the Germans placed into service what was to be unanimously considered by both sides the best fighter of World War I. The Fokker D-VII proved to be such an outstanding weapon that it was the only airplane specified by type to be surrendered to the Allies under the terms of the armistice. It was powered by a 180-hp Mercedes engine that gave it a top speed of 125 mph, and it was armed with the usual two Spandau machine guns. This aircraft had a rugged airframe that allowed it to withstand pullouts from steep dives without losing its wings. The sturdiness of the design also made for a very stable gun platform—the D-VII was unaffected by the recoil from the twin Spandaus. This had been a problem on earlier Fokker designs, including the DR-1, which shook violently during any prolonged burst.

Steadiness while firing is extremely important. A stable platform makes it easier for the pilot to keep his sights on the target and to adjust the bullet impact point as required. This is not as simple a task as it may seem, because, in a hard-turning fight, the airplane itself is bouncing around considerably—the incipient stall leads to airframe buffet. Flying through numerous slipstreams in a fight compounds this problem. The added sighting difficulties created by gun recoil only attest to the marksmanship of the early tigers.

The D-VII was a relatively easy airplane to fly, with excellent maneuverability and good control sensitivity all the way up to its ceiling of 22,000 feet. In ability to maneuver at low speeds and high altitude it outdid most of the opposition. The aircraft climbed well, although not as quickly as the DR-1, and had excellent stalling characteristics, with plenty of warning before the actual stall. And the D-VII did not have the DR-1's tendency to enter a spin from a stall or a nose-high turn.

It is amazing to note the multiplicity of designs and models that were produced by each side in World War I. New types of aircraft were arriving at the front every five or six months. New ideas or improvements on existing equipment were rushed through production. The hectic pace was summed up in a statement by Sir Thomas Sopwith: "Development was so fast. We literally thought of and designed and flew the airplane in a space of about six to eight weeks. Now it takes the same number of years. Everything was built entirely by eye. That's why there were so many structural failures. We didn't start to stress airplanes at all seriously until the Camel, in 1917."

These rapid manufacturing processes and apparent lack of attention to detail were the cause of the many failures of the Fokker DR-1 and gave the basic design an unwarranted bad reputation.

Fokker D-VII——this aircraft so outclassed its rivals during acceptance trials in January, 1918, that the manufacturers of the competing aircraft were *ordered* to produce the D-VII under license.
(Photo courtesy National Air and Space Museum, Smithsonian Institution)

Considering the complexities of aircraft building and the facilities and technology that were available, it is surprising how many airplanes were actually produced during that period—8,500 Spads, 5,500 Sopwith Camels, and, in six and a half months' time, 3,000 Fokker D-VIIs. The succession of new designs during the war brought the airplane from not much more than a powered box kite to a significant military factor by 1918. From the 60 mph of the first combat planes, speeds had increased to about 150 mph, and ceilings of around 20,000 feet were common.

Although more has been written about the fighters and their pilots, by far the most important class of airplanes during the war was the two-place observation plane. Once the tactics of employing fighter screens to protect these aircraft were developed, most aerial battles were a direct result of efforts to destroy, or to prevent the destruction of, observation planes. The surface-oriented thinking that was prevalent in the military of that day is demonstrated by the fact that the German General Staff once tried to *discourage* the development of faster aircraft. They were stuck on the idea of using airplanes strictly for reconnaissance, and were convinced that faster aircraft would mean less accurate observation. Fortunately, this head-in-the-sand attitude did not prevail, and by 1918 the initial glimmerings of the integration of the airplane into the overall scheme of warfare was apparent. For the first time, the British employed their various types of aircraft in a full program of tactical and strategic operations. The primary mission of the fighters was *not* to shoot down enemy planes in general. Fighters were directed to attack only those hostile aircraft that tried to interfere with the squadrons involved with bombing, reconnaissance, artillery spotting, and trench strafing. Engaging and destroying the German Air Force was not an end in itself, but only the means to an end. Enemy fighters had to be destroyed so that the tactical squadrons could carry out their mission of direct support of the ground forces. Although both sides recognized the importance of this type of integrated air-ground operation, only the Royal Flying Corps was successful in putting it into practice.

Thus, by the end of the war it could be said that the airplane, as a weapon, had arrived. Those with an eye to the future could see that this was just a beginning, that we had barely scratched the surface of the airplane's vast war potential. All that was needed were the lighter metals, stronger fabrication, and more powerful engines that the near future would provide.

World War I: Looking Back at the Spad

In 1964, a new airplane appeared on the flight line at Selfridge Air Force Base. It looked a little out of place among the supersonic F-106 interceptors. A group of civilians who worked as base technicians at Selfridge had finished a labor of love that had lasted many years—a complete restoration of a World War I Spad to flyable condition. Looking as if it had just rolled out of the factory, with its spanking new paint job complete down to the 94th "Hat in the Ring" insignia, the bird was certainly a tribute to the master craftsmen who gave new life to this important part of the 94th's history.

The wing commander, Colonel Converse B. Kelly, made the first flight, which lasted about 15 minutes—as did nearly all of the other flights, due to an engine-overheating problem. Later, Lieutenant Colonel Joe Martin, who was commander of the 94th at the time, had a chance to take the Spad around the flagpole a few times. His impressions of the flight, and of the general handling characteristics of the airplane, are as follows:

"The pervading thought in my mind at the time, now in distant retrospect, was, what an embarrassment it would be to 'prang' this museum piece. Therefore, I remained in the traffic pattern close to the field—well within gliding distance to a safe dead-stick landing, should a mishap occur. As I recall, about 150 to 160 mph was the top speed I saw, and the response to throttle movement was instant and pronounced. It occurred to me that compensating for the associated torque would demand nimble coordination and practice, particularly if one wanted to remain in a coordinated state in pursuit of a target. Visibility was good, but a little hard to evaluate in a sterile traffic-pattern environment. It was easy to land, but in taxiing, as with most conventional single-engine landing gear types, one needed to 'S' in order to safely see ahead.

"In a more personal vein, I recall that having donned the leather helmet and goggles to protect my eyes from wind and my ears from noise (this gear had no other usefulness, i.e., no radio or other electronic equipment), I omitted the 'luxury' of fastening the chin strap, which dangled eight to ten inches below my left jaw. You guessed it—on the first takeoff, at about tail lift-off, my face began to pay the penalty of this omission. In the propeller wash and windblast of takeoff velocity the strap became a whip in the hands of the ghosts of flying safety officers of generations past and present. At this critical juncture I could do nothing but endure it until reaching a safe altitude where I could—and did—fasten it. To abort the takeoff because of my error was an option involving embarrassment—my ego rejected it out of hand.

"In summary, I can certainly say that throttle, rudder and aileron coordination was a definite challenge, and that responses and sensitivity in all three were immediate and abrupt."

The Spad did not remain long at Selfridge. Because of its unique historical value, it was quickly shipped to the Air Force Museum in Dayton, Ohio, where it remains on display to this day.

World War I: The Rickenbacker Solution

During the mid 1960s, I had the privilege of being assigned to the 94th Fighter Squadron, which at that time was located at Selfridge Air Force Base, Michigan. The 94th, and its famous "Hat in the Ring" insignia, gained notoriety in World War I through the exploits of America's leading aces of that period, especially Captain Eddie Rickenbacker, who commanded the unit during the last few months of the war. "Captain Eddie" visited the squadron a few times during the '60s, and naturally was bombarded with questions about how it was in the old days. As one would expect, there were frequent comparisons of the performance and rocklike solidity of modern fighters to the 120-mph speed and relative fragileness of the Spads of his day. Survivability in combat was also a big topic, in view of the lack of parachutes in the First War, and the absence of armor plating around the cockpits of the early pursuit ships. The added weight of these "niceties" imposed too much of a penalty in performance, even on the more powerful aircraft that became available toward the end of the war. Figuring that an attack in the blind area beneath his airplane would be the only way he could be surprised too late to take evasive action, Captain Eddie neatly solved the armor problem by slipping an iron stove lid underneath his seat cushion.

Spad VII——restored to a flyable condition at Selfridge AFB in 1964, this plane is now on display at the Air Force Museum in Dayton, Ohio. (Photo courtesy *Aerophile* Magazine)

World War I: To Survive, Innovate

A description by Van Ira of a patrol on which Major Edward "Mick" Mannock, leading British ace of World War I with 73 victories, shot down four German scout planes:

"In his first fight, which commenced at 12,000 feet, there were six Pfalz scouts flying east from Kemmel Hill direction. One he shot to pieces after firing a long burst from directly behind and above; another he crashed—it spun into the ground after it had been hit by a deflection shot; the other, a silver bird, he had a fine set-to with, while his patrol watched the Master at work. It was a wonderful sight. First they waltzed around one another like a couple of turkey cocks, Mick being tight on his adversary's tail. Then the Pfalz half-rolled and fell a few hundred feet beneath him. Mick followed, firing as soon as he got into position. The Hun then looped—Mick looped, too, coming out behind and above his opponent and firing short bursts. The Pfalz then spun—Mick spun also, firing as he spun. This shooting appeared to me a waste of ammunition. The Hun eventually pulled out; Mick was fast on his tail—they were now down to 4,000 feet. The Pfalz now started twisting and turning, which was a sure sign of a 'wind up.' After a sharp burst close up, Mick administered the coup de grace, and the poor old fellow went down headlong and crashed.

"I asked Mick after he landed why he fired during the spin. He replied, 'Just to intensify his wind up.' This was the first occasion that I have ever seen a machine loop during a fight. It was obvious to us, watching, that to loop under such circumstances is foolish. Mick managed, however, to keep behind him, although it was obvious by his maneuvers after he came out of the loop that the Pfalz pilot was all at sea, for he twisted and turned his machine in a series of erratic jerks, just as if he was a dog stung on his tail. Mick says he only looped as well for the fun of it, as he felt his opponent was 'cold meat.' He says what he should have done instead of looping was to have made a zooming climbing turn as the Pfalz looped, then half-rolled and come back on his tail as he came out of the loop. By this means he would have been able to keep the Hun in sight all the time, while he would not have lost control of his machine, as the Hun did coming out of the loop.

"Mick's other Hun was a two-seater which he shot down after a burst at right angles. The old boy crashed into a tree near La Couranne, south of Vieux."

World War I: The Possum Technique

A remarkable story of nerve and airmanship is told about Albert Ball, a British ace of the First War who had a total of 47 victories. While on patrol one afternoon, he spotted two Albatrosses, and on his initial attack he inflicted some damage on both German aircraft. Choosing discretion over valor, the Albatrosses headed for home—with Ball in hot pursuit. Ball continued to make passes until he ran out of ammunition. Undaunted, he once more pressed the attack, using his service revolver, but the Albatrosses were able to escape and land safely. Ball was furious and disgusted that any airman could behave in so cowardly a fashion, and decided to issue a challenge right on the spot. Writing on the note pad that all pilots carried on patrol, he dared his two former adversaries to meet him over their home base the next day at the same time, so that the fight could be finished. He then wrapped the note around a weight and dropped it on the enemy airfield.

The next day, Ball approached the German airdrome on time, and was quite pleased to see the two planes circling over the field, waiting for his arrival. He immediately flew at the closest bird, hoping to unnerve him by his apparent collision tactics. However, before he was close enough to fire, he heard machine-gun fire from his rear. In his eagerness to do battle, Ball had disregarded the by-word of the day—"Watch out for the Hun in the sun"—and had flown into a trap. Chandelling hard to the left, he looked back to see three more enemy aircraft diving to the attack.

Now facing odds of five to one, Ball planned to keep dodging and weaving while attempting to pick off one or two; however, the Germans were old hands at the game, and managed to keep pretty much out of harm's way. Their plan was to box him in and then administer the coup de grace. Ball maneuvered frantically for a good shot, but was always forced off his run by one or two of the Albatrosses getting behind or above him. The German tactics were successful, and he was reduced to taking quick bursts at long range and at undesirable angles, while at the same time taking quite a few hits on his own aircraft. He was unable to make a break for his own lines, because a couple of the Germans always positioned themselves between the dogfight and Allied territory.

Eventually Ball ran out of ammunition, and by all rights everything should have been over in a few minutes. But, keeping a cool head, Ball devised what was probably the most daring scheme ever thought up by a trapped fighter pilot. He spotted a large open field nearby and immedi-ately threw his bird into a wild spin, which he allowed to continue until he was close to the ground. He then broke it and staggered his Nieuport in for a landing.

Naturally, the Germans figured that one of their shots had hit home, and that the wounded pilot had just narrowly averted a crash. Since they knew that the pilot was the British ace Albert Ball, they realized that capturing him would be more of a feather in their caps than shooting him down. The German flight leader signaled two of his planes to land and take Ball into custody; and, as they were about to touch down, the other three flew triumphantly over the field, wagging their wings scornfully at the Englishman's brashness.

After their pass, the three Ger-mans pilots headed for home to spread the news of their victory, and of the renowned ace who was now their prisoner. All this while Ball was slumped over in the cockpit of his Nieuport (whose engine was idling), giving the impression that his last conscious effort had been to land his machine and bring it to a stop. Ea-gerly the German pilots climbed out of their planes and ran toward Ball's Nieuport, anxious to claim the prize of their perfidious game. Ball waited until they were fairly close, and then suddenly jammed the throttle wide open and roared down the field and into the air, leaving the hapless Ger-mans in a cloud of dust and dismay. Mercifully, history does not record the charges and countercharges that were hurled back and forth at the German officers' mess that evening.

CHAPTER 2

REFINEMENTS, WITH MORE POWER: WORLD WAR II

The years between the wars saw dramatic advances in every area of aviation technology. The wood and fabric box kite of World War I evolved into the modern fighter plane, whose speed, armament, and performance outstripped the Spads and Fokkers by many orders of magnitude. Unfortunately, the development of tactics to employ these new fighters successfully lagged far behind. The lessons so painfully learned between 1914 and 1918 had been forgotten.

When England again went to war in 1939, the RAF had no tactics that were suitable for modern air combat. The peacetime years had been used mainly to practice precision formation flying—great for air shows, but completely useless in an air-to-air engagement. Since you fight the way you train, the British used these close-formation techniques in the opening encounters of the war—and quickly found that they were operating at a considerable disadvantage.

The Germans, on the other hand, came into the war in a very strong position. They already had a viable, proven, tactical doctrine, which had been developed for modern warfare in the late 1930s during their involvement as the Condor Legion in the Spanish Civil War. It was in Spain that the Germans introduced the wide-open combat formation, in which the intervals between individual aircraft were increased to about 200 yards (the turning radius of the Messerschmitt Bf-109), and the distance between two elements was twice that much. Boelcke's original concept of the line-abreast formation was retained, and an altitude differential was established between the elements, as well as between the flights if more than one flight was involved. This spread-out, vertically separated formation offered a number of valuable tactical advantages: the search area covered by the flight was increased considerably; each pilot within the flight could contribute to the visual coverage, because he did not have to concentrate on flying close formation; the initiative to take the bounce was retained down to the element lead with no loss of collective strength; and better mutual coverage by each member of the flight resulted in reduced vulnerability. The increased visual coverage afforded by this expanded formation was particularly important when opposing flights approached each other head-on. The high closing speeds in this type of situation made it imperative that the enemy aircraft be spotted and identified in time for the leader to maneuver the flight into a good attacking position.

Refined flight tactics were not the only benefit derived from the Condor Legion's participation in the Spanish Civil War. Another was the development of an army–air force plan for joint operations under centralized control—the first successful approach to this type of combined warfare. The product was *Blitzkrieg,* or Lightning War, in which massed armor was supported by dive bombers, which in turn were covered by large numbers of fighters to insure air supremacy. The effectiveness of these new tactical doctrines is shown by the rapidity with which the Germans overran Europe in 1939 and 1940.

Messerschmitt Bf-109——the G model pictured here marked the beginning of a decline in the operational effectiveness of the 109 series. Design changes prompted by Luftwaffe demands for increased firepower and additional equipment seriously hurt the aircraft's flying characteristics.
(Photo courtesy National Air and Space Museum, Smithsonian Institution)

A remarkable new airplane was under development during these years in Spain, and it was destined to become the mainstay of the Luftwaffe during all of World War II. The Messerschmitt Bf-109 (popularly called the Me-109) was quite an advanced machine for its day, incorporating various high-lift devices such as leading-edge slats, slotted ailerons, and slotted flaps. This resulted in a very stable bird that had good stalling characteristics and was capable of high-G turns. It was powered by a 1,550-hp Daimler Benz engine that gave it a top speed of 452 mph, and, above 25,000 feet, superior performance to both the Hurricane and the Spitfire. It also possessed a higher ceiling and better armament than these British fighters. The advantage in armament came from its two 20-mm cannon with 60 rounds per gun, plus two 7.9-mm machine guns with 1,000 rounds per gun, as compared to the normal armament of eight machine guns for the Spitfire and Hurricane. But the Bf-109 did have some problems resulting from the leading-edge slats mentioned above, which affected its stability as a gun platform.

The leading-edge slats were small, partial airfoils running along the outer half of each wing's leading edge. At low speeds they extended by gravity along tracks to a position slightly forward of, and a little lower than, the main wing section. In this position, airflow between the slat and the wing was directed over a high-lift airfoil. As airspeed increased after takeoff, the additional air pressure slowly forced the slat up the track to the closed position, creating a high-speed, rather than a high-lift, wing.

The stability problem occurred during the high-G turns that are basic to any dogfight. The slat on the high wing had a tendency to open slightly due to the disturbed airflow over the highly loaded wing surface. This caused the high wing to suddenly generate more lift than the other wing, producing a rolling action that had to be corrected for. Then, just as suddenly, the slat would close, and the correction had to be taken out. Often the high wing slat would pop in and out several times, which would play havoc with the pilot's attempts to keep the pipper on the target.

Another characteristic of the Bf-109 that added to the pilot's aiming problems was extreme heaviness on the controls, especially in dives, where considerable stick forces were required to pull out. Given these control problems, and considering the state of the art in the early 1940s, it is hard to imagine why a cockpit-controlled trim system was not installed. However, the aircraft had only ground-adjustable tabs available, and the lack of rudder trim curtailed its ability to turn left at high speeds. A few other bad features of this bird were a cramped cockpit with poor rearward vision, a short radius of action that allowed, for example, only 20 minutes in the combat area over Britain, and weak landing gear. This poorly designed gear, coupled with a tendency toward left wing heaviness on takeoff, caused five percent of the 33,000 Bf-109s produced to be written off due to accidents.

In spite of these difficulties, the Messerschmitt was a formidable combat weapon during the early years of the war. It could outdive any other plane in service. This diving capability was enhanced by a fuel-injection system that allowed a pilot to nose the aircraft over sharply and utilize negative Gs to dive away. British pilots, flying with Merlin engines that had a float-type carburetor, could not follow this maneuver. Their engines would cut out due to momentary fuel starvation. The carburetion problem on the Merlin engine was not remedied until late 1941.

Another important breakthrough that the Bf-109 helped to pioneer was the use of radios in fighter planes. The rapid exchange of information between members of the flight that the radio made possible increased the formation's offensive and defensive potential manifold. Radios also provided better air-to-ground coordination and control, an essential ingredient in the fighter's expanded role in supporting rapidly moving ground operations. It certainly afforded a better means of calling the Tally Ho! than did earlier methods of signaling—shooting flares, or rocking the wings.

Until the Allies gained air superiority over continental Europe in the latter phases of World War II, the role of the fighter squadrons on both sides of the Channel could be viewed as mostly defensive. Either they were defending their turf against incoming bombers, or they were defending their own bombers against opposing fighters. The massed fighter sweeps over Europe by the Allies, the purpose of which was to seek out and destroy the last remnants of the Luftwaffe, were not feasible until later, when the following conditions had been met: First of all, sufficient resources had to be available to mount such missions without depleting the supply of fighters needed for bomber escort and for homeland defense. Next, effective and coordinated resistance by the Germans had to be reduced to the point where our losses on these missions would remain acceptable. And last, some method of augmenting the range of the fighters had to be found, so that deep penetration into occupied France and Germany was possible. Drop tanks were the solution to this latter problem, and more will be said about them later on.

Since defense was the name of the game, the tactical employment of fighters in both the offensive–defensive escort posture and the purely defensive interceptor role took on enormous proportions. As the number of bombers in each raid increased, the number of protective fighters also escalated, until there were literally hundreds of fighters above and around the bombing force. To counter these large raids, the defenders usually scrambled two or three squadrons of 12 aircraft each, and then followed with other units as the situation dictated. The clash of these opposing forces produced an awesome spectacle, with many hundreds of airplanes maneuvering for a split-second advantage in one gigantic life-and-death struggle.

Obviously, the sheer weight of numbers played an important part in this type of operation; however, there was a practical limit to the number of birds that could be controlled when engaging a large enemy force. Although opinions varied somewhat, the consensus was that 24 aircraft were the optimum that could be worked in the air without their getting in one another's way. Arguments against larger units were that they were too unwieldy to maneuver quickly, and that such a large number of airplanes was too easy for the opposition to spot.

World War II brought about the refinement of a new role for fighter aircraft, in addition to their traditional employment against enemy air forces. This new mission developed from the need to destroy difficult, pinpoint targets, as well as the need for accurate and responsive close support for ground troops—thus was born the fighter/bomber. Another important factor in assigning the close support mission to fighter aircraft was that they were the only type of bird suitable for bombing and strafing when enemy fighters were present. If they were hard pressed by the enemy before finishing the close support mission, they could always jettison their bombs and engage the opposing fighters on an equal basis.

The basic concepts of close air support were worked out during the First War; however, with the advent of faster airplanes, better weapons, and improved methods of communication and control, this phase of aerial tactics was fast becoming a science of its own. The unique requirements of the close support mission demanded first-class communications between the grunts and the aircrews, as well as specialized training for the latter. Accurate and positive target identification by both air and ground participants was absolutely essential in joint operations, because in many cases the targets were within a few hundred yards of friendly troops. Although the principles were known from the outset, the truly close, intimate cooperation between ground and air forces was not fully realized until the Desert Air Force and the British Eighth Army teamed up against Rommel's Afrika Korps in 1942.

Soon after the outbreak of the war, the RAF realized that definite changes of tactics were required if they were to compete successfully against the Luftwaffe. They were reluctant to abandon entirely the drill-like procedures that were practiced between the wars, and some attempts were made at formalized techniques for combat. This was a rigid, attack-by-the-numbers scheme—each member of the flight was directed to begin his attack from a highly stylized approach to the target. This might have worked on a gunnery range, but was totally unusable in an air battle of any kind. Another tactic that lasted a little longer, but was also discarded, was the line-astern formation, which provided everyone with great coverage to the rear—except number four.

Soon it became patently clear that the old rules of "Boelcke's Dicta" still applied. Fighter tactics must be kept simple because pilots who wished to survive had no time to execute elaborate maneuvers. Control of even a small formation is quickly lost when a lot of complicated maneuvering is involved, because the flight rapidly splits up into individual engagements, and mutual coverage and coordinated action become impossible.

The trial-and-error period lasted until mid-1941, when the RAF Fighter Command belatedly realized that it was lagging far behind the German Fighter Arm tactically, and decided to adopt the enemy's line-abreast formation. This reinvention of the wheel had decided advantages over the line-astern formation that was in vogue at the time, particularly in the area of mutual coverage, which had suffered badly due to the restricted visibility afforded by enclosed cockpits. The RAF had learned, albeit the hard way, that the basics were still valid. Victory was achieved by the man with altitude, airspeed, and position, and not by a series of ritualized maneuvers.

Along with the Few, owed so much by so many, one of the major factors in the RAF's success in the Battle of Britain and subsequent operations was the technological breakthrough achieved by the introduction of radar. Even though the original radar system was quite limited, and in many ways seems primitive by today's standards, radar had a profound and lasting impact on the grand tactics dealing with the employment of an entire air defense force. In this context, radar had two roles—the detection and reporting of hostile raids, and the control of fighters scrambled to intercept these raids. While the bombers were still too far away to be intercepted, their position was continually tracked to determine the probable target area. Then the fighters responsible for the defense of the area were alerted to stand by for their scramble orders. As the bombers neared the maximum intercept line, the fighters were given their airborne orders, and since by this time the size of the raid was more accurately known, additional units were brought up to readiness as the situation required. When the squadrons became airborne and formed up into flights, the leader checked in with the radar control center, which was now plotting both the bombers and the fighters on its scopes. The interceptors were ordered to fly a heading that would lead them to the attacking force, and told to climb to an altitude that would put them above their targets. On the way in, the fighters were briefed on the size of the raid, probable altitude, fighter cover, and any other pertinent information that was available. The fighters were given corrected headings and altitudes as the interception problem continued, until the squadron leader had visual contact with the enemy bombers. From that point on, the more individualized tactics of attack and defense came into play.

The real-time intelligence provided by the radar system allowed the battle commander to conserve his forces until the target was known, and then to concentrate the maximum number of fighters against the main threat. This economical use of limited fighter resources multiplied fighter strength several times.

Fighters operating in an area of radar coverage were not free to roam about looking for targets of opportunity; they were constantly under the control of the battle commander in the radar center. This tight rein on their freedom of action did have its advantages. In this situation, the preflight briefings given the British pilots were continually updated with the latest information; the German aircrews, on the other hand, had to rely on data that was three hours old. Another disadvantage the Germans worked under was that their only assessment of the tactical situation was based on what they could actually see.

Radar, which was probably the biggest gun in what Winston Churchill called the "wizard's war," was not exclusively a British advantage. The Germans also had a radar warning system. Fortunately, theirs was not as highly developed as the English system, having a range of only about five miles, as compared to the 120 miles of the British radar. Later in the war, German radar was improved to the point where it could be used for both the detection of incoming raids and the control of fighters.

When the Luftwaffe changed its strategy to concentrate on the nighttime bombing of English cities, the RAF had to develop a defense to counter the attacks.

What evolved was the first major offshoot of fighter tactics since they were crystallized by Boelcke and Immelmann. An entirely new approach to the task of shooting down bombers came into being—an approach whose concepts were quite radical and seemingly in direct opposition to the proven tactics of daytime operations. Gone were the squadron-size scrambles, the close teamwork within and between flights and elements, and the wild maneuvering commonly associated with dogfights. Instead, the new tactics revolved around a single aircraft operating under radar control, and utilizing techniques quite different from those of daytime fighting. These techniques called for a high degree of proficiency in instrument flying, complete dependence on ground radar control, temperaments suited to lone-wolf operations. From these requirements the night fighter was created—a specialized breed of fighter pilot whose forte was the destruction of bombers alone at night and/or in bad weather. For this new kind of mission, an aircraft had to be designed around the unique requirements of nighttime interception. Airborne radar equipment was a necessity; so was heavy and concentrated firepower.

Bristol Beaufighter——the first of the all-weather fighters, this plane played a prime role in defeating the Luftwaffe's nighttime "blitz" in 1940–41. (Photo courtesy National Air and Space Museum, Smithsonian Institution)

The initial attempts to produce such a bird were not the success they should have been, equipment-wise. The RAF used a day fighter and tried to adapt it to night operations by hanging the radar equipment on it wherever it would fit. Like most jury-rigged affairs, this did not work too well, and the first true night fighter did not appear until the Bristol Beaufighter made its debut in September, 1940. This plane was specifically designed as a weapons system for the night mission, with radar, navigation equipment, and radios matched to the airframe and engines. An additional crew member was added to operate the radar set, and the armament was awesome indeed—four 20-mm cannons and six .30-caliber machine guns.

When radar picked up enemy bombers, a night fighter was scrambled. It worked with a radar control center near the takeoff point; the center would direct the pilot to climb to the altitude of the bombers as determined by its radar system, and would also give him headings to fly that would bring him in behind the bomber formation—about five miles in trail. The pilot would then fly the same course as the bombers and close on them from behind until the radar operator could pick them up on the airborne intercept radar in the Beaufighter. (The maximum range of the airborne set was about four miles.) Once the target was on the scope, the radar operator took over the job of giving the pilot headings that would bring them in directly astern of the selected bogey. At the minimum range of the radar, about 200 yards, the pilot would be able to see the bomber, and all that remained was to center it in the gunsight and hose it down.

Once the procedures and techniques for night interception were refined and aircrews had adequate training in the use of the equipment, the success rate of the night fighters improved steadily. However, the system *was* limited, because the ground controller could handle only two aircraft at the same time (given the state of the art in those days, this was not to his detriment), and the system quickly became saturated during large raids. The night fighters also had to contend with airfield facilities that were inadequate for bad-weather operations, particularly with respect to runway and approach lighting, and navigational aids.

When the tide of the war turned against the Germans, they too had to counter nighttime bombing raids, as had the English a few years earlier. In the development of radar, the Germans lagged considerably behind the British, and their version of airborne intercept radar seriously degraded the speed, range, and handling characteristics of the aircraft in which it was installed. German ground-based radar was fairly effective in its own area of coverage, but problems developed when the ground controllers attempted to pass raids, and the intercepting fighters, from station to station. From these meager beginnings emerged the modern air defense interceptor, which is now backed up by a sophisticated communications and control system that can provide effective air defense for half a continent.

Of all the fighter planes that have come down the pike since World War I, the only one to achieve legendary status is the RAF's Spitfire. This mainstay of the Battle of Britain was the embodiment of England's spirit of resistance during the dark days of the early '40s, and became the tangible symbol of her final victory over Germany. Originally introduced in 1938, the Spitfire was particularly noted for its good handling qualities. It was very light on the controls, had excellent turning and maneuverability characteristics, and gave plenty of warning of an approaching stall. Unlike the Bf-109, it did have a trim system, and by proper adjustment it could be flown hands-off.

The Spit did, however, have a problem with aileron heaviness at high speeds, and this was only partially corrected on the Mark V models used in the Battle of Britain. Of the more than 22,000 Spitfires built, more Mark Vs were produced than any other model. This bird had a maximum speed of 369 mph when equipped with a 1,440-hp Rolls-Royce Merlin engine. The normal armament on the Mark V was either eight .303-caliber machine guns, or four of these guns plus two 20-mm cannons. Initially, some pilots objected that the cannons jammed too often; nevertheless, the two-cannon, four-gun configuration was pretty much standard for Spitfires other than the Mark V. Later models were powered by numerous versions of the Griffon engine, with horsepowers ranging up to 2,200, which resulted in top speeds approaching 450 mph.

Supermarine Spitfire——this plane's taxi time had to be minimized because the gear leg disrupted the airflow through the glycol radiator, causing the engine to boil over unless the bird got airborne quickly.
(Photo courtesy *Aerophile* Magazine)

Since a Spitfire could out-turn a Bf-109 at medium and low altitudes, a favorite German tactic to escape from a turning engagement was a sudden nose-over into a steep dive. The Messerschmitt could dive faster than the Spitfire, and had the added advantage of the head start provided by its fuel-injection system, which was unaffected by the negative Gs of this maneuver. As mentioned before, the Spitfire could not hang in there during such a pushover.

A handy feature found on the Spitfire was a control column with a circular handle on the top, which must have made the plane a lot easier to fly left-handed. This would have been especially convenient in the earlier models, in which you had to pump the gear up and down manually with a two-foot handle located on the right side of the cockpit.

Technological advancements came forth in ever-increasing numbers during World War II. The introduction of radios has already been mentioned, and although these sets were limited to a comparatively small number of preset frequencies, they made a significant contribution to the art of aerial combat. Armor plating around cockpits and self-sealing fuel tanks were instrumental in saving innumerable aircrews. Quite a few stories tell of pilots trying to nurse crippled fighters back to the home drome and getting bounced by the enemy. In many cases, their birds were so shot up that they could not take evasive action, and they just had to sit there, huddled behind the armor plate, while the enemy fighters hammered them. The chances of fire or explosion were minimized by the self-sealing tanks, and the armor afforded the pilot enough protection to enable him to bring the bird home.

As the bombing missions against Germany assumed strategic proportions, the only way to keep losses down to acceptable levels was to provide a fighter escort during the entire raid. This prompted the design of external drop tanks for fighters—light, bomb-shaped containers to carry the additional fuel the fighters needed to accompany the bombers all the way to the target and back. These tanks were hung beneath the fuselage and/or the wings, and each held about 108 gallons. The fuel in the drop tanks was used first. As soon as enemy fighters were encountered, the tanks were jettisoned so that the fighters could operate clean, without the weight and drag of the tanks impeding their performance.

Drop tanks were also used to extend the range of massed fighter sweeps against ground targets once the Luftwaffe had been eliminated as a viable force. If a very lucrative target was expected on one of these sweeps, the fighters would use only about one-third of the fuel from each drop tank. Then, as the first flight made their initial strafing pass over the target, they would drop their partially full tanks into the target, saturating it with gasoline. The next flight would set the gas on fire with their incendiary ammunition, and also release their tanks as they closed on the target, to add to the conflagration.

An innovation that provided the solution to a strictly local problem was the "clipped and cropped" Spitfire used in the desert war. Fighter operations in Africa consisted mainly of close air support missions and the required fighter cover for these attacks. Since most of this action took place at 10,000 feet or below, the Desert Air Force "clipped," or squared off, the elliptical wing tips of their Spitfire Vs to give them better low-altitude rolling characteristics. The supercharger on the Merlin engine was also adjusted, or "cropped," to give maximum engine power at 8,000 feet. These two modifications allowed the Spitfires to fare much better against the far superior Focke-Wulf FW-190s.

Although these and many other improvements certainly gave the World War II fighter pilots better tools to work with, there were other problems that hardware modifications could solve only partially. Two of the primary difficulties were the high speeds of modern fighters, and the poor marksmanship common to most single-engine drivers. The first problem dictated the use of hit-and-run tactics in a large dogfight, which meant less time for aiming and firing—which in turn meant that marksmanship went from bad to worse. It quickly became obvious that corrective action had to be taken to achieve a knockout punch with the shorter bursts of fire allowable in modern combat. The equally obvious solution took a two-pronged approach—better gunsights, and heavier guns.

The sighting problem was solved by using a modern version of René Fonck's gunsight of World War I—the reflector sight. This device projected a circle of light with a dot or a cross at the center onto a flat glass plate mounted behind the windshield, directly in the pilot's line of vision. Also projected on the glass plate were two movable range bars, which allowed the pilot to set into the sighting mechanism the wingspan of the aircraft he expected to encounter. Thus, if Bf-109s were the target, the sight would be set for a little over 30 feet, the wingspan of the Bf-109. Then, when the Messerschmitt's wings filled the space between the range bars, the plane was at the "harmonization" range of the attacker's guns; that is, at the optimum firing distance. Harmonization was a technique employed on fighters with wing-mounted guns to help solve the problems of poor shooting and lack of a knockout punch when using a short burst. The wing guns were adjusted to fire inward at a slight angle, so the paths of the bullets would cross at a distance of about 250 yards in front of the aircraft. This distance was the harmonization range for that bird. The net result was about 500 yards of the concentrated, lethal envelope of fire that was desired. Of course, firing *out of range* with this system almost guaranteed a miss, because the paths of the bullets diverged beyond the harmonization range. But since the convergence point was determined by a mechanical adjustment of the gun mounts, there was some latitude for the preferences of individual pilots who always flew the same aircraft.

The .30-caliber machine guns used during the opening months of the war were soon deemed not heavy enough. As newer aircraft were produced, the .50-caliber gun became the standard, with six or eight guns the normal complement for most fighters. An alternative to this array of .50s was a pair of 20-mm cannons mounted in each wing. These produced tremendous hitting and explosive power even when fired in short bursts.

The Germans, too, were confronted with the problem of getting more lead on the target, particularly when they were working against the B-17, which proved to be a tough customer to knock down. In order to stay beyond the range of the Flying Fort's .50-caliber guns, the Germans installed an extra 20-mm cannon in a gondola beneath each wing of the Bf-109. (These extra guns hung on the

Messerschmitt did exact a severe penalty in performance. Birds thus modified were intended only for hit-and-run attacks against bombers.) Then, in order to bring this firepower to bear on the bomber's weakest defensive area, they resorted to head-on attacks, hoping to get a kill before coming under the B-17's defending fire. This must have been one of the hairiest games of "chicken" imaginable, with formations of fighters and bombers approaching one another head-on at a combined speed of approximately 600 mph, with all guns blazing. Small wonder that the more experienced German squadron leaders complained that the younger troops were firing out of range and breaking off the attack too soon.

Special missions required even heavier guns on some types of aircraft, as can be seen by the two 40-mm cannons installed on Hawker Hurricanes used in the desert. Although it took a little time to learn how to control the aircraft against the recoil of the guns, the cannons were very effective against tanks. In a last-ditch effort to stop the indomitable B-17s, the Germans tried 50-mm cannons on the Me-262 jet aircraft introduced in August, 1944. One round from these guns could destroy a bomber; however, by this time, the Luftwaffe and Germany were crumbling, and it was a case of too little and too late.

While any of these cannons could destroy an aircraft that was a little over half a mile away, the chances of a hit at that distance were quite small. Therefore, even when the planes involved were equipped with cannons, the old tried-and-true rule of aerial combat still applied—get in close before opening fire. Another cogent reason for holding your fire until you were fairly sure of a hit was the limited ammunition supply for the large-bore guns. Most fighters could carry only enough ammunition for a total of six seconds of firing time with 20-mm guns—hardly enough time to correct your aim by using tracers during a long burst.

A year or so before the war in Europe ended, a new type of gunsight was introduced that was the best answer thus far to the problem of poor marksmanship. This was the gyroscopic sight. It still utilized a flat piece of glass, or the flat bulletproof windshield itself, on which to project an image. It also retained the range-setting capability of the earlier sights, but instead of two movable range bars, it used a ring of six small diamonds of light projected on the glass. The diameter of this ring could be adjusted by the pilot to correspond to the wingspan of the target, as with the range bars in reflector sights. However, this circular arrangement of the range marks made it easier for a pilot following a rolling target to estimate the proper firing distance. The major improvement offered by the gyroscopic sight was that it solved the problem of deflection shooting.

Before the gyroscopic sight, a lack of skill in deflection shooting, and the tendency to fire out of range, were the two major causes of bagging a "probable" instead of a "kill." The image *or* circle of light projected by the reflector sight could be used to estimate a deflection shot, but it was just that—an estimate. However, the new sight took the guesswork out of computing the proper lead on a target that had some relative movement with respect to the longitudinal axis of your airplane. Now it was no longer necessary to get dead astern of your adversary, where proper range was the only problem, to be sure of scoring some hits. The light image projected on the windshield was not fixed, as in earlier sights, but was able to move about three inches in any direction from center. The movement of this image was controlled by gyros within the sight that sensed the aircraft's rate of turn about the pitch and roll axes. In a hard-turning fight, the output from these gyros would tilt the gimbal-mounted reticle used to produce the sight picture in the proper direction and in the proper amount to provide the pilot with the correct lead angle.

As an example, let's assume you're following a guy in a hard-diving right turn and you're close enough to fire, but the nose of your bird is pointing right at his tail. Naturally, if you fired in this position, your bullets would go behind him, because by the time they got there, he would have moved farther to the right. In this situation, the image from the gyroscopic sight would be near the lower left-hand corner of your windscreen. The harder the turn, the greater the displacement in this direction. In order to get the pipper (the dot of light at the center of the image,) on the target, you would have to pull harder to get your nose pointed out in front of your opponent's aircraft. Once the pipper was on the target, you could hose him down with reasonable certainty of scoring a kill. Unfortunately, this is not as easy as it sounds, because your target is probably gyrating all over the sky in an attempt to shake you off his tail. This means that unless you're exactly matching his every move while pulling lead, the geometry of the sighting problem is constantly changing. This in turn means the sight picture is continually moving around on the windshield, thus necessitating more than ever your trying to hold the pipper on the target for an instant while hosing off a quick burst. Of course, the longer you hold the pipper on the target, the more accurate will be the solution furnished by the gunsight.

Although the Spitfire, the Messerschmitt Bf-109, and the Mitsubishi Zero, which will be discussed later, all could be considered outstanding fighters of World War II, there is one aircraft that is universally acclaimed as the premier fighter plane of the piston-driven era—the P-51 Mustang. This bird outclassed anything with a prop, and, as the sports saying goes, "It had all the moves." The Mustang initially saw combat in August, 1942, with an RCAF unit, and in December of the following year the first American outfit was equipped with P-51s. The "D" model with the bubble canopy was the most heavily produced of the line—nearly 8,000 were made. This version was powered by a Packard-built Merlin engine with 1,450 hp, which gave it a top speed of 437 mph. Armament consisted of six .50-caliber Browning machine guns. In some of the earlier models, the ammunition feed system jammed under high-G conditions. This was because the guns had to be canted 30 degrees in order to fit into the thin, laminar-flow wing. On the "D" model the wing was redesigned to allow upright gun installation, and the jamming problem was cured.

The P-51 had everything a fighter pilot desired—excellent maneuverability, a small turning radius, and a high rate of roll. In these departments, the Mustang was the equal of any other aircraft in the war, and surpassed most. The wide-tread landing gear made takeoffs, landings, and taxiing easy, and in the air the bird had honest stalling characteristics that gave plenty of warning. The P-51 was a forgiving airplane, and it took a real ham-fisted jock to get into trouble flying one. The bird flew well in instrument conditions, and still had positive feel and control response at 40,000 feet.

While flying at normal combat speeds of 300 to 420 mph, the P-51's controls retained their good feel, and they were manageable even at extremely high speeds, though under these conditions a sensitive hand at the helm was required. In vertical dives with the engine wide open, the controls stiffened appreciably in the region of 500 to 650 mph. Recovery from dives like these was best accomplished by using the trim system, because manual back pressure on the stick had a tendency to produce compressibility stalls.

The Mustang's ability to dive at very high speeds quickly negated the Bf-109's favorite defensive tactic, diving for the deck. Any bogey within reasonable range could be caught by a P-51 if the pilot elected to chase it with determination. If a Mustang pilot was at 30,000 feet and spotted a Bf-109 5,000 feet below him and already in its dive, he could catch the Messerschmitt by the time it reached 15,000 feet.

There were two features of the Merlin engine that P-51 drivers particularly enjoyed—an automatic supercharger and an automatic mixture control. Both of these items were controlled by a barometric switch that cut them in and out at the proper altitudes, and thus they allowed the pilot to keep his attention on tactical problems. The power plant also had a "war emergency setting" at which the engine developed absolute full power, but its operation in this range was limited to five minutes, and this top setting was intended to be used only for getting out of tight situations. The five-minute limit was imposed to prevent engine damage, but in one extreme case the emergency setting was used for 45 minutes without causing an engine failure.

The Mustang was the first fighter with truly long legs, and if it was equipped with two 108-gallon drop tanks, its escort range was increased to 850 miles. This gave round-trip fighter protection to bombers going to targets deep within Germany. A bird that was fitted out for one of these missions, with a full combat load plus drop tanks, did have some stability problems with fuel in the aft fuselage tank. This extreme rearward CG condition gave the airplane a tendency to spin unless it was flown very carefully.

The rugged construction of the Mustang allowed pilots to utilize a technique that made this very maneuverable fighter turn even better. Even at the speeds encountered in a dogfight, the P-51 driver could drop some flaps in order to reduce his turning radius. An enemy fighter trying to turn inside a Mustang that was using a tad of flaps would usually spin out. Although this worked well against the Bf-109 and Focke-Wulf FW-190, a new air-to-air tactic had to be developed when the Germans introduced the Me-262 jet fighter. In order to combat this faster bird successfully, the P-51 had to initiate a diving attack from a higher altitude to gain the speed necessary to close with the target. This dive had to be timed just right to catch the jet before it got close enough to a bomber to open fire. Defending against the Me-262 was less of a problem than keeping it away from the bombers, because P-51s could easily out-turn and outmaneuver the faster jets.

Two American aces, Don Gentile and John Godfrey, developed the team concept to a high level of perfection while flying P-51s. They would allow an enemy

P-51D——The only airplane the Mustang could not outmaneuver was the Spitfire, but, in contrast, the P-51 offered advantages in speed, range, comfort, ground handling characteristics, and stability on instruments that the Spitfire pilot never knew. It was the "sports model" of all the World War II fighters.
(Photo courtesy National Air and Space Museum, Smithsonian Institution)

fighter to get almost into firing range, and then they would each execute a hard break into a climbing turn—in opposite directions—and come back down to the attack. You can imagine the confusion of the German pilot—looking for an easy kill after his apparently undetected approach, he finds suddenly that everything has turned to worms and he has become the attackee.

The war in the Pacific did not bring about any significant changes in the area of fighter tactics. By the time the Allies could devote sufficient men and materiel to take the offensive in this theater, their pilots were well versed in the concept of team fighting, and in the proven value of the Fluid Four, or Fingertip, formation. Airspeed and altitude were still the keys to success, especially against the more maneuverable aircraft flown by the Japanese.

Like Germany, Japan had an opportunity to develop tactics and sharpen skills in aerial combat before entering World War II. The Sino-Japanese conflict, which began in 1937, mirrored Germany's success in Spain—a quick string of victories in which air power played a key role. However, another parallel between these two wars must be noted: both the Condor Legion and the Japanese fought against an enemy whose air force was outgunned, out-trained, and out-equipped.

In contrast to these similarities, one surprising dissimilarity emerges. In tactics, the Japanese were as far behind the times as the British had been in 1939. The Vee, rather than the Fingertip, was the standard formation that came out of the war with China.

Eventually what proved to be the Japanese's greatest failing was their failure to learn the need for teamwork between individual members of the flight. It was common practice, once the engagement had started and the Vee formations had been broken up by the initial onslaught, for each pilot to strike off on his own against a single target. The wild free-for-all that ensued resembled the large dogfights of World War I. Probably this penchant for meeting the enemy on a one-to-one basis resulted from the widespread Japanese belief in the absolute superiority of their fighters against all comers. In their book, maneuverability was a fighter plane's most highly valued characteristic, and the ability to out-turn an opponent was the most prized quality of all.

The Japanese based their fighter tactics on their demonstrated effectiveness during the war with China, which only served to entrench them more deeply. However, these techniques were of little value when the opposition refused to mix it up in a turning engagement. Given that maneuverability was the prime consideration in Japanese aircraft design, the Zero fighter was the logical outcome. This aircraft proved so effective during the early days of the war that it developed a mystique of invincibility. In fact, its reputation during that period was not unwarranted. The American P-40 Warhawk and the P-39 Airacobra both were capable of high diving speeds, and the F4F Wildcat possessed good maneuverability; but none of these birds had the overall performance of the Zero. When the P-38 Lightnings appeared on the scene, they too were manhandled when they tried to fight the Zero's brand of war—a hard-turning dogfight at medium or low altitude.

The secret of the Zero's success was its unusually light weight—it was only 6,026 pounds fully loaded. Comparing this with the P-40's 8,500 pounds, and the P-39's 7,500 pounds, and considering that these planes both had engines of approximately the same horsepower as the Zero's, it is easy to see where the advantage would lie. However, this benefit was not achieved without paying a price. In order to lighten the Zero, its designers eliminated armor plate and self-sealing fuel tanks. And in an effort to save even more weight and reduce drag, pilots had the radios and antenna masts removed from their airplanes. The Zero was powered by an 1,150-hp engine that gave it a top speed of 346 mph, and it was armed with two 20-mm cannons and four machine guns.

In performance, the Zero's main weaknesses were a limited ability at altitude, aileron heaviness at high airspeeds, and no capacity for high-speed dives. On the other hand, the American fighters in the Pacific were excellent performers at high altitude, and had engines and airframes that produced and allowed dives near the compressibility limit. The Americans quickly adopted new tactics to make the most of these advantages, and the scales of battle tipped to their side, for they could remain at altitude and choose the exact time and place of combat.

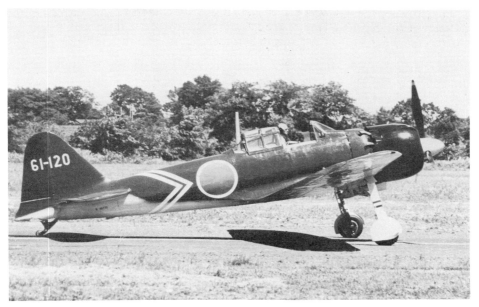

Mitsubishi Zero——master of the Pacific until the Battle of Midway, in June, 1942. After that, the Zero's effectiveness declined steadily to the low point of its career—flying lead in the kamikaze missions.
(Photo courtesy *Aerophile* Magazine)

The most successful tactic against a group of Zeros was a high-speed formation dive from high altitude to scatter the enemy, followed by a second-wave attack from altitude into the disorganized Japanese. A cardinal rule for the attackers was: Never let your speed get below 300 mph. This rule capitalized on the fact that above that speed, the Zero began to experience aileron heaviness.

Of all the birds that fought against the Zero, the F6F Hellcat was the only one that could hold its own with it in a fighter-versus-fighter dogfight. Designed in direct response to the threat posed by the Zero, the Hellcat outperformed it in just about every category—it had an engine twice as powerful as the Zero's, coupled to a lighter-than-usual airframe.

Despite the lack of armor and self-sealing tanks, the pilots who flew the Zero scorned the use of parachutes. They claimed that the chute straps restricted their movements in the cockpit too much in an air battle. But there was also another, and probably more important, reason they did not carry parachutes in their birds. The Zeros fought the majority of their battles near or over Allied installations, where bailout meant capture; capture was against the samurai code, and any fighter pilot who allowed himself to be taken prisoner brought disgrace to his family.

In retrospect, the rise and fall of the effectiveness of the Zero symbolized the fortunes of the Japanese empire. The Zero provided the Japanese with a tangible national reflection of their prowess in battle, in victory and then in defeat.

One of the most effective fighters used by the Allies in the Pacific campaign was the F4U Corsair. This "Bent-Wing Bird," as it was called, was unanimously considered the finest naval fighter of World War II, and in many respects it closely rivaled the P-51 for the honor of being the best piston-driven fighter of the war. Its all-around great performance was achieved by wedding the most powerful reciprocating engine ever designed for a fighter to one of the largest props ever used. A 2,000-hp Pratt & Whitney engine swung a three-bladed prop that was over 13 feet in diameter. Such a combination gave the Corsair a top speed of 415 mph. In an emergency, the horsepower could be boosted to 2,250 for a maximum of five minutes. The standard armament for the Corsair was six .50-caliber machine guns, with 391 rounds each.

F4U Corsair——the F4U was the first single-engine fighter in the United States to break the 400 mph barrier. This speed proved to be its greatest advantage over the Zero. The proper use of speed dictated the fighter tactics of the day.
(Photo courtesy *Aerophile* Magazine)

The inverted gull wing neatly solved the problem of how to utilize so large a prop and yet retain the short, sturdy landing gear needed for carrier operations. The early F4Us had difficulties with carrier landings because of poor forward visibility (due to the long nose), too-stiff landing gear that resulted in a "built-in bounce," and a tendency to swing badly on touchdown. These were corrected by raising the cockpit to give better visibility, increasing the height of the tail-wheel leg to improve directional stability, and using a longer-stroke oleo strut with a low rebound ratio to solve the bounce problem. In the air, the Corsair had good handling characteristics across the board—maneuverability and rate of roll were good, and the plane had no undesirable tendencies at either high or low speed. However, it gave little or no warning of a normal stall, and when it did stall, the left wing often dropped sharply. This was later corrected by adding a spoiler to the right wing.

In normal flight attitudes, the F4U's cockpit visibility was good, particularly beneath the airplane, for the pilot sat behind the trailing edge of the wing. The F4U

F4U Corsair——the effectiveness of the Corsair in the close air support role and the distinctive noise produced by the airflow through the wing-root oil coolers prompted Japanese troops to nickname this bird "Whistling Death."
(Photo courtesy *Aerophile* Magazine)

had to be flown every minute it was airborne, especially under instrument conditions and at high altitude, and it was common practice for the pilot to be trimming constantly, even during maneuvering flight.

A couple of unusual features found on this bird were landing gear that could be used as a dive brake (though its use was not too wise a move in combat), and a floorless cockpit, which gave one the impression of sitting on the edge of a deep hole.

The Corsair was in production for 13 years, longer than any other American fighter, and proved to be a rugged workhorse that could be used with equal effectiveness on air-to-air and close support missions. In the former category, it achieved an enviable victory/loss ratio of 11.3 to 1. Like the Mustang, the Corsair was active in a ground-support role in the Korean War.

As the curtain fell on World War II, the era of the piston-driven fighter was replaced by that of the jet. The new designs flew at speeds and altitudes unheard of only a few years earlier, yet they caused little change in basic fighter tactics. What would later be called the Fingertip formation along with the techniques of fighting in pairs were still as valid as they had been in the days of Boelcke and Immelmann. One thing had changed, though—the fighter's role in the overall scheme of war had been firmly established. The fighter was no longer just an adjunct to ground operations, but now played an essential part in both the tactical and strategic phases of any campaign.

The development of nuclear weapons posed a new problem to those in the fighter business. The defense against bombing raids of the future had to be perfect— if even one bomber got through, the devastation it could wreak would be incalculable. So the jet interceptor was developed, and military men continued to refine that new branch of fighter tactics utilized against the night bombing raids of the Luftwaffe. The radar-equipped interceptor, operating under radar control, was to become the predominant weapons system of the 1950s and 1960s.

In contrast to the large number of fighters of different design that saw action during World War I, only about 20 individual types were used by the United States, England, and Germany combined during the second flap, and these figures include night fighters. This was to be expected, however, because the design of the reciprocating-engine fighter reached its zenith in the latter days of the war, and significant improvements were few and far between as the state of the art neared perfection.

How the fighter pilot in World War II plied his trade is best summed up in a briefing given by Colonel Hubert Zemke to his P-47 pilots in the 56th Fighter Group, known as the "Wolfpack," which destroyed 1,006 enemy aircraft during their tour in the European theater. Zemke himself accounted for 17.75:

"A fighter pilot must possess an inner urge to do combat. The will at all times to be offensive will develop into his own tactics. If your enemy is above you, never let your speed drop, and don't climb, because you'll lose too much speed. If you're attacked on the same level, just remember you can outclimb him. Beware of thin cirrus clouds—the enemy can look down through them but you can't look up through them. Don't go weaving through valleys of cumulus clouds, either with a squadron or by yourself. The enemy can be on your tail before you know it. When popping down out of a cloud, or up, always do a quick turn and look back. You may have jumped out directly in front of a gun barrel. When attacked by large numbers of enemy aircraft, meet them head-on. In most cases half of them will break and go down. Handle all those remaining in an all-out fight until you're down to one—then take him on."

World War II: Beating the Odds

An account by Lieutenant Dean Caswell, USMC, flying off the USS *Bunker Hill* in the Pacific; 7 total victories:

"April 26, 1945, in the Okinawa campaign. We were providing air cover 150 miles north of Okinawa for three radar picket destroyers. A vital part of the radar warning net of Vice Admiral Marc A. Mitscher's famed Task Force 58, these destroyers had been having fits as a result of kamikaze attacks. Action began with my three F4U Corsairs vectored toward a bogey coming in high. Up we went for the enemy, clawing for altitude at full throttle. There was a bad haze that got worse as we gained altitude, and we couldn't see a thing. We were high, on oxygen, and it was extremely cold up there. 'Many bogies dead ahead, twelve miles,' rasped the controller's voice in our headphones. If we couldn't see any better than this, we were going to miss them. Everything was a dirty yellow haze. We heard a 'Tally Ho!' from nearby friendly planes and almost immediately saw aircraft going down in flames about two miles to starboard. It was quite a show. Suddenly I felt my stomach tighten and I got an ominous feeling of hostile presence.

We had run right smack into 20 to 25 Jap fighters in the haze. We were no longer spectators enjoying someone else's flamers.

"Initially we tried to fight by the book. The lead F4U did a split-S after a Zeke, and I was left with the third man of the flight, First Lieutenant John McManus, USMC. You might say we were left holding the bag, the bag being a sky full of Zekes and Tonys (Zeros and Kawasaki Ki-61s). Things happened fast. I was on their tail. Then they were on mine. Some of those Japs were good pilots. Round and round, tight, high-G turns and milling confusion. In this melee I steadied on a meatball target and it exploded in orange flames as I pulled the trigger. This was not a new feeling, for I had done it before, but each time my exultation barely overcame the paralyzing fear that grips the vitals when you are fighting overwhelming odds. There were plenty of targets. The Japs were going round and round and we were in the middle. The battle sorted itself out into that kind of thing. Mac got one, and I saw it flame out of the corner of my eye. I got another one. We began to weave, Mac and I, protecting each other, until I got caught between two fires, a Zeke in front and a Tony in back. In much less time than it takes to say it, my six .50-calibers blew the Zeke apart and Mac got the Tony hugging my tail.

"We again pressed the attack. Our only salvation lay in aggressiveness and in keeping the enemy confused, and confused they were now. They had lost seven aircraft in as many minutes and were in danger of shooting each other down in their efforts to get at us. All of their losses had been huge, terrifying flamers, those colossal gouts of fire that so often ended the lives of Japanese pilots. In the haze, these livid firebursts were heightened in effect. It probably tipped the balance in our favor that they did not get us and yet two Corsairs, full of fight, kept coming at them and scoring flamers. Mac and I continued to hustle, and our shots were soon snap bursts at fleeing Japs. We actually turned the rest for home, with my Corsair riding herd on two Zekes. I put one of them in my sight and drew a blank. No ammo. I signaled to Mac and he took over, sending another Jap down in flames."

World War II: The Ingredients of Victory

"**G**" is a term used to indicate the force of gravity. A 4-G turn forces a pilot into his seat in such a way as to make his body seem to weigh four times its actual weight. Thus, a 200-pound pilot for the duration of his 4-G turn weighs the equivalent of 800 pounds. Enduring a physical strain like that while manipulating a gunsight and throttle controls, and monitoring the radio require almost phenomenal concentration. Keeping the aircraft at the proper speed and in the proper attitude are added to this burden. On top of it all, during battle, is the never-ending watch for the enemy. Some pilots cannot do all these things simultaneously, and as a consequence fail to survive. These tasks as handled under heavy Gs are graphically described in Lieutenant Colonel Clarence Anderson's story (his total was 16.25 victories):

"We were escorting bombers to the Ludwigshafen-Mannheim area on May 27, 1944. Our group was equipped with P-51s.

"We were flying a group formation with my squadron on the right flank, and as we rendezvoused with the 'big friends' (B-17s) at around 27,000 feet, we crossed over the bombers and started to make a lazy turn to the left. The group leader identified our bombers and then immediately someone called over the R/T that a large number of enemy fighters was about to attack the bomber formation immediately in front of ours. We released our drop tanks and turned sharp left to engage these fighters. At this point the flight I was leading was placed on the outside of the turn, and therefore was vulnerable to attack from the rear. Before I could look behind, my element leader, First Lieutenant Edward K. Simpson, Jr., of Hampton, New Jersey, called out that four Me-109s were diving on our tails from five o'clock high.

"My element turned sharply into the Me-109s as we fell into a close string formation. The lead German was a sharp customer, but his attack was thwarted by our sharp turn. The four Germans pulled up and began circling with us. At full throttle and rpm we were able to maintain our turn inside them. Climbing to 29,000 feet, we equaled them and began to gain a little on them on each turn. The Germans decided to try something else.

"Turning east, three of them flew level at 29,000 feet while the number-four man climbed as quickly as possible in the same direction. Lieutenant Simpson and his wingman pursued the climbing Me-109. With my wingman, I continued to chase the other three enemy aircraft. They were at full throttle, as we could see black exhaust pouring from their engines. Our own throttles were clear to the firewalls, and we slowly crept up behind the last German. Holding my fire until about 250 yards dead astern, I fired a short burst and got some good hits around the wing roots and fuselage. More black smoke began to pour from his aircraft, only this time it wasn't exhaust. He rolled over on his back and flew upside down in an attempt to shake me, but I stayed level and fired another close-range burst. Chunks flew off and he burst into flames and

began spinning lazily down to the deck.

"We closed in now on the remaining two Germans, who saw us coming. The leader pulled up sharply into a climbing turn, and his wingman rolled over and went diving for home. We cut across the leading German's climbing circle, which he tightened. I was forced to pull up sharply to avoid hitting this German because he now reversed his turn and was pulling his nose up for a shot at my wingman, Lieutenant Skara. Skara threw his Mustang into a spin to avoid being shot, and as he descended the Me-109 followed him down. I followed. As I closed the range, the German broke violently into a climbing left turn and I had to pull up sharply again. The German reversed his turn, pulling up steeply for a short burst at me. He was very close, and I could see the detail and color of his highly polished aircraft. Luckily, he couldn't get his nose high enough to get a shot at me. He stalled just before I did, and as we both nosed down to gain speed I was again behind him. Once more he pulled up into a tight left climbing turn. This time I throttled back slightly and stayed inside his turn. He saw that I wasn't going to overshoot him this time and he pulled almost straight up. Following, I was able to get in a long burst which connected in his cockpit and engine. He burst into flames and smoke, rolled slightly, and then dove straight for the earth from 30,000 feet."

CHAPTER 3
THE NEW TECHNOLOGIES: KOREA AND VIETNAM

The Korean War did not bring about any radical new developments in fighter tactics. The basic concepts of World War II remained valid in the era of jet propulsion. The primary mission of the fighter squadrons on both sides of the Yalu was the same—to gain and keep air superiority over the combat area—and their efforts to achieve this goal followed similar, and familiar, patterns.

In this discussion I will only consider the two premier fighters of the Korean War, the F-86 Sabre and the MiG-15, the birds that were mainly involved in seeking air superiority. The United Nations forces used other fighters, including the F-80, F-84, F9F, P-51, and F4U, but theirs was mostly the ground support mission.

The Fingertip, or Fluid Four, formation was flown by both the MiGs and the F-86s, and the basic fighting unit was still the element of two aircraft, with the leader doing the shooting and the wingman the looking. During an engagement, the wingman would move into the fighting wing position, which was the same distance out from the leader, but a little farther back. The idea was that the wingman would be free to maneuver within a 60-degree cone extending from the leader's tail while the leader worked to get in a shot or shake off a bogey. Of course, the best position for the wingman was on the edge of the cone, where visual coverage to the rear was maximized; however, in a hard-turning fight, the wingman would often spend more time trying to stay with the lead and out of his way than providing much lookout behind the flight.

The faster airspeeds of the new fighters, coupled with the extreme altitudes at which they normally operated, required that the spacing between individual aircraft be increased to 1,500 feet, and that between elements to 3,000 feet. The thin air at 35,000 to 40,000 feet, and the inherent characteristics of jet engines at those altitudes, posed unique problems with respect to formation flying and aircraft handling during an engagement. Power settings in jet aircraft are not established by using manifold pressure, or direct engine rpm, as in piston-driven fighters. Instead, they are set on an rpm gauge that measures percent of full engine rpm, rather than actual revolutions of the turbine. Nearly all the effective power of a jet engine is delivered only in the last 20 percent of full rpm—that is, from 80 to 100 percent. Therefore, in a combat area, the formation leader would normally set his power at 96 percent, in order to keep his airspeed as high as possible and still give the wingman something to play with. As you might guess, this 4-percent was not sufficient to allow the wingman to catch up if he fell even a short distance behind during a turn. Maintaining position in tactical formation in jet aircraft requires the utmost in judgment, and no small amount of finesse, during the constant maneuvering that is the key to survival in a hostile area. Once the "Tally Ho!" was called, all throttles immediately went to 100-percent power, and the guy who was out of position at that point really had his work cut out for him. His only hope of regaining position was if the turn into the attacking force was made in his direction.

Other factors that compounded the problem of maintaining good formation at high altitude were the slow response time of jet engines, and the extreme aerodynamic cleanness of modern jet fighters. When the throttle of a reciprocating-engine fighter is advanced quickly, you get more or less instantaneous response in the form of increased airspeed. Not so with the jet! If you were cruising at 92-percent power and firewalled the throttle to 100 percent, it would take a few seconds for the turbine to build up to that speed—the increase in airspeed would definitely be slower than with a prop. Assuming you were at full power in an attempt to catch up with your flight lead, and you were just about in the proper position but did not correctly anticipate when to ease off on the power, your new problem would be even worse than your old one. Because of their designed-in lack of air resistance, jet fighters do not slow down quickly when the power is reduced by a small amount, and you keep on sailing for what seems like forever out in front of your lead, until your speeds synchronize. In a combat situation, where flight integrity is an absolute must, each pilot had to constantly consider the acceleration lag and deceleration lead that were the facts of life in jet aircraft.

At the altitudes where the Sabres and MiGs were operating, airspeed is measured not in knots or miles per hour, but in Mach number, which is the relationship of the speed of the aircraft to the speed of sound at that altitude. If the Mach meter indicated .85 M, the bird was traveling at 85 percent of the speed of sound.

Mach number is a more useful measure to the pilot at high altitude than indicated airspeed, which might register in the neighborhood of 250 knots (290 mph) while true airspeed would be near 550 knots (635 mph). Knowing how close you were to Mach 1.0, the speed of sound, was also important, for aircraft of that era that could go supersonic usually had some undesirable handling characteristics in the trans-sonic region (.95 M to 1.05 M) that had to be anticipated.

Cruising in a jet airplane at high altitude with a relatively low indicated airspeed put a limitation on the number of Gs you could pull if you were bounced. The rapid bleed-off of airspeed experienced during a hard turn at these heights could quickly stall the aircraft, and thus make it easy pickings for enemy fighters. Gone was the ability to make the hard 5- or 6-G breaks so common in World War II; and above 35,000 feet, gone also was the ability to make a climbing turn and meet a diving enemy formation head-on. If a break was necessary, it nearly always had to be combined with a dive so that the aircraft's energy level could be kept high. (The concept of energy maneuverability will be discussed more fully in the chapter on basic fighter maneuvers.)

Naturally, the problems of flying and fighting at high speeds and high altitudes were common to both the MiGs and the Sabres. They are presented here as a backdrop of new "givens" against which the aerial combat of the jet age must be considered.

As groups of Sabres approached "MiG Alley," a 100-mile-long area running down the northwest coast of what is now North Korea, they were arrayed in what was called a "train formation." This mass formation allowed the greatest number of fighters to come in contact with the MiGs, and also considerably lessened the chances of a surprise attack on any individual flight of Sabres.

The "train" consisted of six flights of four aircraft each, arranged in a loose trail formation, with about a mile of separation between flights. This kept all flights within easy supporting distance of each other, and yet permitted each individual flight, which was in Fingertip formation, a maximum of maneuverability and offensive flexibility. Approaching the Yalu, the F-86s leveled off at an altitude just below the contrail layer, which was normally around 30,000 feet. This made spotting the approaching MiGs relatively easy, because they would always attack from a higher altitude, and thus give themselves away as soon as they hit the "con" layer. The Sabres also stayed at around 30,000 feet because they had better maneuvering capability at this altitude than at 40,000 feet.

Once the MiGs were sighted, the F-86s jettisoned their drop tanks and took on the enemy in flights of four, or in elements of two. Since the game was being played on the MiGs' home field, the enemy did have one big advantage—radar coverage of the battle area. The inbound flights of Sabres were picked up early enough to allow the MiGs plenty of time to scramble and climb to an altitude above the 86s, and to position themselves favorably for the attack. Thus, the MiGs were able to choose the time and place of combat, or, if the odds were not right, to avoid a fight altogether.

With their superior altitude, the MiGs initiated the bounce about 70 percent of the time, and the tactics of the 86s revolved around this fact. If the Sabres were surprised, the best move was a hard-diving turn to gain some room to maneuver for a better position. If the enemy was picked up some distance out, the 86s swung to meet them head-on and break up their attack formation.

Some engagements in the Korean War started out at around 35,000 feet and ended up right on the deck, with fighters still turning and twisting in an attempt to get behind the opposition. Most of the passes, however, were of the hit-and-run variety, because of the extremely high closing speeds and the large amount of airspace it took to turn a jet fighter around at these speeds. In nearly all cases, the MiGs employed the hit-and-run attack, which usually took one of the following forms: a diving attack for one firing pass and then a sharp pull-up into the sun to exploit the MiGs' exceptional rate of climb; a group attacking from an orbit 5,000 to 6,000 feet above the Sabres, with MiGs diving singly and then zooming back up into the orbit; and, after the fall of 1951, when MiG pilot proficiency and gunnery were noticeably poorer, a one-pass attack by large groups of MiGs from altitude from either side of the route used by the F-86s, followed by a run for the Yalu at full blower.

The team fighting concept had apparently been not too well learned by the MiG pilots, because early in the war they made their attacks individually, with no protecting wingman. The hard lessons being taught by the Sabre jocks over the Yalu eventually hit home, and later the North Koreans adopted the element as the fighting unit.

The home-field advantage also gave the bad guys another big plus—more time in the combat area. The MiGs were operating relatively close to their home bases, while the Sabres had to fly 250 miles just to get to MiG Alley, which allowed them only about 25 minutes of patrol time in the area. If an engagement took place, this time was even shorter, because at full throttle a jet's rate of fuel consumption is prodigious, and the rate of fuel consumption increased as the fight worked down to lower altitudes. The Sabres normally had to head for home with one-third of their fuel (about 275 gallons) remaining, and if the weather was bad, this amount had to be increased accordingly. Naturally, there were many times in the heat of battle when a break-off for minimum fuel could not be accomplished easily. The only recourse for a pilot in this situation was to break off the fight at the first opportunity, climb as high as the bird would go, and, when safely out of the combat area, shut the engine down to save fuel and glide part of the way home. The idea was to save just enough gas to light up the engine as you neared the field and have one shot at a power-on approach and landing. Many times it didn't work out that way, and there would be two or three birds in the flameout pattern, making deadstick approaches to the field.

The high rates of closure mentioned above, often exceeding 1,200 mph during a head-on pass, became the norm for combat between jet aircraft. This, in turn, necessitated split-second timing in maneuvering and shooting by the pilots on both sides, and the need for instantaneous decisions was complicated by the fact that, at a quick glance, the MiGs and the Sabres looked quite a bit alike.

Although the Korean War did not engender significantly new tactics, aircraft design and performance, as typified by the F-86 and the MiG-15, took a quantum leap forward. Overall, these aircraft were pretty much evenly matched, but each of them had characteristics that gave it a slight edge in certain situations. The engines in both the MiG and the Sabre delivered approximately the same amount of thrust (about 5,900 pounds), but the MiG weighed around 6,000 pounds less than the F-86. This weight difference allowed the MiG to outclimb the Sabre at all altitudes, and particularly at high altitudes. Conversely, the 86 could outdive the MiG, because above 25,000 feet it had no limiting Mach number, whereas the MiG

MiG-15——while light and maneuverable, the MiG-15 had instability problems, poor spin characteristics, and gave no warning of an approaching stall.
(Photo courtesy National Air and Space Museum, Smithsonian Institution)

was limited to .92 M. The MiG incorporated an interesting feature to insure that this Mach number would not be exceeded—at .92 M the speed brakes automatically extended. This must have really watered the eyes of the MiG drivers as they raced for the sanctity of the Yalu with a Sabre on their tails and saw their speed creeping above .91 M. About all they could do here to dodge the silver bullet was to convert their speed into a high-altitude zoom—one of the MiG's more outstanding capabilities.

Below 25,000 feet, the Sabre still had a higher red-line speed than the MiG, because at medium to low altitudes the MiG suffered from poor lateral and directional stability at high speed. Loss of control was a possibility under these conditions. Once these shortcomings were known, the high-speed dive became the best evasive tactic for the F-86s.

Later versions of the MiG were allowed to go to .98 M in a dive, but were not supersonic. The North Korean defector who brought the first MiG-15 to the UN forces stated that a Russian pilot had tried to go through Mach 1 in a MiG, but the wings had collapsed.

The MiG's control problems, plus a slow rate of roll, gave the Sabres a slight edge in a very high-speed turning engagement. At slower speeds the turning radius of both birds was about equal; however, the Sabres were equipped with full-span leading-edge slats, and these would occasionally cause the same problem they had caused on the Messerschmitt in World War II. A redesigned, solid leading edge that was lengthened chordwise by a few inches solved this difficulty, and also improved the Sabre's top speed, range, and high-altitude maneuverability.

The tremendous progress in aircraft design after World War II was not matched by similar advances in armament systems. Both the Sabre and the MiG had combinations of guns and sights that were not altogether suitable for aerial combat in the jet age. The F-86s still used the gyroscopic sight that had been developed late in World War II; however, it now had a new feature that provided the last piece to the pilot's sighting puzzle—range. A small radar set mounted in the upper lip of the intake duct automatically locked on to any target directly in front of the Sabre and provided the pilot with exact range information.

Although the aiming problem was solved, the F-86 was not well enough armed to maximize the advantages offered by the sight. It still carried six .50-caliber machine guns, and although their rate of fire was good, they lacked the knockout punch of a cannon. The limited aiming and shooting time available in modern air combat, which had prompted the use of cannon-armed fighters in World War II, was even more of a problem with the jets in Korea. But in spite of the known advantages of 20-mm guns, the six .50s remained the standard Sabre armament until the end of the war.

The MiG's problems in this area were just about the opposite of the Sabre's. MiGs were equipped with three cannons, two 27-mm and one 37-mm, but their rates of fire were too slow for a fighter-versus-fighter engagement. The MiG had a gyroscopic sight, but it did not have the radar-ranging capability; this, coupled with the low rate of fire and poor gunnery, put the North Koreans at a considerable armament disadvantage against the Sabres. An improvement in gun installation over the arrangement found in World War II was made by both sides; the guns were now mounted in the fuselage, which gave a better concentration of fire and eliminated the harmonization problem.

Combat at high speeds and high altitudes necessitated many developments that had been unheard of or rejected as unnecessary luxuries in World War II. Ejection seats, which enabled a pilot to get out of a disabled bird despite windblast and high G forces, became standard equipment. The extremes of temperature that jets operated in (ranging from 90 degrees F on the ground to –60 degrees F at altitude) dictated a cockpit air-conditioning and defrosting system in addition to the normal pressurization system. Flight controls were now hydraulically operated, because the air loads on the control surfaces at high speeds prevented their being moved by the conventional cable-and-bell-crank setup. Now, moving the stick merely repositioned a hydraulic control valve that metered the correct amount of fluid to the actuating cylinders. Of course, this did away with the normal feedback from the control surfaces that gave the pilot a "feel" for the aircraft in any given flight condition. This sensation now had to be artificially induced by bungee cords, or spring mechanisms, attached to the control system.

The MiGs were a little more austere than the Sabres. They had no provisions for G suits, had cramped cockpits, and lacked an adequate canopy defrosting system. The cockpit layout seemed almost primitive when compared to that of the F-86, and the profusion of pipes and valves resembled a plumber's nightmare. The sophistication of the Sabre's cockpit, from the standpoint of handiness and ease of operation, is clearly evident in a comparison of the two.

Considering the numerous complex systems required to operate a modern jet fighter, one would assume that it would be terribly vulnerable to hits in any area. But, in fact, with fewer moving parts overall, a jet aircraft is pretty tough to shoot down. Because it was designed to fly 200 mph faster than the typical World War II fighter, the jet fighter had to be more ruggedly constructed, and made of stronger materials, than its predecessors. Fighters in the Second War had very thin outer skins and used a large amount of internal bracing to carry the main structural loads. Jets, on the other hand, had relatively thick skins and less internal bracing, which spread the structural load over a greater area and minimized the damage caused by enemy fire. Both the Sabres and the MiGs could absorb a considerable amount of battle damage and still make it back to the home drome.

F-86——the fighter beneath the skin. It was necessary to cram as much as possible into the shallow area of the frame just beneath the external skin, because the interior of the fuselage had to contain the air duct, the engine, and the major fuel cells.
(Photo by Frank J. O'Brien)

F-86——this model of the Sabre incorporated the "flying tail." Both the elevator and the stabilizer moved in response to control stick inputs. This new system provided greater control effectiveness plus retention of control sensitivity at high Mach numbers.
(Photo courtesy National Air and Space Museum, Smithsonian Institution)

One of the primary reasons for the lopsided score run up against the MiGs by the Sabres was the superior training, teamwork, and aggressiveness shown by the American pilots. Nearly always flying against considerable odds, they carried the fight to the enemy whenever and wherever he appeared. "Attack!" was the byword, and this outlook gave rise to the concept from which the title of this book came— every man a tiger! Tigers they were, with the experienced veterans of World War II leading, teaching the new guys the techniques of the art of war. The high degree of teamwork proved that tigers are made as well as born.

The MiG pilots, on the other hand, were for the most part the antitheses of the tigers in the Sabres, and displayed a surprising lack of professional skill. Unless they greatly outnumbered the F-86s, they were averse to accepting a challenge. If the Sabres bounced a small number of MiGs or had them boxed in, the MiGs quickly tried as a group to make a dash for home. If a MiG found a Sabre on its tail, it tried every means to escape, using cloud cover, violent maneuvers, or a run for the Yalu, rather than attempting to turn the tables in its favor. Their poor teamwork and lack of concern for their squadron mates is shown by a statement made by the North Korean defector, Lieutenant Ro Kum Suk, who said that he often saw Sabre pilots take great risks in trying to drive a MiG off another Sabre's tail, but that in all the time he flew for North Korea, he never once saw a Red pilot try to save another's life.

When all the dust had settled after the war, the numerous big and small advantages of the Sabre over the MiG added up to one big plus in the win column. A total of 839 MiGs were shot down during the war, 800 of them by F-86s, while only 58 Sabres were lost—which gave the 86s an enviable 14:1 win-loss ratio. The Korean Conflict proved not only that the characteristics of successful fighter pilots had not changed in 35 years and three wars, but that the demands of jet combat had made these characteristics even more important.

While the Korean War was in progress, there was a growing realization in America that we urgently needed an effective air defense system. The Russians had The Bomb, and the rapid growth of their strategic bomber force, coupled with a variety of muscle flexings around the world, made it apparent that developing one was our only course of action.

Because of the destructive capability of nuclear weapons, the proposed air defense network had to be airtight—capable of detecting, tracking, and stopping every inbound hostile raid. This stringent requirement brought into being a program whose scope, complexity, and cost were a bit staggering, but which was essential to our national survival.

What eventually resulted were three radar defense lines guarding the approaches from Russia to the North American continent. The farthermost was the DEW Line, with 64 radar stations stretching from the Aleutians, across extreme northern Canada, through Greenland to Iceland. The Mid-Canada Line was next; and along the northern border of the United States was the Pine Tree Line. An elaborate communications system, utilizing tropospheric scatter, connected all of these sites, and would allow target information to be passed southward as a raid progressed. The majority of the installations on the first two lines were early warning sites, but the radar stations of the Pine Tree Line could control fighters; it was in their area that the first interceptions would take place.

The requirements for the aircraft that would operate within this system seemed farfetched, given the existing fighter designs of the day. The air defense interceptor had to have a quick reaction time—that is, it had to be capable of getting airborne in two to five minutes after the scramble order was given. It also had to be designed so that when the mission was over, it could be refueled and rearmed in 30 minutes or less. The bird had to have a rate of climb that would enable it to get to 40,000 feet in six to eight minutes, and it had to be able to cruise at a high Mach number once it got up there. Long range was another requirement, so the fighter could engage the enemy at a considerable distance from American cities.

Naturally, the plane had to have airborne radar that could locate and track a target, and supply the pilot with steering information that would fly him through the correct attack geometry. (In some interceptor designs, the job of handling the radar was given to a crew member whose cockpit was behind the pilot's. He eventually became known as the "GIB," or the "Guy In Back.")

Because the air defense interceptor would have to operate at night and in all kinds of weather, guns and cannons were not a practical armament system. Instead, to insure one-pass killing capability and to minimize the interceptor's exposure to defensive guns, rockets (and, later, missiles) were the weapons put in all of these birds. Because of these weapons' relatively long effective range, the interceptor could fire its armament and break away from the target before coming within range of the bomber's guns. The requirement for all-weather operation also dictated the need for navigation and communications gear that would normally not be found in the fighter aircraft of that period.

When all of these requirements were wrapped up in three different designs—the F-86D, the F-89, and the F-94—the teeth were finally added to our air defense system. These birds were based mainly at fields along the eastern, northern, and western borders of the United States; some were deployed into Canadian provinces.

The teamwork between and within elements that was typical of day-fighter tactics proved to be of little use to the all-weather interceptor. It would be strictly a one-man show; each aircraft would be under individual radar control, and it would be a one-on-one contest between him and the bomber. If more than one bird was committed to the same target, there would be no attempt at mutual support; the interceptors would be kept at least three to five miles apart by the radar controller. The rationale behind this was that the air defense game would be played against the enemy's strategic bomber force, and all the action would take place far beyond the range of any fighter cover. So convinced were the planners that the interceptors would operate in an environment free of hostile fighters, that air-to-air tactics were not taught to interceptor aircrews. It was also felt that becoming proficient in the interpretation and operation of radar, along with learning to fly the aircraft, was in itself a full-time job. Of particular importance was instrument flying; this skill had to be developed to the point where it was almost subconscious. During nearly every phase of a typical intercept mission, the pilot had to devote a considerable amount of his attention to the radar scope; therefore, cross-checking the gauges had to become an almost peripheral action.

The high-side gunnery pass, so dear to the hearts of the day-fighter troops, was replaced by tactics better suited to the armament of the interceptor and to operating under instrument conditions. Until missiles came along in the late '50s, all rocket armament was designed to be launched in a wings-level attitude, with no Gs on the aircraft. To satisfy these conditions, and to maximize the chances for a kill, the 90-degree beam attack was developed. The attack geometry, as seen from above, is depicted in this sketch:

The interceptor is vectored by ground radar to a position about 50 miles in front of, and to one side of, the target (position 1). At the correct time, the interceptor is turned toward the target so that their extended flight paths will cross at a 90-degree angle. During this turn, the target should start to appear on the interceptor's

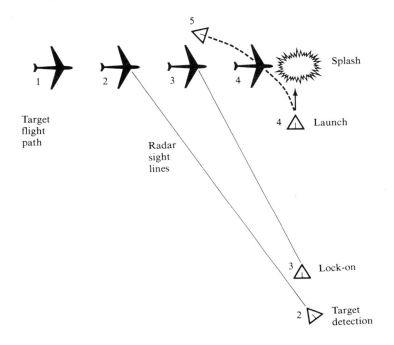

The 90-degree beam attack

radar scope (position 2), and when he rolls out on his final attack heading (position 3), the radar can be locked on the target and can begin to supply the pilot with accurate steering information. The radar system then computes a firing distance (position 4). The weapons will be launched toward a point in front of the target; and the hope is that both of the principals in this last phase of the attack will arrive at one point at the same time. Immediately after the launch, the interceptor breaks away to the rear of the target (position 5).

Modifications of this optimum attack were of course possible, with the extreme case being a direct head-on. The high closing rate generated by this situation only made things tougher for the interceptor crew, because at high speed it was much more difficult to achieve a lock-on, and the steering became quite a bit more critical.

In the late 1950s, the gods of war smiled on the defensive side of this contest, as bombers that could fly above 40,000 feet and maintain a respectable Mach number became available. The performance of the fighters of the period began to taper off above that altitude, so a variant was developed. This tactic was called the snap-up maneuver; it employed the same attack geometry as the 90-degree beam or frontal attack, but the interceptor stayed 10,000 to 15,000 feet below the target's altitude, where its maneuvering potential was higher. Target acquisition and lock-on were accomplished by tilting the radar antenna so that it would look up rather than straight ahead. Elevation steering was ignored until the last few seconds before firing, when the aircraft was pulled up smartly into about a 45-degree climb, and the weapons were fired at their precomputed time.

In order for the snap-up to be successful, the offense had to come up with some technological advances of its own. Enter guided missiles developed to replace the unguided rockets. Their ability to steer out the final errors of the attack resulted in a very high kill probability.

Another area that required special tactics, as well as a high level of coordination between ground radar, the interceptor crew, and other birds running on the same target, was working against the strike force flying at a low level in an effort to escape radar detection. Working against a target at 1,000 feet nearly always meant that the 90-degree beam attack had to be converted to a stern approach when the interceptor was about five miles from the target—an approach much like the one the Beaufighter pilots used in World War II. Low-level intercepts at night or in bad weather demanded the utmost proficiency in both instrument flying and ability to interpret a radar scope saturated with ground clutter.

Naturally, the bad guys in the bombers would not be just sitting there waiting for the interceptors to hose them out of the sky. They had their own bag of tricks to use against radar-equipped interceptors that, when used skillfully, could make it a long day or night for the fighter jocks. The oldest, and yet one of the most effective, was chaff, or "window," as it was called by the British, who first used it against German radar in mid-1943.

Chaff is small pieces of aluminum foil, cut to precise lengths and dropped out of the bombers in bundles, each bundle about the size of two packages of cigarettes placed end to end. When the bundle opens in the airstream, the foil forms a small cloud that reflects radar beautifully, and presents a very inviting blip on the scope of an interceptor.

Electronic jamming is another very effective method of denying the interceptor target location or range; it can also be used to trick the interceptor's radar into believing the target is in a completely different position in space than it actually is. A bomber can also take evasive action to confuse approaching interceptors (this works especially well at low levels); and the confusion factor can be multiplied if the target uses spoofing techniques, as was common when all interceptors were controlled by voice commands from ground radar operators. If radio contact with the intercept director was poor or intermittent, the fighter could be given false headings or altitudes by the bomber crew; if this was done cleverly, it could ruin the entire intercept attempt, and in many cases it allowed the target to escape completely.

The introduction of Semi-Automatic Ground Environment (SAGE) in the late fifties pretty well nullified this ploy, but best of all it allowed the air defense battle to be conducted more efficiently. Radar control centers were now able to handle more fighters over a larger area, thanks to the development of Data Link. This subsystem of SAGE eliminated the need for voice contact between the intercept director on the ground and the aircrew. A ground computer, tracking both the interceptor and the target, solved the intercept problem and sent coded electronic commands to the fighter, giving the necessary headings, altitudes, and airspeeds to complete the intercept. The commands were decoded by an airborne computer and displayed on the instrument panel, along with information on the target's heading, altitude, distance, and relative bearing from the nose of the aircraft. If the aircrew so desired, an autopilot could be engaged, and the ground computer's commands would be acted upon automatically—all the pilot had to do was move the throttle to maintain the proper airspeed, select the weapons, lock the radar on the target, and hold the trigger down until the system launched the missiles. With this setup, it was possible to climb out, intercept the target, shoot it down without ever seeing it, return to the base, and make a letdown and approach, all without touching the controls, or a word's being said. Spooky stuff! And it really worked!

Of all the many aircraft designed to meet the challenge of modern air defense up through 1970, the F-106 was by far the best produced anywhere. It was originally put into service in 1959, and is still being used by some National Guard units. The "Six," as it was called, was a big airplane for a single-seat fighter—over 70 feet long, and weighing in fully loaded for combat at nearly 42,000 pounds. It was equipped with an engine that delivered 16,100 pounds of thrust, and this jumped instantly to 24,500 pounds when afterburner was selected. This engine and airframe combination was a pilot's dream, because the throttle seemed to be connected directly to the airspeed indicator. If left in burner, the F-106 moved on out to better than Mach 2 in no time at all. In a clean configuration, the bird has an extremely high rate of climb that enables it to go from brake release to 40,000 feet in less than three minutes. A max performance climb at night in weather is a hairy experience that is probably best described as hanging on rather than flying. The Delta Dart was a pleasure to fly in any flight condition—very responsive and light on the controls, with good stability throughout the flight envelope.

Another great feature of the F-106 was its long legs. When equipped with the normal 360-gallon drop tanks, and flying a cross-country type mission, it could go over 1,600 nautical miles and still have enough gas for a letdown and landing. The 106 had a very sophisticated radar system that was nearly immune to jamming and was extremely effective for every type of air defense mission. It was also equipped with an infrared detection and tracking system that allowed the pilot additional tactical options and increased the flexibility of the entire weapons system.

The F-106 carried guided missiles, plus an unguided rocket with a nuclear warhead. The bird also had an autopilot and was capable of flying the fully automatic

F-106A——this extreme nose-high landing attitude is normal for the Delta Dart, and is held as long as possible during the landing roll to maximize the effects of aerodynamic braking. (Photo courtesy *Aerophile* Magazine)

mission with Data Link I've just described. However, by means of its onboard computer, the 106 could go the auto mission one better. The target information being sent to the fighter was stored in its computer, and if Data Link and radios were lost, the airborne computer could pick up the problem automatically, and continue to give attack instructions to the pilot.

Along with all this exotic equipment, the Six also had one of the cleverest gadgets to come down the pike since the days of Wilbur and Orville. This was the Tactical Situation Display Indicator (TSDI), and it was certainly a boon to single-seat drivers as they were muckering through the clag and were asked by the ground controller, "What's your present position?" This was usually asked just after all the navigation gear had broken lock on the station, and all a pilot could offer the controller was an embarrassed silence. The TSDI solved this problem by giving the pilot a picture of his position over the ground at all times. The apparatus projected a slide of a map of the area selected on a ten-inch circular screen mounted in front of the stick, between the pilot's feet. Superimposed on the screen was a triangular image representing the 106, which pointed in the direction the plane was flying, and moved over the map at the same relative speed that the plane moved over the ground. The maps could be changed to show a 400-, 200-, or a 50-mile radius around the selected Tacan (Tactical air navigation) station; the ground features shown were appropriate for the scale selected. On the 50-mile map there were also penetration and approach plates, just as depicted in the jet letdown book, along with airfield data and approach minimums for the field.

During the intercept phase of the mission, the target's position was indicated on the TSDI by an X with an arrow going through it; the arrow showed the target's direction of flight. This symbol also moved and turned to reflect the target's actual flight path, speed, and heading. If there was a failure of Data Link or Tacan, the 106's onboard computer kept the symbols moving by means of dead reckoning.

Our worldwide commitments in the middle to late '60s meant we needed the ability to provide worldwide air defense on relatively short notice. The F-106 was just the bird to fill the bill. It was modified so that it could be refueled in midair; and, since global operations might very well result in the bird's being flown within range of enemy fighters, Air Force brass decided to investigate just how well the 106 would perform against other fighters. The results were startling, to say the least. We'd had a sleeper right under our noses for nearly ten years. The F-106 proved to be outstanding in an air-to-air engagement, even though it was not designed for this kind of service. If flown to fight the kind of battle it was best suited for, it could take on the best fighters of the day and win. This was proven time and again in mock-combat engagements against the F-4 Phantom and the F-104 Starfighter.

These impressive results led to two new modifications that made a good bird even better. The first of these was a one-piece canopy with bulged sides that improved upward and rearward visibility. (The old canopy, with its solid metal bar at the top, was a serious disadvantage in a dogfight.) The other was the installation of a 20-mm multibarrel cannon inside the armament bay, with just the lowest barrel protruding. (I will say more about this type of weapon shortly.) These improvements, plus the bird's exceptional speed and maneuverability, and its long range and superior radar, made the F-106 one of the best fighter planes in the free world until the F-15 Eagle came upon the scene.

The political restrictions placed on nearly every phase of air operations during the war in Vietnam had a decided impact on the use of fighters in that conflict. Strategic attacks by large bomber forces were outlawed, and the approved targets were normally small in size and required pinpoint delivery techniques rather than area coverage. Therefore, the primary mission of our birds in Vietnam was that of fighter bomber. In its traditional role, establishing air superiority, the fighter was needed over North Vietnam only in the general area of Hanoi and Haiphong; this was the area where all but one of the MiG bases were located.

North Vietnamese fighters from the MiG fields were used strictly for defense of the area, and were not employed in the ground support role. The aggressive MiG reaction to our raids required that strike aircraft be protected by flights of birds specifically designated to take on the MiGs until the bomb carriers were off target.

F-4——Originally developed for the U.S. Navy in the mid-fifties, the F-4 became the back-bone of the tactical air forces of the U.S. and many of its allies. Over 5,000 Phantoms have been delivered since the prototype first flew in 1958, with more than half going to the USAF. (Photo courtesy National Air and Space Museum, Smithsonian Institution)

On these missions, just about every aircraft was a fighter; however, some were configured with bombs, some with missiles and a gun for air-to-air work, and others with countermeasures equipment. Once their bombs were gone, the strike aircraft had some capability of defending themselves in case of a bounce, but at this point the best defense was a high exit speed from the area.

On targets other than those in North Vietnam, it was exclusively a fighter bomber show, for the MiGs rarely ventured far from their local area. These missions involved nearly every type of weapon and delivery technique—dive-bombing with conventional bombs; radar bombing; low-level attacks with napalm; use of anti-personnel weapons and high-drag bombs; loran (long-range navigation) bombing; night dive-bombing under flares; strafing; and others.

There was another type of mission for which fighters were needed throughout Southeast Asia—the Search and Rescue (SAR) effort. This was really something to see in operation. Once word was received that an aircrew was down anywhere within the operating range of the rescue forces, the war literally took a back seat until the rescue operation was terminated. SAR fighters from every base that could reach the area of the downed crew were at the disposal of the rescue commander, and configured with whatever weapons he felt were necessary for the success of the mission. These birds were kept on an alert status that allowed them to be airborne within five minutes for as long as the rescue operation was in progress. There is no jock who ever flew a mission in Vietnam who would not agree that the rescue troops who drove the Sandys (A-1Es) and Jolly Greens (HH-53s) were the gutsiest bunch of individuals who ever strapped on an airplane. Tigers all!

In Vietnam the Fluid Four was still the best bet in a MiG threat area, although now the wingman had a little more freedom to initiate the attack when he got the first radar contact on the enemy. Airborne radar that could locate and track hostile aircraft, and also provide range information to the gunsight display, was an innovation that brought about significant changes in the way an engagement was conducted. Radar information on the location, size, and heading of the enemy threat, received well before the enemy could be seen, allowed the flight to maneuver to maximize their position with respect to the bogies. In most cases, this resulted in a head-on pass with closing rates approaching Mach 2. The combination of radar and missiles made this type of attack not only possible, but practical. If radar contact was made far enough out, and the contacts were distinct enough, it was possible for each member of the attacking flight to lock on to a separate target and for the flight to make a clean sweep on the first pass. As the fight developed, however, the best idea was still the oldest—get behind your opponent, where you can control the situation. (Then, too, the heat-seeking missiles were only effective from astern of the target.) As in earlier days, after the first pass the flight was usually broken down into the basic fighting unit—the element of two aircraft.

The MiGs in North Vietnam, like those in Korea before them, had the advantage of being vectored into the strike force by an elaborate ground radar network covering their area. The only counter to this radar system that the United States had was the EC-121 "Big Eye." This was a Lockheed Constellation extensively modified to carry long-range search and height radar. It orbited over the Gulf of Tonkin during strikes on the north. The main purpose of this bird was to warn the strike force when MiGs were airborne from a certain base, and, as the MiGs approached, to give their approximate distance and bearing from the strike force. Even information as sketchy as this was a big help to pilots trying to maneuver into the proper position to intercept the MiGs before they could reach the bomb carriers. Later in the war, a picket ship, code-named "Red Crown," provided these MiG warnings.

Although MiGs were a problem during attacks on the Hanoi–Haiphong area, by far the most serious threat to the strike force came from surface-to-air missiles (SAMs), and from antiaircraft artillery. The massive concentration of these weapons around the North Vietnamese capital made this area one of the most heavily defended targets in the history of aerial warfare.

SAMs were controlled by a ground radar station that tracked the target until the last few seconds of its flight, when the missiles' internal guidance systems took over the final steering. There was virtually no ceiling on the effective range of these missiles; however, the target had to be above 1,500 feet for proper tracking by the ground station.

SAMs worked so well that their avoidance or suppression was a major consideration on each mission, and eventually fighter aircraft in Vietnam were equipped with an electronic device that told the pilot when he was being tracked by SAM radar, and the relative bearing of the ground site. Knowing the general direction in which to look, the aircrew could take evasive action once the missile was spotted—it was possible to outmaneuver a SAM and cause it to overshoot if it was sighted early enough. However, the evasive action required was fairly violent, and no small amount of judgment and timing was demanded for it to be successful. Multiple SAM firings from a variety of directions and/or in quick succession tended to nullify continued evasive action by the fighter.

For a strike mission to be successful, the ordnance had to be placed on the target, and not jettisoned prematurely as each bird gyrated around the sky, avoiding SAMs. Fighter pilots were helped greatly by the introduction of the Electronic Countermeasures (ECM) pod, which was about the size of a small drop tank and was hung beneath the wing in place of a bomb rack. The pod was filled with electronic gear designed specifically to jam the radar used by the SAMs for tracking and guidance. The ECM pod worked very well.

For maximum effectiveness against SAMs, the Fluid Four formation had to be closed up to what amounted to a "loose" close formation. Unfortunately, in this formation the flights were unable to maneuver and provide the mutual cover that was so essential in a MiG environment. But since SAMs were a greater threat than MiGs, the pod formation was retained, and flights of fighters configured for the air-to-air mission accompanied the strike force as their high cover, or MiGCAP.

Another wrinkle was thrown in on these raids to confuse the intercept direction and SAM radars. Just ahead of the strike force, a number of birds dispensed a continuous stream of chaff while they were in the high-threat area. These chaff drops, plus the jamming done by the ECM pods, proved to be pretty much the answer to the SAM problem. With MiGCAP taking care of the defending interceptors, and ECM pods suppressing the SAMs, all the strike force jock had to worry about now was flak, which in the Hanoi area was thick enough to walk on.

Since flak of some variety could be expected around nearly every target in Southeast Asia, pilots quickly developed the habit of "jinking" while they were in the target area. Jinking was making random, rapid movements of the aircraft so that its flight path could not be predicted long enough for a gunner to establish the proper lead. Rolling in on the dive-bomb run on the target was also done from random directions so as not to establish a pattern, and it was *de rigueur* to jink once or twice while going down the chute. Diving speeds had to be a minimum of 450 knots to give the gunners a tougher problem, and on low-angle bomb runs for napalm or high-drag bombs, 500-plus knots was even better, if a lot of ground fire was reported. Naturally, high approach speeds and jinking allowed precious little time for target acquisition and aiming, which in turn dramatically affected the Circular Error Probable (CEP) of bombing in Vietnam. The CEP is a measure of accurancy given in terms of the radius of a circle, whose center is the aiming point, so that on the average half the bombs will strike inside the circle, and the other half will fall outside. Under ideal conditions—for example, on a bombing range, with no enemy to worry about—CEPs as low as 100 feet can be achieved. In combat, however, a more typical figure would be about 250 feet.

For a while, the guys flying MiGCAP had their problems when it came to target identification. Even if the aircrew had a radar contact in the area where Big Eye or Red Crown had warned of approaching MiGs, they could not open fire without positive visual identification of the target as a hostile aircraft. There were two reasons for this: the very large number of friendly aircraft involved in strikes on the area defended by MiGs, and the imprecision of Big Eye or Red Crown in picking out fighter-size targets at the distances involved. Later in the war, MiGCAP had an easier time of it; a system for identifying the good guys electronically was introduced.

The raids into North Vietnam brought back a problem familiar to fighter pilots since World War II—long distances to the target. The distance to Hanoi from most bases was better than 250 miles, and this was quite a haul, considering how the bird's performance was affected by the weight and drag of bombs, plus the operational necessity for using afterburner in the target area. With the burner going for any length of time, fuel consumption skyrockets, and it seems as if you can almost see the fuel gauge indicator moving downward. The fuel problem was solved by placing tankers in orbit just outside the North Vietnamese border, and having the attack force join up for both pre- and post-strike midair refueling. The availability of fuel just outside the hostile area certainly allowed the mission pilots more flexibility, and permitted more aggressiveness when tangling with MiGs than would otherwise have been possible. This benefit was particularly helpful when a bird received battle damage to its fuel system, and was definitely hurting by the time it made it to the tankers.

Although many different fighters were employed in Southeast Asia, the two that were involved in the majority of air-to-air engagements were the F-4 Phantom and the MiG-21. As in Korea, the birds doing the dogfighting were pretty well evenly matched, with each having some disadvantages that could then be exploited by the other.

The MiG-21 was a radar-equipped bird designed specifically for the air superiority role. (It eventually became the most widely used fighter in the world.) It was capable of speeds up to Mach 2; however, its armament consisted of only two heat-seeking missiles, which limited the number of passes it could make, and the direction from which the attack could be initiated. As I mentioned before, heat-seeking missiles are only effective in the rear hemisphere of the target, so the missiles can get a good look at the jet exhaust plume and the hot spots in the engine on which they rely for guidance. Of course, in Vietnam everyone in the fight operated in full afterburner, and the infrared missiles had excellent heat sources to home in on.

The lack of a radar-guided missile denied the MiG frontal attack capability, which put it at quite a disadvantage during the first pass of an engagement. Even with the minimal radar information available from Big Eye or Red Crown, MiG-CAP birds could usually turn to meet the MiGs head-on, or at enough of an angle off their nose to prevent the heat-seeking missiles from "seeing" a good target. Another limitation of the MiG was its lack of a gun to be used as a follow-up weapon, in case the missiles missed the target. (These armament deficiencies were corrected on later models of the MiG-21 by the addition of radar missiles, a 23-mm cannon, and improved search-and-track radar.) This bird also had relatively poor visibility from the cockpit, and a gunsight whose gyros tumbled at just under three Gs, making it pretty much useless in a hard-turning fight.

Despite these shortcomings, the MiG-21 was a tough opponent in a hassle. It was more maneuverable than the F-4, and very hard to spot because of its small size and the lack of a smoke trail from its engine. MiGs were usually employed in pairs, and the pilots displayed more adeptness at teamwork than their counterparts in the Korean War had. The secret of the MiG-21's excellent performance, even when powered by an engine of modest output by American standards, was its light weight. A fully loaded MiG-21 weighed in at 18,740 pounds—which, curiously enough, was only a few hundred pounds heavier than the weight of the *fuel* carried by an F-4 equipped with drop tanks, which was the normal configuration for these birds when they were flying MiGCAP.

F-4D——in Southeast Asia, the Phantom II was all things to all people. A good weapons system, in-flight refueling, and the ability to carry a big load made it the number-one bird for air superiority, close air support, interdiction, air defense, gunship escort, and long-range bombing. (Photo by Frank J. O'Brien)

The F-4 Phantom II was the only bird used by the good guys in Vietnam that could compete effectively with the MiG-21. The F-4 was a big machine, about twice the size of the MiG-21, with aerodynamic lines that made it look as if it had been put together by a committee. Although to the aesthetic eye it was a little on the ugly side, it was a real goer, capable of speeds in excess of Mach 2, and it could carry just about anything you could hang on it. The Phantom could out-accelerate the Mig-21, and this capability, plus a higher maximum speed, provided an effective counter to the MiG's better turning ability. The F-4 also had a better armament and weapons system than the MiG. Carrying both infrared and radar missiles, plus a Gatling gun, it could utilize the full potential of a versatile radar system. With the GIB handling the radar, as the additional crew member, the F-4 had the edge of another pair of eyes in a dogfight, and the pilot could concentrate on flying the bird. In case of an emergency, the GIB could also bring the bird home—he had a duplicate set of controls and instruments in the back seat.

The performance of the F-4 would have been even more outstanding if, like the MiG, it had been designed just for the air superiority role. However, it was a multimission bird with weapons attachment gear and numerous pylons that added both weight and drag. Despite these encumbrances, the Phantom could carry quite a load, and for most ground support missions it was equipped with 12 500-pound

MiG-21——the cone-shaped centerbody in the air intake houses a search-and-track radar with a range of approximately 12 miles. This centerbody is also movable to control airflow in the inlet duct. (Photo courtesy National Air and Space Museum, Smithsonian Institution)

bombs and two 360-gallon drop tanks. This 14,000 pounds of external stores on a fighter is quite remarkable when you consider that the normal bomb load for the B-17G in World War II was around 10,000 pounds.

If weather became a factor on missions against area targets such as supply depots or bunker complexes, the F-4's inertial navigation system and radar combined to give it an offset bombing capability. This allowed the bombing of one point by using radar fixes on another, letting the onboard computer solve the geometry problem.

Vietnam did for weaponry advances what Korea had done for aircraft improvements over World War II designs. Now the primary weapon in the fighter-versus-fighter arena was the guided missile. This type of armament required a slight change in gunnery tactics, in that now the problem was not how to get in close to your opponent to insure a kill—instead, you had to fire *before* reaching a certain minimum range, or the missile would not have time to arm itself before reaching the target, and thus would be a dud.

The increased emphasis on protection from SAMs brought into being a special missile that homed in on the SAM's ground radar transmitter, and packed enough of a punch to put the whole site out of commission. Another innovation in this area was the so-called "smart bomb." These weapons were conventional iron bombs, weighing 2,000 or 3,000 pounds, that were fitted with guidance and control devices that permitted them to be steered to the target during their fall. The guidance systems utilized either reflected laser energy or television to provide steering information right down to impact. The accuracy of these bombs was phenomenal, so they were used primarily on critical targets that were small and/or hard to hit by conventional dive-bombing methods.

Perhaps the most significant air-to-air weapon that came out of this era was the aforementioned Gatling gun, which solved the age-old problem of getting a lot of highly destructive projectiles onto the target in an extremely short period of time. This gun was also an excellent weapon with which to follow up a missile attack. It was a 20-mm cannon with six barrels that rotated as a unit around an axle mounted to the breech mechanism. Each barrel fired once during each revolution, when it was at the lowest point of the circle. This arrangement produced a rate of fire of 6,000 rounds per minute. As you can well imagine, this allowed a pilot to put a terrific amount of lead into a target with even a very short burst.

When fired, the Gatling gun did not make the familiar rat-a-tat or chug-chug sound normally associated with machine guns and rapid-fire cannons; rather, it made a continuous roaring sound. On strafing runs against area targets such as truck parks or a network of prepared positions, the effect of this weapon was truly awesome. Slightly longer bursts were possible in this situation, and if the aircraft was yawed gently back and forth during the run, the bullet pattern cut scythe-like across the target area. Short of a death ray or some kind of laser disintegrator, this gun was about as close as you could get to the ultimate weapon for close-in work during a hassle.

View through an F-4 gunsight on a 60-degree dive-bombing run in Vietnam. (Photo by Frank J. O'Brien)

Looking back over the developments in the fighter pilot's world during the last four wars, it is quite evident just how correct is Group Captain J. E. Johnson's assessment that combat tactics have come full circle. Although weapons and the aircraft that deliver them have improved immensely since 1914, the basic tactics developed by Boelcke have proven to be as timeless as the pyramids. Many variations have been tried, but when tested in the crucible of combat they invariably yield to the superior qualities of the basics. However, a thorough knowledge of the fundamentals is but the first step toward success for the modern fighter pilot. Today, in order to win at the air-to-air game, a pilot has to know considerably more about his business than his predecessors did. Armament systems geared to handle anything from guns to complex missiles, and offering countless options and counteroptions as the situation dictates; radar, whose proper operation and interpretation is a science in itself; the tactics and delivery techniques to satisfy each weapon's parameters—all have to be brought together at the right place and right time.

Round-the-clock fighter operations, typical of the war in Vietnam, required that pilots be jocks of all trades—a counter air mission today, dive-bombing tomorrow, and, another time, night bombing under flares with midair refueling on the way.

As aircraft and weapons systems became increasingly sophisticated, the success of the mission depended more and more upon aircrew specialization in some specific form of weapons delivery. While technology is the key element in most phases of the fighter business today, the connection between the stick and the seat is still the prime factor. The critical interaction of man and machine is best summed up by the wartime leader of the Luftwaffe, General Adolf Galland, who said, "Only the spirit of attack borne in a brave heart will bring success to any fighter aircraft, no matter how highly developed it may be."

Korea: The Sucker Maneuver

An account by Col. Harrison Thyng; 14 victories:

"Once again the Commie leaders have taken up our challenge, and now we may expect the usual numerical odds as the MiGs gain altitude and form up preparatory to crossing the Yalu. Breaking up into flights, we stagger for altitude. We have checked our guns and sights by firing a few warm-up rounds as we crossed the bomb line. Oxygen masks are checked and pulled as tight as possible over our faces. We know we may exceed eight Gs in the coming fight, and that is painful with a loose mask. We are cruising at a very high Mach. Every eye is strained to catch the first movement of an enemy attempt to cross the Yalu from their Manchurian sanctuary into that graveyard of several hundred MiGs known as MiG Alley.

"Several minutes pass. We know the MiG pilots will become bolder as our fuel time limit over the Alley grows shorter. Now we see flashes in the distance as the sun reflects off the beautiful MiG aircraft. The radio crackles, 'Many many coming across at Suiho above 45,000 feet.' Our flights start converging toward that area, low flights climbing, yet keeping a very high Mach. Contrails are now showing over the An-tung area, so another enemy action is preparing to cross at Sinuiju, a favorite spot. We know the enemy sections are being vectored by GCI, and the advantage is theirs. Traveling at terrifically high speed and altitude, attackers can readily achieve surprise. The area bounded by the horizon at this altitude is so vast that it is practically impossible to keep it fully covered with the human eye.

"Our flights are well spread out, ships line abreast, and each pilot keeps his head swiveling 360 degrees. Suddenly MiGs appear directly in front of us at our level. At rates of closure of possibly 1,200 mph we pass through each other's formations. Accurate radar range firing is difficult under these conditions, but you fire a burst at the nearest enemy anyway. Immediately the MiGs zoom for altitude, and you break at maximum G around toward them. Unless the MiG wants to fight and also turned as he climbed, he will be lost from sight in the distance before the turn is completed. But if he shows an inclination to scrap, you immediately trade head-on passes again. You sucker the MiG into a position where the outstanding advantage of your aircraft will give you the chance to outmaneuver him. For you combat has become an individual dogfight. Flight integrity has been lost, but your wingman is still with you, widely separated but close enough for you to know that you are covered.

"Suddenly you go into a steep turn. Your Mach drops off. The MiG turns with you, and you let him gradually creep up and out-turn you. At the critical moment you reverse your turn. The hydraulic controls work beautifully. The MiG cannot turn as readily as you and is slung out to the side. When you pop your speed brakes, the MiG flashes by. Quickly closing the brakes, you slide onto his tail and hammer him with your .50s. Pieces fly off the MiG, but he won't burn or explode at that high altitude. He twists and turns and attempts to dive away, but you will not be denied. Your .50s have hit him in the engine and slowed him up enough so that he cannot get away from you. His canopy suddenly blows and the pilot catapults out, barely missing your airplane. Now your wingman is whooping it up on the radio, and you flash for home, very low on fuel."

Korea: The Wrong Move

An account by Major James Jabara, the first jet ace; 15 victories:

"If we're outnumbered, or the fighting gets too rough, then we maneuver around waiting for the enemy to make a mistake. Thank God he makes more than his share of them. Like the one he made in a big scrap on April 12. I was at 25,000 feet and he was 5,000 feet beneath me, heading for the B-29s. That advantage in altitude was my break and I used it to get speed. I caught him just as he was in range of the B-29s. The bullets saddle-stitched his fuselage, but he went into loops and rolls. He was badly crippled. Another burst got his engine and I saw him crash trying to leg it across the Yalu.

"The numerical odds were against us on April 22, when our 12 Sabres were outnumbered three to one. With Captain Norbert W. Chalwick flying protection for me, I took my time getting behind a couple of MiGs and hit them both with short bursts. I had to pop my dive brakes to keep from running into one. I was still firing as he rolled on his back. I followed him down but I didn't realize how close to the ground I was until he crashed. I had a hell of a time pulling out of my dive. The cockpit dial showed nine Gs before I blacked out. Fortunately my eyes focused in about three seconds and by instinct, I guess, I was headed upward. That was my fourth kill. The first one was on April 3, when Becker was flying wingman. We were two against two. We saw the MiGs first at 7,000 feet and I used 1,200 rounds damaging the engine of one MiG that flamed out and crashed about ten miles from its home field. I damaged the other.

"On April 10 we were MiG hunting again in the Alley. We let down to 36,000 feet through the overcast and broke out in the clear at 10,000 feet. We saw six of them at 5,000 feet and bounced them from the 7 o'clock position. Four of the MiGs broke up into the overcast and two broke down toward the ground. They just shouldn't have done it. I took after them. The leader scampered away, leaving his wingman wide open. After three Lufberys [360-degree turns] I scored hits on the wingman.

I used up my 1,800 rounds of ammo but stayed with the MiG for about 30 seconds, meanwhile radioing my wingman, Lieutenant Otis Gordon, to start shooting. This proved unnecessary, as the enemy pilot suddenly bailed out about 30 miles south of Sinuiju. I was flying almost at the speed of sound and couldn't see too much, but he had a light blue parachute, a black helmet, and a light gray oxygen mask."

Vietnam: When the Enemy Doesn't Run

Captain Steve Ritchie (5 victories) from Reidsville, North Carolina, was leading a flight of F-4 Phantoms. His four aircraft were protecting a strike force as it departed a target near Hanoi and headed for Udon Thani Royal Thai Air Force Base, Thailand. A "Big Eye" EC-121 radar support aircraft offshore warned the F-4 crews that MiGs were aloft. The information, however, was too late to help the F-4s carrying chaff dispensers. Enemy radar had vectored a MiG-21 pilot in behind the chaff aircraft. He moved in rapidly, fired an ATOLL heat-seeking missile, and broke away to safety. The ATOLL hit the left engine of one of the chaff escorts. With a badly crippled F-4, the pilot headed out of the target area while transmitting his position, heading, and altitude on the radio guard channel.

Meanwhile, another pilot flying cover for the benefit of the strike force also had to depart—his plane had an engine fire. Captain Ritchie, knowing that North Vietnamese

ground radar controllers would direct their MiGs against crippled aircraft, descended to about 5,000 feet above ground. Learning from Navy radar and the orbiting EC-121 that two MiGs were two miles north of the flight, Captain Ritchie turned north to intercept them. Within seconds he made visual contact with the lead aircraft—he was close enough to see a silver MiG-21 with bright red star markings. Recalling that a common North Vietnamese tactic was to send a single MiG out front as a decoy, Captain Ritchie refused the baited trap, rolled his aircraft, and dove closer to the ground. Soon he saw the second MiG pass overhead approximately 10,000 feet behind the first.

The ploy of the MiG pilots had failed; now they were the hunted. Captain Ritchie began a hard-slicing 6½-G turn to get into position behind the second MiG fighter. He had the MiG in his gunsight and the radar was locked on, providing range information; after several seconds he squeezed the trigger twice, firing two

Sparrow radar missiles. The first missile exploded in the center of the MiGs fuselage; the second missile went through the fireball.

Usually when MiG pilots worked in pairs, the remaining pilot fled when his companion was in trouble. But this time, the red-starred MiG leader stayed in the fight and tried to shoot down the number-four aircraft in Captain Ritchie's flight.

In response to number-four crew's request for assistance, Captain Ritchie descended to gain speed and made another hard turn just in time to get into firing position as the MiG pilot was maneuvering to destroy the number-four aircraft. The MiG pilot sensed his danger and initiated a hard turn back into his attacker. There was time for just one missile to come off Ritchie's F-4. It shot straight out, made almost a 90-degree turn, and smashed dead center into the fuselage of the MiG-21. The enemy aircraft disintegrated in a huge fireball.

Vietnam: The Arsenal

I was serving as mission commander of a force of F-4C, F-104, and F-105 aircraft performing a planned fighter sweep in the Hanoi area. Fourteen flights of F-4s, six flights of F-105 "Iron Hands," and four flights of F-104s participated in the sweep, supported, in the normal fashion, by B-66s with ECM pods, Big Eye, and KC-135 tankers. The B-66s were provided escort by additional F-4C aircraft. As mission commander, I flew lead position in Olds flight, first in the stream of F-4Cs that was to converge on Phuc Yen airfield. TOT (time on target) was 1400G (Greenwich), and was made good. No definite radar contacts were made as we ingressed on a heading of 145 degrees. Weather at the time was solid undercast, tops estimated at 7,000 feet, ceiling unknown.

I led Olds flight past Phuc Yen for approximately 14 to 18 nautical miles, then turned so as to cross Phuc Yen again on a reciprocal heading. As the turn was completed, Olds 3 picked up a radar contact low at 12 o'clock, high closure rate. He gained a lock-on and was instructed to attack. Steering dot information put the flight into a 10- to 15-degree dive. Just as we neared the top of the undercast, radar broke lock. The target was under or in the murk and had passed beneath us on an opposite heading.

I led the flight on past the airfield once again, called incoming F-4 flights Ford and Rambler that missiles free was no longer in effect, and turned my flight back southeast. Just as we again crossed Phuc Yen, Ford flight arrived on time. Then everything happened at once.

Ford called a MiG-21 closing an Olds flight at their 7 o'clock. Olds 2 saw the MiG simultaneously. Additional MiGs were popping up through the clouds. I initiated a left turn of sufficient intensity to throw off the attacking MiG's aim, but without breaking Olds flight integrity. A defensive split by elements was automatically taken.

After 90 degrees of turn in this modified break, I sighted an aircraft at my 11 o'clock in a left turn, slightly low, about a mile and a quarter away. I closed on this target for positive identification—I had never actually seen a MiG before and by now was uncertain of the exact location of all members of Ford flight. The target was positively identified as a MiG-21, silver in color, too distant for markings to be seen. I instructed the GIB to go bore sight and put the pipper on the target, and called for lock-on and full-system operation. I was setting us up for an AIM-7 attack.

Closure was enough to necessitate haste in establishing the proper attack parameter. We achieved the steering dot (interlocks "in") and pressed-released, pressed, and held the trigger. Two AIM-7s launched and appeared to track. At that moment we lost radar lock-on, having pressed beyond minimum range, and the missiles had no chance to guide. I quickly selected HEAT, put the pipper on the MiG as he was disappearing into the overcast, received an indistinct missile growl, and fired one AIM-9, knowing the missile had little chance to guide.

During the first encounter, Olds 2 was busily engaged in pursuing the MiG-21 that had originally closed behind my flight. In addition, as I closed on the MiG that had vanished in the cloud deck, I had another in sight at my 10 o'clock, in a left turn

and just above the clouds. I turned my attention to this second MiG. I pulled sharp left, turned inside him, pulled my nose up about 30 degrees above the horizon, rechecked my missile switches and ready panel, switched fuel to internal wing transfer, barrel-rolled to the right, held my position upside down above and behind the MiG until the proper angular deflection and range parameters were satisfied, completed the rolling maneuver, and fell in behind and below the MiG-21 at his 7 o'clock position at about .95 Mach. Range was 4,500 feet, angle off 15.

The MiG-21 obligingly pulled up well above the horizon and exactly downsun. I put the pipper on his tail pipe, received a perfect missile growl, squeezed the trigger once, hesitated, then squeezed it once again. The first Sidewinder leapt in front of my bird, and within a split second turned left in a definite and beautiful collision-course correction. I did not take my eyes off the first Sidewinder and consequently did not see precisely what the second missile did. It appeared to have guided also. The first missile went slightly down, then arced gracefully up, heading for impact.

Suddenly the MiG-21 erupted in a brilliant flash of orange flame. A complete wing separated and flew back in the airstream, together with a mass of smaller debris. The MiG swapped ends immediately, and tumbled forward. Then it fell, twisting, corkscrewing, tumbling lazily toward the top of the clouds. The plan form view of the aircraft was clearly visible during many separate instants. The bird was minus one wing and the other presented the wedge-shaped, sharply swept leading edge and the straight trailing edge characteristic of the MiG-21.

I continued my left turn, looked for other MiGs, checked my fuel gauge, and gave the order to egress, knowing that Olds 4, not having obtained fuel from his centerline tank, was then at bingo. An account by Col. Robin Olds.

Vietnam: The SAM Break Maneuver

The techniques for evading SAMs were basically the same as those used in a fighter-versus-fighter engagement. When he was under attack by a SAM or another fighter, the defender's actions were all designed to accomplish one thing—make the enemy overshoot.

Surface-to-air missiles are airborne vehicles, just like fighter planes, and as such they have definite G-loading and turning limitations. The name of the game for the fighter defending against a SAM was to capitalize on these limitations and, in essence, out-turn the missile during the final phase of its flight. Although this maneuver could be tried at any altitude, the sequence normally started with the fighter at about 25,000 feet, the usual ingress altitude for an F-4 carrying 12 500-pound bombs.

For the maneuver to be anywhere near successful, the aircrew had to spot the SAM very soon after it was launched. A cockpit warning device assisted the crew in this area by indicating direction from which the missile was coming. Once the SAM was spotted or the crew knew that one was headed for their bird, reaction had to be immediate and positive. The stick was jammed forward and maximum afterburner selected, to get the aircraft in a steep, high-speed dive. This pushover usually put about two to three negative Gs on the bird—inducing a highly uncomfortable sensation and also making it very difficult to reach switches on the forward and lower panels in the cockpit.

As the aircraft was nosing over, it had to be turned as quickly as possible to put the rising SAM off one wing tip or the other. Next, the pilot had to somehow reach the "panic button" on a forward sub-panel and jettison the bomb load, to decrease drag and lighten up the aircraft for more maneuvering potential.

The situation was now this: the fighter was diving steeply and turning just enough to keep the SAM on its wing tip; the missile guidance system sensed this change of direction by the target and caused the SAM to start arcing over from its climb. By now the fighter was well below the missile, and as the ground started to become a factor, the pilot began to ease out of his dive. He continued to turn to keep the SAM at his 3 or 9 o'clock position. The missile had now completed its turn and was coming back down at the fighter, which by this time should have been level at a low altitude and going like a scalded dog.

The missile was now fast approaching the point at which its own radar would acquire the target and provide terminal guidance for the SAM. The hope was that the profusion of ground clutter the missile's radar was forced to look into would mask the target and prevent a good lock-on. However, because of the SAM's proximity fusing, this final guidance was not always essential to achieve a kill, and at this point the pilot had to decide exactly when to initiate a hard-climbing turn into the missile. This turn would generate the largest possible angle off from the tail of the fighter to the missile. The missile would be unable to match such a turn, and it would pass astern of the fighter and thus lose any chance of a lock-on.

Carefully planned and executed, the SAM Break was an effective counter against the deadly missile; however, the timing of the final turn into the missile was extremely cru-cial—if the pilot turned too early, the missile would have time to react; too late, and the fighter would be within the lethal blast radius when the SAM passed and detonated. Further, when the fighter completed the SAM Break, it was at a relatively low altitude and, probably, at a comparatively low airspeed. Its lack of energy maneuverability left the fighter very few options if it encountered another SAM right away. North Vietnamese gunners often did fire three SAMs at the same airplane in rapid sequence. If the cockpit warning device gave continuous indications of SAM activity in the vicinity, the best tactic was to exit the area at as high an airspeed and as low an altitude as possible. In this way, the fighter stayed below the minimum acquisition altitude of the SAM radar, and also minimized its time in the high-threat area.

PART 2
The Prerequisites of Mock Combat

CHAPTER 4
BASIC ACROBATICS

The first step in making every man a tiger is getting people who are basically straight and level pilots to handle themselves competently in situations that are everything but straight and level. Before trying any of the basic fighter maneuvers to be discussed in Part 3 of this book, a pilot should feel completely at home in his bird while it is on its back, in a high-G turn, or in a vertical dive with the throttle wide open. A thorough knowledge of basic acrobatics and how your aircraft reacts under these conditions is an essential prerequisite to learning any of the fighter pilot's tricks. Maneuvering around the sky in a hassle with another bird is not the time for your first experience at being on your back in a climb, or for running out of airspeed, altitude, and ideas all at the same time. The chase itself will provide enough moments like this; and it's quite reassuring at these times to know that you've been there before, and that your knowledge and experience with acrobatics will allow you to make a safe recovery.

There are a lot of reasons for trying your hand at acrobatics other than the fact that they are there. First of all, these maneuvers help you to build confidence in yourself and your airplane. This confidence, in turn, enhances your ability to instinctively handle the unusual attitudes that inevitably crop up in flying from time to time. Acrobatics also provide an opportunity for learning to fly your bird within more exacting parameters. Flying good acrobatics requires attention to detail and precision handling of the controls at all times. Once mastered, these techniques all become second nature and need only an occasional brushing up. But keep in mind that this chapter is about *basic* acrobatics, and the descriptions of the maneuvers are just that—basic instructions on how to perform normal acrobatics in a safe manner. They are *generalized* techniques that pertain to no particular airplane, and are definitely not intended to teach competition aerobatics, which is an area of flying that is a science in itself. Only work with a qualified instructor *in the air* can fully prepare a pilot for acrobatic flight.

There are some common denominators for all acrobatic missions that should be thoroughly understood from the outset. Here I may appear to be belaboring the obvious, but these things are too important to be left unsaid. Before trying any acrobatics, be sure you know which maneuvers are permitted by your owner's manual or design specifications, *and* which ones are prohibited. Also, make sure that your bird is certificated for the G loads you will encounter, and that your engine can handle momentary inverted flight. If any G force less than one causes your mill to quit dead, and if air starts present a problem, then by all means stick to the simpler maneuvers, or modify your engine to carry you through overhead acrobatics.

A thorough briefing, preferably by an instructor, or an in-depth self-study session is an absolute requirement for every mission. Know which maneuvers are to be performed, and what to look for in every phase of each—and this includes knowing and flying the recommended entry airspeeds. These airspeeds can make you or break you on an acrobatic mission—if you go too fast, you won't test your ability to perform the maneuver correctly; too slow, and you'll stall out halfway through the maneuver, usually in a nose-high inverted position. The recommended entry airspeeds for each permitted maneuver are normally found in your owner's manual.

If no manual is available, the following rules of thumb should be used as guidelines to compute entry airspeeds. All loops, barrel rolls, slow rolls, vertical recoveries, and Cuban eights have an entry speed of two and a half times the stall speed of your aircraft; the Immelmann and cloverleaf require three times the stall speed because of the half rolls involved. Except for certain split S's, all of the maneuvers described here are done with the power set in the high cruise position.

Along with entry speeds, you should have in mind the airspeed at which your engine hits the maximum permissible rpm with the throttle wide open. Knowing this airspeed will give you one less instrument to monitor during acrobatics; this will be even more important when you get into basic fighter maneuvers.

When you begin to fly acrobatics, start out with the easier maneuvers in order to build your confidence and skill level, and to help yourself gradually feel out your aircraft's responses under various new conditions. The recommended sequence for learning these maneuvers is the order in which they are presented here. Proceed slowly and get each maneuver down pat before proceeding to the next—*don't* try vast undertakings with half-vast preparations. The best possible procedure to follow, if the equipment and qualified personnel are available, is to fly a couple of dual acrobatic missions with an instructor who will demonstrate the proper execution of each maneuver.

A commonsense rule to follow is to practice acrobatics only in the designated area, where other birds will be more or less expecting the unusual attitudes you will be in. Be sure to clear the area adequately before every maneuver with a good look *all around* you, especially to the rear. A couple of quick S turns using a high angle of bank should let you throw an eyeball over the entire area of your intended maneuver.

Speaking of acrobatic practice, it is definitely not too swift an idea to try these maneuvers under conditions of restricted visibility—for example, when there is a broken cloud deck or haze. Inflight visibility should be at least five miles so you can see and *be seen* during all your gyrations. This is particularly true if other birds are using the area for acrobatics at the same time you are. Nothing is more disconcerting than to be coming over the top of a loop and to look back to pick up your section line for reference, only to see another bird in the same position. You should also avoid practicing acrobatics in the area around cumulus clouds with a lot of vertical development. These buildups seem to fascinate all throttle benders, and some guy may suddenly come around the corner of one of them just as you're in the middle of one of your maneuvers. In this situation, you may be able to do nothing except go into the cloud, and such a sudden transition to instrument flight while in an unusual attitude would tax even the instrument cross-check abilities of a bat.

A preflight item that could make a lot of difference when you need it most is cleaning the cockpit floor and stowing all loose items. If you fall out of a maneuver, there is a good chance that you will apply some negative Gs to your bird, and then everything that's loose will start to float around the cockpit. This is no time to have your attention diverted from the proper recovery procedures by maps, pencils, dirt, and other junk flying around the cockpit.

When you start flying acrobatics and you're not used to the higher G forces and the unusual and/or inverted attitudes involved, eat just a light meal before flying. If you have an inclination toward airsickness, it's a good idea to carry a barf bag in your pocket for the first few missions. It's sure a lot easier than cleaning out the cockpit after you land.

Each jock should know the stalling characteristics of his bird, and the airframe noise and vibration warnings that it gives when it's approaching a stall. Something that comes into play more noticeably during acrobatics, and something you have to remember to compensate for on every maneuver, is torque. If you have an offset fin to counteract torque at normal cruise, its effect will be proportional to your airspeed; therefore, your rudder pressures will have to vary, and perhaps alternate, during a maneuver.

An item that is really helpful in getting the most out of overhead maneuvers is a G meter—it allows you to adjust your pull-ups and pullouts precisely to the recommended G loadings. It's also nice to know when you've laid just a few too many Gs on the bird, so you can check for popped rivets, cracks, wrinkles, or other signs of structural damage after you land. If you inadvertantly over-G a bird during any type of maneuver, don't continue with the mission, because more stress may aggravate the situation. Take the bird home and give it a good looking over before the next flight.

Speaking of G forces, don't get the impression that it is necessary to load the bird up to the max G limit for every maneuver. Basic acrobatics are not designed to completely wring out an airplane by flying it at the featheredge of controllability. Stick to the entry and minimum airspeeds and fly the patterns in the proper manner, and acrobatics will be entirely safe and comfortable, and probably a lot of fun.

Any time you are flying acrobatics, be sure to observe a safe minimum altitude.

Plan on completing all maneuvers at or above an altitude from which you can safely recover from a spin or a vertical dive. Should you fall out of an overhead maneuver or misjudge the pullout, it's nice to have a little insurance cushion available.

In the discussions of individual maneuvers that follow, I make reference to having a constant power setting. By this I mean that once the power is set at the proper rpm or manifold pressure, it should essentially be left there. This does not preclude slight adjustments to maintain rpm as airspeed changes during a maneuver. But leaving the power set in approximately one position puts the burden on you to use the proper airspeeds and G loadings to execute the maneuver correctly. It is more important to learn to fly a loop in the proper manner than to rely on power to drag you through the pattern despite a sloppy entry and pull-up.

Naturally, if you see that you won't be able to complete a maneuver safely, use whatever power is available to start a recovery before your airspeed gets too low. Don't try to finish an overhead maneuver if things start turning to worms before you're over the top. There's not too much to learn from a maneuver that was improperly executed from the start, so initiate a vertical recovery and try it again, the right way.

Something else you'll find in the following descriptions is a lot of discussion of reference points and other criteria you should look for in each maneuver. These are meant only as aids to the learning process. After you get the mechanics of a maneuver under your belt, you'll find that you'll refer to them subconsciously and that they won't occupy your attention as much as they did initially.

As your proficiency in acrobatics increases, all the considerations I've outlined will become second nature, and you can sit back and enjoy the fun of acrobatics all the more. But before each mission, you should consult the Acrobatics Briefing Guide and Form in Appendix B of this book. I can't say too often that solid preflight preparation is of paramount importance.

The Chandelle

The chandelle is probably the most basic acrobatic maneuver having definite parameters. A chandelle has no real practical application to other aspects of flying; its main value is that it offers an excellent vehicle for practicing precision flying— pretty much a case of learning to do it right because it's there. The chandelle is a 180-degree climbing turn, often called a "bank and yank," that has a definite entry and a definite exit speed. Hitting the proper exit airspeed at exactly 180 degrees of turn is more important than any specific amount of altitude gained. During this maneuver, the nose of the aircraft (as seen from the cockpit) describes a 45-degree line with the horizon. Once this climbing attitude has been established, it should be kept more or less constant throughout the turn.

To perform the chandelle, turn to a cardinal heading, or, if you don't have a directional gyro, line up with a section line or a straight piece of road that can easily be picked up when you turn around. After clearing the area, set the power and start a slight dive to pick up airspeed. As soon as you hit the proper speed, roll smartly into about a 60-degree bank and then apply back pressure to establish a moderate climbing attitude. From this point on, it's pretty much a judgment call as to just how much back pressure to maintain—continually play the amount of turn remaining against the airspeed you have to lose to hit the desired minimum at the top. If you yanked too hard at the beginning, you'll probably have to ease off on the stick a little to complete the 180 degrees of turn before running out of airspeed. Conversely, if you didn't put enough muscle into the initial pull-up, you'll find yourself all the way around and still going like a scalded dog. It takes a little practice before you can feel just how much back pressure will give the smooth, constantly rising flight path you are shooting for, with no dips or humps to correct for improper airspeed loss.

As you proceed through the turn and reach a point about 30 degrees from the desired rollout heading, start decreasing your bank angle smoothly so as to arrive at the wings-level position at the same time you complete 180 degrees of turn. At this point, your *exit* airspeed should be about half your entry speed. While rolling out of the bank, your wings will effectively generate more lift, so you may have to ease in just a hair of additional back pressure to keep the airspeed decreasing at the rate you want. On the other hand, the additional lift may provide you with a little cushion if you happen to be a tad slow at this point.

Because the chandelle is a precision acrobatic maneuver, with specified entry and exit airspeeds, there are a number of things that could be called common errors associated with it. Too high an entry speed will increase your exit speed, or require a too-steep climb angle to compensate for it. Too low an entry speed will mean you probably won't make it all the way around before hitting your minimum airspeed unless you flatten out your climb quite a bit. Too much bank at the outset may get you around more quickly, but, because you won't have as much effective lift, your airspeed will bleed off more rapidly and you won't be able to achieve the desired 45-degree climb line. If your bank is too shallow and the proper back pressure is maintained, you'll run out of airspeed before you're even close to the 180-degree point in the turn.

Once you start the chandelle, your bank angle should remain constant until you begin the rollout. The primary method of controlling the progress of this maneuver is varying the back pressure. As I mentioned before, you'll have to work on this for a while before you can expect to do a succession of chandelles with any degree of respectability.

The Lazy Eight

Another maneuver that has no real practical use, except during formation training, is the lazy eight. This maneuver requires more skill and concentration to fly properly than the chandelle, and is a good test of a pilot's proficiency in controlling his bird with smoothness and precision. The ham-fisted stick handler need not apply here. What makes the lazy eight more demanding than the chandelle is constantly changing airspeed, angle of bank, and altitude; all three are necessary to meet the maximum and minimum parameters for the maneuver.

The only things that are relatively constant in the lazy eight are the power setting and the overall rate of turn. Since there is almost no additional G loading on the bird during a lazy eight, the maneuver can be performed by nearly all types of airplanes. This maneuver is a series of 180-degree turns, incorporating a climb in the first 90 degrees, and a dive in the second 90 degrees, with a change of direction after each 180 degrees of turn is completed.

The object of the maneuver is to hit the airspeed and altitude parameters at each 90-degree point at the proper bank angle while leaving the power setting constant. Select a long stretch of straight road, or a long section line, and clear the area. Position yourself on one side of the road, on a heading that is perpendicular to the road (position A). After you set the power, entry into the lazy eight is made by starting a shallow dive that will bring you across the road at the higher of the two airspeed limits for this maneuver. Hold your heading until your wing tip crosses the road (position 1), and as it does, note your altitude, for it becomes the base altitude for the rest of the maneuver. Then, smoothly apply enough back pressure to get the aircraft into a gentle to moderate climb; at the same time, begin to feed in aileron and rudder to establish a smooth, coordinated climbing turn. The idea in the first half of a lazy eight is for the bank angle to increase smoothly and steadily until you have completed 90 degrees of turn and are parallel to the road (position 2). At this point, you should be in a 90-degree bank, and at the lower airspeed limit for the maneuver—about 60 percent of your entry airspeed. Here, again, note your altitude; this figure becomes the maximum for the rest of the maneuver. Do *not* pause at this peak altitude and 90-degree bank position, even if you haven't achieved the desired airspeed—the 90 degrees of turn is the key.

Once this first half of the turn is complete, release a little of the back pressure and allow the nose of your bird to drop slightly, to set up a gentle descent. At the same time, start reducing your bank angle slowly but steadily, so that you keep the turn going, but at an ever-decreasing rate. What you are aiming for in the second half of a lazy eight is to recross the road at a 90-degree angle, at the base altitude you noted earlier, at the upper airspeed limit, and with the wings level (position 3). This sounds like a tall order, but, as with the chandelle, it amounts to playing airspeed to be gained against degrees of turn to go. In the lazy eight, you have the added problem of hitting the right altitude in a wings-level attitude.

As soon as you cross the road, the whole procedure is repeated in the opposite direction—that is, you start a climbing turn to arrive at the maximum altitude and the lower airspeed limit, in a 90-degree bank, parallel to the road (position 4); then you descend again to cross the road at a 90-degree angle (position 5).

This maneuver can be repeated until the road makes a turn or you run out of section line. After a little practice, you'll find that the properly flown lazy eight is a graceful, easy, floating type of maneuver, yet one that can still provide a challenge. When the lazy eight is flown according to the book, and all the airspeeds and altitudes are hit right on the money, the aircraft is in constant motion with respect to pitch and roll. The wings and the nose are moving in one direction or the other at all times; if you have to pause and hold either or both in a certain attitude in order to make your parameters, you have misjudged something along the way.

Never depend on power to help you out if you're not hitting your airspeed and altitude marks. Once set, the power should be left alone, except for minor adjustments to keep the rpm within limits. Leaving the power alone means you'll learn the most from practicing lazy eights—that is, precise control of airspeed, altitude, and direction by means of maneuver alone.

Both the chandelle and the lazy eight are good jumping-off points for acrobatic training. They introduce you in an easy, controlled way to aircraft attitudes and procedures not normally encountered in everyday flying around the local air patch. Additionally, they demonstrate the necessity of hitting the proper airspeed at the correct point in space, which is probably one of the most important facets of acrobatics.

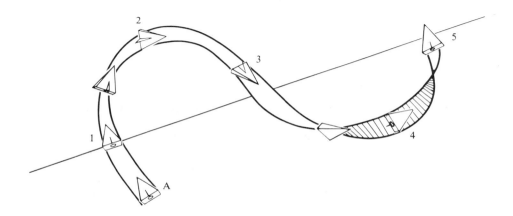

The lazy eight

The Slow Roll

The next step in acrobatics is to get you used to being on your back in an airplane, and this is done by means of the slow roll and the barrel roll. In contrast to the chandelle and the lazy eight, these acrobatics have a practical application, both as maneuvers in their own right, and as part of other, more complex aerobatic maneuvers.

The slow roll is a rotation of the aircraft around its own longitudinal axis, keeping the nose aimed at some distant reference point. This reference point should be something that is easily recognizable, such as an isolated cloud or a prominent mountain peak. In a way, using this point is slightly academic, because the maneuver goes fairly quickly, and the point is only used as a reference after the fact— that is, to see if you rolled out a little off your original heading.

Clear the area and adjust the power to bring the aircraft to the desired entry airspeed. Point the aircraft at the selected reference point and pull the nose up to about 15 to 20 degrees above the horizon. Then apply a moderate amount of aileron in the direction you want to go, and hold it until the roll is completed. Don't use full aileron on your first few tries, because this will generate a fairly high roll rate.

Initially, you just want to feel out the bird's rolling characteristics and find out what you have to do to complete the maneuver successfully. The higher the roll rate, the easier it is to become disoriented, so take it easy until you get the hang of the thing. On the other hand, don't be a pussycat and roll it so slowly that your grandmother could beat you around.

As you roll through the inverted position, your lift is acting downward, and if this effect is not taken into consideration, you will complete the roll in a nose-low attitude. Countering this nose-dropping tendency while inverted is the purpose of starting the slow roll with a slight climb. This compensation allows you to roll out in a fairly level attitude.

While doing the slow roll, start to neutralize your ailerons when you have about 30 degrees of roll left to go, to stop the roll in the wings-level position; while rolling out, use rudders as required to stay coodinated. During this last segment of the roll, check how you're doing in relation to your reference point. If it looks like you're going to be off in one direction or the other, now is the time to feed in a little of the appropriate rudder to bring you back on the mark.

If you insist on giving your grandmother a run for her money and trying this maneuver using a slow rate of roll, the nose-dropping tendency while inverted will be more pronounced, because you'll be spending more time on your back. An alternate method of compensation in this case would be to apply just a tad of forward stick for the second or two that you are upside down. Although it gives you one more thing to think about during the maneuver, it makes for a better-looking slow roll than does an increased climb angle during entry. Conversely, on a slow roll with full aileron, you'll probably go all the way around without noticing any appreciable nose drop. The maneuver utilizing a high rate of roll is more properly called an aileron roll.

It's a good idea to practice slow rolls and aileron rolls to the left and to the right, in order to learn to recoginize and compensate for the positive and negative effects of torque. (This holds true for nearly all other acrobatic maneuvers, too.)

The Barrel Roll

Our next rolling maneuver is the barrel roll, which is somewhat more precise than the slow roll, and as such demands more attention to parameters and reference points. The barrel roll is another easy, smooth, floating type of maneuver; during it you describe a circle around a reference point on the horizon, and end up back at the entry altitude. If it's done properly, you shouldn't put too much more than one to two Gs on the bird all the way around. If you have a two-seater, a good test of whether you've flown the barrel roll correctly is to do one while your passenger closes his eyes. With the exception of a slight increase in Gs during entry and recovery, he should not be able to tell that he was in anything but straight and level flight. The secret here is keeping at least one G on the bird during the entire maneuver, even when inverted, in order to maintain seat pressure.

Before starting the barrel roll, select a reference point that is (or appears to be) near your altitude. This could be a cloud or a distant mountaintop, but if these are not available, use the point where a road or a section line intersects the horizon. You can really use anything that is far enough in front of you that you can keep an eye on it throughout the maneuver.

Clear the area and adjust the power to bring the bird to a speed that is a little slower than the desired entry airspeed. Then start a gentle dive straight toward the reference point to pick up the remaining airspeed for entry. While you're in the dive, note the relative distance your nose is below the point. This distance can be used as a rough measure of the radius of the circle you want the nose to describe around the reference point. Assuming you're going to make the barrel roll to the left (most fighter pilots prefer left-handed maneuvers), note your altitude as soon as you hit the desired speed, and then start a turn to the right. As soon as your nose is about 30 degrees to the right of your reference point, in one, smooth, continuous motion stop your right turn and roll into a 30- to 45-degree bank to the left, while simultaneously feeding in back pressure to get the bird into a moderate climb. Keep the roll going as you arc up and around your reference point, using the ailerons to control the "roundness" of the circle you are describing on the horizon. If your circle is tightening up, ease off a little on the roll rate to flatten it out. If you're starting to slip outside the ideal circle, put a little more aileron into the roll.

As I mentioned above, the barrel roll is an easy, floating type of maneuver; therefore, after the initial pull-up there is little need for back pressure until the recovery is started. In fact, as you float over the top, you'll probably find that neutralizing the elevators works best to preserve the "roundness" of your circle. If you're doing a very large barrel roll, in which your upside-down time is a little more prolonged, a slight amount of forward pressure may even be needed at the top to keep the pattern symmetrical.

After completing 270 degrees of roll (your right wing should be pointing straight down in a roll to the left), start reapplying back pressure and adjusting your roll rate so that you will finish the maneuver at the altitude you noted during entry. At this completion point, you should also be in a wings-level attitude and heading straight for your reference point.

Naturally, every barrel roll does not end up right on the money. The time to make a "how goes it" check is at the 270-degree point. If it looks like you're going to end up below your original altitude, start adding back pressure right away, along with some left rudder if you're rolling to the left. Don't use ailerons to correct for this situation, because even though a tighter roll may allow you to catch the altitude in time, you'll be off your reference point to the left (see Figure 1 below).

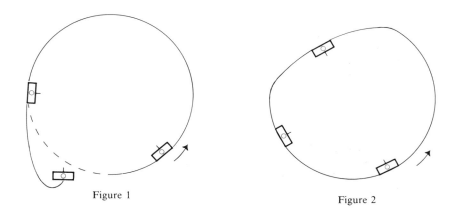

Figure 1   Figure 2

Correcting your altitude coming out of a barrel roll

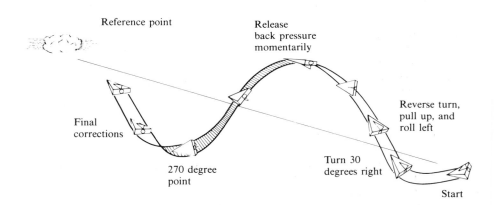

The barrel roll

If, on the other hand, you tightened up the roll going over the top, and you will finish the barrel roll above your base altitude, take out a tad of aileron to flatten out your arc, and add a little right rudder to bring the nose down quicker (see Figure 2). You will recognize that the application of bottom rudder while in a moderate bank is the same control action needed to slip the aircraft. The slip under these conditions does the same job as it does on final approach—it results in a rapid loss of altitude without a lot of lateral movement or increase of airspeed.

Both of these corrections should be just momentary applications of control pressure to make a one-shot attempt to salvage the maneuver. Any correction must be made quickly because you must start the recovery from the barrel roll at the 270-degree point or you'll overshoot your mark by quite a bit. A sketch of the entire barrel roll maneuver is shown opposite.

The Vertical Recovery

The vertical recovery is not by itself a specific acrobatic maneuver, but I cover it here in order to give you a definite procedure to follow in case you fall out of an overhead maneuver before you're over the top. Like parachuting, the vertical recovery does not lend itself very well to practice or simulation. *Do not* try to set up actual conditions for practicing the vertical recovery. It is usually needed to effect a safe, controlled righting of the airplane from an inverted, nose-high position, and purposely trying to stall an aircraft in this attitude, and then adding rudder to recover, is asking for a spin—probably an inverted one. The best procedure for learning the vertical recovery is to fly a straight-ahead approach to a stall, using about a 45-degree climb angle; when your airspeed *approaches* the stall point, start your vertical recovery.

Early recognition of the need for a vertical recovery is the best guarantee of success with this maneuver. The problem is an actual or incipient stall, or a loss of airspeed at a rate that will produce a stall shortly. The usual cause of this problem is too low an entry airspeed for a contemplated maneuver, and/or excessive Gs on the pull-up to overhead aerobatics, causing a rapid bleed-off of airspeed too early in the maneuver. You will generally encounter this problem after completing about 120 degrees of turn in the vertical plane during an overhead maneuver, or while you are inverted and still climbing at a 30- to 45-degree angle. A too-easy pull-up that does not get the bird over on its back soon enough and prolongs your time in the vertical plane can also bring about a rapid loss of airspeed and a need for the vertical recovery.

If you find yourself in this situation and things are turning to worms in a hurry, *don't try to complete the maneuver*—you'll only aggravate the condition. Here, discretion is the better part of valor; chalk one up to experience and start the vertical recovery immediately.

Since the problem is a stall, your corrective action should be anything that re-

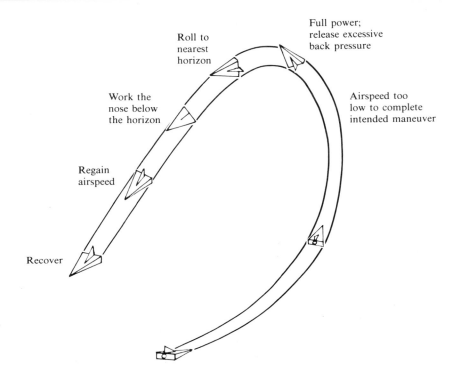

The vertical recovery

lieves the stall and helps you regain flying speed. First of all, get full power on the bird and release any excessive back pressure on the stick; at the same time, start a coordinated roll to the nearest horizon. Don't neutralize the elevators in this case unless you're really stalled out and have to break it in a hurry. It's best to keep a little back stick in if you can, to help get the nose down below the horizon. Applying a little rudder at the same time will also help to bring the nose down quicker without aggravating the stall.

If your wings are level with the horizon when you start the vertical recovery—in a loop, for example—the choice of which rudder to apply is up to you. However, a lot of planes, as they approach the stall, have a tendency to drop one wing. If this happens while you are inverted, pick the rudder on the side of the wing that's pointing at the ground. Don't jam in full rudder all at once, but ease in a moderate amount and see how the bird responds.

When you release excessive control pressures and use the rudder to start the nose down, the plane's inherent stability will cause it to slowly assume a gentle gliding attitude. This is similar to the recovery following a straight-ahead stall. Don't worry about being in a near vertical bank as you recover—your first job is to work the nose below the horizon and pick up some airspeed. When things are more under control, you can roll the wings level and try 'er again!

An important thing to remember while doing a vertical recovery is to go *smooth and easy* on the controls. Don't try to horse the bird around—you're too close to a stalled condition to begin with, and ham-handing the controls will only make things worse. Fly it by feel, and let gravity and the bird do their thing, with an assist in the right direction from you. Unless you're eyeball to eyeball with the trees, don't be in a hurry to pull out of the steep dive that will most likely result from a vertical recovery. Trying to pull up before you have sufficient airspeed could result in a secondary stall. Then you'll be back where you started, only lower.

The Loop

With the techniques of the vertical recovery well in hand, we're ready to start talking about overhead maneuvers. The first of these is the loop. This maneuver, or some portion of it, has a lot of applications in both acrobatics and combat tactics: therefore, you should be very familiar with it. The loop is a 360-degree turn in the vertical plane; if done properly, it should describe a circle in that plane. Although this doesn't sound like a real big deal, the rub lies in entering and exiting the loop right on the reference line, and at the base altitude.

In this maneuver, hitting the entry airspeed is critical; in fact, it doesn't hurt to have a little cushion of a few knots over this speed on your first few attempts at a loop—or, for that matter, any other overhead maneuver. Clear the area, set your power, and line up right over a section line, with your nose pointing in the same direction as the section line. A cloud or some reference point on the horizon won't hack it during a loop—you need a ground reference that you can pick up and align yourself with as you come over the top and down the back side.

Start a moderate dive straight along the section line until you pick up your entry airspeed. At this point note your altitude, because this altitude is what you'll be shooting for on the recovery. Begin a smooth, wings-level pull-up, and keep the back pressure coming in until you have about 3.5 to 4 Gs on the bird. Keep this amount of back pressure constant as long as you can, especially during the first 90 degrees of the loop, because slackening off here will just set you up to fall out of the loop before you get over the top. As you pass about 135 degress of turn in the vertical, your airspeed will have decreased by quite a bit; consequently, you'll have to add a little more aft stick to keep the bird turning at the desired rate. But don't overdo it at this point, because too much back stick here will force an early stall.

When you approach the top of the loop and your nose is at or near the horizon,

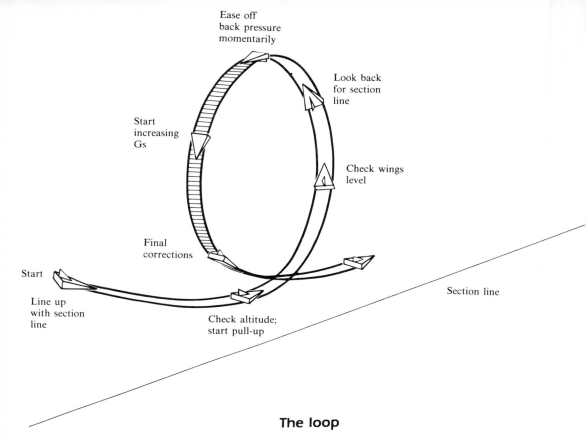

Ease off
back pressure
momentarily

Look back
for section
line

Start
increasing
Gs

Check wings
level

Final
corrections

Start

Line up
with section
line

Check altitude;
start pull-up

Section line

The loop

you can ease off the back pressure momentarily and let the bird float for an instant. Then start to feed in back stick as the nose starts down the back side of the loop. The control pressures in this 90 degrees of the loop are very similar to those needed in the second quarter of the maneuver—from 90 to 180 degrees of turn—except that they are applied in reverse order. As you come through the vertical dive position, your airspeed will be picking up rapidly, making your elevators more effective. The idea from here to the completion of the loop is to adjust the back pressure so as to end up the maneuver in level flight at the base altitude you noted during entry.

Using pitch control to keep the maneuver perfectly round is only half the battle where a good loop is concerned. Ideally, you should stay exactly over the section line during the entire maneuver. Therefore, this reference must be used as much as possible throughout the loop. Fly the entry dive and initial pull-up right down the line, and, as your nose rises to the point where it blocks out the section line, start checking how your wings line up with the horizon. If they are not parallel with the horizon, make a quick adjustment to level them out because you'll lose this horizon reference shortly. As you go through the vertical and start over on your back, it's pretty much "by guess and by God" as to what a wings-level attitude is. The only thing you can do here is to concentrate on keeping the ailerons neutral until you can pick up the section line again. When your nose is still about

30 degrees above the horizon as you approach the inverted position, throw your head back as far as you can to look out the top rear portion of the canopy. You should be able to pick up the section line, and this gives you a chance to cheat a little. If you notice that you're pointed off to one side or the other, ease in a little rudder to swing the nose in the desired direction.

By making small corrections early in the maneuver, you'll have less error to correct for later, and you won't have to make a large and obvious correction turn during the down side of the loop. Keep working to get realigned with the section line as you go over the top and down the back side, so that by the last 90 degrees of the loop you'll be right in the groove. If you have stayed in the vertical plane of the loop, you will hit your own prop wash as you level out at the base altitude.

A G meter installed in your bird makes flying the loop a lot easier. At the entry point you simply add back pressure until you're reading 3.5 to 4 Gs on the meter, and hold it there. As before, when you slow down in the second quarter of the loop, you'll have to add more aft stick to hold the Gs in as long as you can without approaching a stall. Over the top, the G meter can be pretty much ignored until you start to pick up airspeed on the down side. Then begin to reapply back pressure until you hit 3.5 to 4 Gs again, and peg it there until you reach the level flight position. Using a G meter this way will give you a perfect loop every time—if you keep your wings level with the techniques I mentioned above.

The Cuban Eight

The next of the four overhead maneuvers is the Cuban eight, a loop in which a half roll is performed on the back side so that recovery is made on a heading 180 degrees away from the entry heading. It teaches you to keep yourself oriented and the bird under positive control during both inverted and rolling flight.

The first half of a Cuban eight is exactly the same as the first half of a loop— the same references, techniques, and speeds apply to both. With this in mind, we'll pick up the action at the top of the loop in the inverted position. Once again, try to make whatever corrections you can to get back over the section line. Continue just as in a loop until your nose is 30 degrees below the horizon. Then feed in aileron and rudder to make a smooth, coordinated half roll to the upright position. This roll should be done smartly—you don't have the airspeed to really wrack it around, but if your roll rate is too slow, you won't be right side up in time to pull out at the base altitude.

When the half roll is complete, you should be in about a 50-degree dive, over the section line with the wings level. About the time you roll upright is when you should start feeding in back pressure to recover from the Cuban eight at your base altitude.

As you approach the base altitude, you should be coming up on your entry airspeed. If you have this speed at your altitude reference, start a pull-up into the second half of the Cuban eight, which is done exactly like the first half. If you're a little shy of the airspeed, you'll have to press on in the dive until you reach it. Don't try to force it just to keep the pattern symmetrical, because you'll most likely fall out of the maneuver at the top of the second loop.

The complete Cuban eight is two of these loops with the half roll, and ends up with the aircraft going in its original direction, over the section line, at the base altitude, in a wings-level attitude. If you find yourself quite a bit off the reference line as you are completing the half roll, adjust your roll rate, tightening up or loosening the roll. In addition to adding or taking out aileron in the final portion of the half roll, you might put in a little rudder in the desired direction to expedite the corrective action. If you do this properly, it will almost look as if you knew what you were doing all the way around.

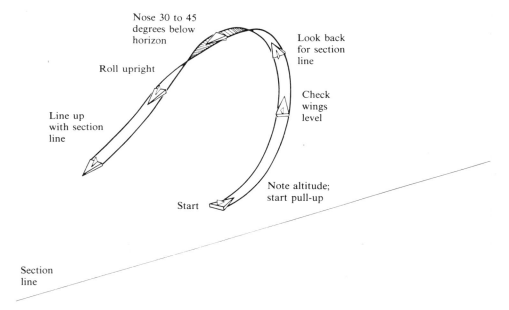

The Cuban eight (first half)

The Immelmann

The Immelmann, the third overhead maneuver, is named after the World War I ace Max Immelmann, who first used this turn in combat—with outstanding effectiveness. (Immelmann ran up a string of 15 victories flying with Oswald Boelcke. He bought the farm when his Fokker Eindecker broke apart during a dogfight in 1916.) The Immelmann turn has applications in both the acrobatic and tactical areas, and particularly the latter; therefore, you should practice this maneuver until you can execute it almost perfectly every time. It is a 180-degree turn in direction accomplished in the vertical plan—or, in other words, a loop with a half roll at the top.

As with the Cuban eight, the first part of the Immelman is exactly the same as the first half of a loop. The difference in the Immelmann comes when you approach the inverted position, when your nose is about 30 degrees above the horizon. About the time you throw your head back to pick up the section line through the top rear of your canopy, release the back pressure and start a smooth, coordinated roll to the upright position. (The direction of the roll is immaterial.)

Since your airspeed is about as low as it's going to get in the maneuver at this point, you must take care not to stall the bird out during the roll. As you feed in aileron to execute the roll, allow the nose to keep coming down to the horizon, just as if you were going to stay inverted and complete the loop. You will find that because of your relatively low airspeed, it will take a fair amount of stick movement to complete the roll. The same will be true with the rudders as you coordinate the roll and try to stay lined up over the section line.

If you do the Immelmann properly, you should be able to finish the roll and stay in level flight at the peak altitude of the loop. However, don't stand on principle if you roll out wings level and find that your airspeed is getting dangerously close to the stall. Bite the bullet and allow the nose to drop a little to regain some flying speed. The maneuver isn't designed for you to come out at the top with a full head of steam, but you should have enough push left to do a little maneuvering without stalling out.

When rolling out of the Immelmann, the objective is smooth, coordinated control movements, and a light hand on the stick, to get and keep the maximum altitude gain from the maneuver.

The Cloverleaf

The last of the overhead maneuvers is the cloverleaf. As with the Cuban eight and the Immelmann, it can add much to your knowledge and confidence in handling your bird precisely while you are in unusual attitudes. It is probably the most difficult of all the basic acrobatics, and as such it requires a little more concentration and planning to execute properly. A sketch of one "leaf" of this maneuver is shown below.

The cloverleaf is basically a looping maneuver with the added twist of a half roll on the front side of each loop. Essentially, you start a loop in one vertical plane, and by means of the half roll on the way up you complete the loop in another vertical plane, oriented 90 degrees to the first. The complete cloverleaf consists of four of these loops.

Once again, all of the entry conditions and techniques for a loop apply to the cloverleaf. However, with the cloverleaf you have more of a problem with reference

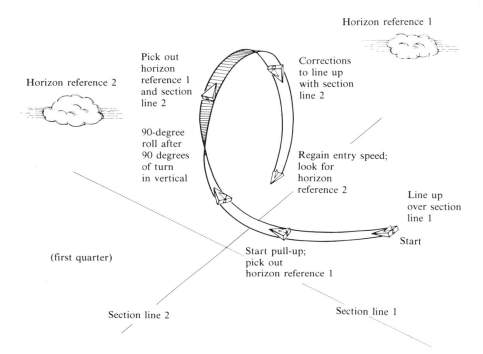

Horizon reference 1

Pick out
horizon
reference 1
and section
line 2

Horizon reference 2

Corrections
to line up
with section
line 2

90-degree
roll after
90 degrees
of turn
in vertical

Regain entry speed;
look for
horizon
reference 2

Line up
over section
line 1

Start

(first quarter)

Start pull-up;
pick out
horizon reference 1

Section line 2

Section line 1

The cloverleaf (first quarter)

points. As with the loop, you need a section line to start out on, but it's a lot handier if you're in an area with section lines that run at right angles to each other. And horizon references such as clouds or prominent landmarks are almost a necessity for the cloverleaf. The best time to practice this maneuver is on a day when you have some fair-weather cumulus clouds in the area to act as these references.

The setup and diving entry for the cloverleaf are the same as for the loop, with one additional requirement thrown in. As you are going down the chute to pick up your entry speed, locate a cloud, horizon reference, or extended section line that is 90 degrees from your present heading and on the side of the cockpit that corresponds to the direction you have planned for your half roll. In other words, if you intend to do a half roll to the right on the way up, select a horizon reference off to the right side of your bird.

When you hit your entry speed, start the pull-up just as for a loop. After you have completed almost 90 degrees of your pull-up turn in the vertical, begin a smoothly coordinated roll in the direction of your reference point. It may take a little head twisting to keep this point in sight as the roll progresses, but you've got to keep an eye on it, because you want to stop the roll when the reference point is at the top of your canopy. However, don't let lining up with this reference point during the half roll occupy all of your attention. You must keep the back pressure in and adjust it to keep the nose coming over the top, just as in a normal loop. By the time you reach the inverted position, the nose of your aircraft should be pointing right at the reference. If you're off a little, use a tad of rudder to correct as you did in the loop.

The remaining half of this "leaf" is accomplished just like the second half of a loop, but, as you start down, you've got to pick up a section line running at a 90-degree angle to the one you used on entry, and use this new one to line up on. Although hitting the base altitude is important, allowing the aircraft to accelerate to entry speed is even more important. Keep on churning down the section line until you have your speed, and then start another pull-up to repeat the entire procedure just described. Remember to pick out a new horizon reference on the same side of the cockpit as the first one, so that you'll have something to line up on during the next half roll. For each of the remaining three "leaves" of the cloverleaf, all the procedures are exactly the same. The important points to remember are: make sure you have entry airspeed before proceeding to the next "leaf;" constantly adjust to your reference lines; pick a horizon reference as you start each pull-up; and try to hit the same base and peak altitudes in each "leaf."

The Split S

The split S is yet another variation of the basic loop. This maneuver is used primarily by fighters in combat situations; however, it does have some application to normal acrobatics. The split S allows you to practice, under controlled conditions, the techniques needed to recover from a somewhat hairy situation you may find yourself in some day—a vertical dive with the throttle wide open. Every jock who intends to get involved in acrobatics or mock combat should know his bird's split S characteristics at all power settings. The most valuable information to be gained from the maneuver is exactly how much altitude your bird requires to do a split S and recover to straight and level flight. Don't try this maneuver at relatively low altitude until you've worked it out higher up and you're completely familiar with the amount of altitude the split S eats up.

The split S is best described as a descending 180-degree turn in the vertical plane—sort of an Immelmann in reverse, or the second half of a loop. Start the split S with the same procedures as for other acrobatics—clear the area and set yourself up over a section line. Retard your power to the low cruise or idle position, and execute a coordinated half roll to the inverted position.

From here on out, the split S is exactly the same as the back side of a loop. Allow the nose to start dropping, and use rudder as required to stay lined up over the section line. Start to put in some easy back pressure, which should be increased gradually to 3.5 to 4 Gs as you progress through the vertical position and on around to level flight. Once the G load is set, hold it there until the bird is level—

the whole idea of a split S is to turn around with a minimum of altitude loss. Be sure to jot down your entry and exit altitudes for reference later.

After you've got a few split S's under your belt and you've got a handle on it, take the bird up to a higher altitude and try a few at a medium power setting. Again note the altitudes. The next move is to take it up to a still higher altitude and get your thrill for the day by trying a split S at max cruise power. Make sure you've got plenty of room under you when you start the maneuver, because the old altimeter will really unwind, and it seems to take forever to get the plane back to a level attitude without over-G'ing it. Also be sure to keep an eye on the rpm and airspeed so that you don't exceed your red lines.

The data supplied by the split S at a high power setting is probably the handiest, because when you start working with basic fighter maneuvers, you will encounter these conditions frequently. Be familiar with them, for, as the first corollary to Murphy's Law states, when something goes wrong, it will be at the worst possible time. Thus, if you suddenly find yourself going straight down with the engine wide open, it's nice to know immediately just what it will take to recover the bird without putting any bends or wrinkles in it. Of course, if you do get caught in this situation, your recovery can be expedited and the altitude loss kept to a minimum by retarding the power to idle, and applying the maximum G load certified for the aircraft.

CHAPTER 5
SAFETY AND BRIEFING—THE CRITICAL FACTORS

No practice of basic fighter maneuvers and mock combat would be intelligent without the pilot's placing a heavy emphasis on safety. Practicing safety is not throwing a wet blanket over the fun and excitement; it is just good common sense. Some sage long ago made an interesting observation that is worth repeating here: "Aviation, like the sea, is not inherently dangerous; but, like the sea, it is terribly unforgiving of any carelessness, incapacity, or neglect." Keep this thought in mind as you work through fighter maneuvers, and insure that you and your wingman regard safety as the *paramount* consideration in every air (or ground) situation. Don't compromise in this area to the slightest degree—make sure that you and your bird are both ready for the proposed mission. Some of the more exciting aspects of dogfighting are also some of its more dangerous—in fact, short of your being shot at, performing basic fighter maneuvers is probably the most dangerous type of flying you can do. You will be dealing with higher speeds, higher rates of closure, higher G conditions, and more unusual attitudes than you have been used to. Add to this the close proximity to other maneuvering aircraft, and you can see how the chances for a ding can multiply. Therefore, know what you're doing when you get into the acrobatics area; proceed slowly, and master each step of a maneuver before proceeding to something more difficult. Consider other people who may be using the area—they will probably not be expecting the type of maneuvers you and your wingman will be practicing, and they should be given a wide berth. Above all, don't bounce someone crossing the area, because he may become so flustered by your actions that he reacts very unpredictably and unconventionally. Remember: a midair can spoil your whole day!

Knowing the Mission and the Bird

As with any other phase of private flying, the safety aspects of basic fighter maneuvers are mainly the responsibility of the individual participants. If established regulations and common sense are disregarded, the chances that someone—including yourself—will buy the farm are greatly increased. Since you will be establishing your own safety program to coincide with local conditions, the following discussion is intended only as a guide to the more important elements to be included.

Before I get into the particulars on safety, I want to repeat one very basic assumption made throughout this book that should never be disregarded. This is the premise that *anyone attempting these maneuvers will be flying a bird that is designed and stressed for acrobatics.* These tactics were developed for high-performance aircraft in a combat situation, and if they are executed near the limits of the performance envelope of your bird, they can produce considerable stress on the airframe and the pilot. (This point will be discussed further in Chapter 6.) Unless your bird can hack the rigors of acrobatics, including inverted flight and/or negative Gs, for slightly longer periods than you are normally accustomed to, basic fighter maneuvers are definitely not recommended.

Careful flight testing of the reactions and capabilities of your bird under high-G conditions is absolutely essential before trying any basic fighter maneuvers. This is the time to establish absolute parameters on maximum and minimum airspeeds, plus and minus G loads, high- and low-speed stalling indicators, inverted flight, and so forth. The safety considerations of having a hassle-worthy bird cannot be overemphasized. Compliance with established limitations has a marked influence on increased longevity.

Although it may seem too formalized when compared with normal pleasure flying routines, *thorough briefings are essential to the success of this kind of flying.* Jot down notes on your kneeboard so that you'll know exactly what's to be done, when, how, and to whom. If your cockpit is too cramped for a kneeboard, try a spring clip attached to the instrument panel to hold your notes. Make sure that everybody on the mission fully understands all phases of it, and the sequence of events that is planned. Don't count on using the radio to clear up any doubtful points after you're airborne. (The topics that are considered a must for briefing any basic fighter maneuvers mission will be outlined in greater detail at the end of this chapter.)

Aircraft preflight is another item that should be emphasized—again at the risk of your appearing slightly unconventional to the other throttle benders around the local air patch. This is particularly true after you've put a few missions on the bird and have subjected it to stress factors not found in day-to-day pleasure flying. Go over the bird with a fine-tooth comb, checking for cracks, popped rivets, loose lines, leaks, and anything else that could be caused by wracking the bird around in a hassle. I'm not talking about a major overhaul inspection every time you're going up to tangle with someone—just a thorough preflight with careful attention to small details. A little time spent here always pays big dividends after you've "slipped the surly bonds of earth."

Your preflight should also include a good look around the cockpit—including under the seat. Remove or stow all loose items that could start floating around and become a hazard during negative G conditions—especially solid objects such as nuts, screws, and pencils that could become lodged in your control mechanism at the wrong time and cause you to end up a statistic. Remember: Murphy's Law applies more to basic fighter maneuvers than to any other type of flying: If something can go wrong, it will go wrong.

Maneuver Area and Minimums

The area in which fighter maneuvers will be practiced usually is the designated acrobatics area for your local airport. If this space is quite large, or you're out in the boonies and have to establish your own area, there are a few points that should be kept in mind to make the whole operation safer. First of all, you should select, if you have a choice, that portion of the acrobatics area that is used the least. Time in the air is too precious to waste waiting for someone to clear the area after you're all set up to go on a particular maneuver. Further, you and your wingman will be utilizing a larger chunk of airspace than is required for single-ship aerobatics; the more remote spots offer less chance of interruption by a transient. If possible, the tactics area should have easily recognizable landmarks that can be used for rendezvous points, or as references for the area boundaries. Rejoins over unbroken, nondescript landscape can be very time-consuming. Open bodies of water beyond easy reference to the shoreline should be avoided for the same reason. Besides, there is nothing more disconcerting than coming out of an overhead maneuver heading away from the shore on a hazy day, particularly if the sun is low. Up and down look the same, as does sideways; such conditions almost require an immediate transition to instruments to make sure you're right side up. If this momentary confusion occurs at a relatively low altitude and you end up in a steep dive, there may not be enough space left to effect a safe pullout.

When selecting an area for performing fighter maneuvers, try *not* to choose one that is a zillion miles from home plate, if you can avoid it. Proximity to the home drome allows you more time to practice on any given mission, and best of all, if an emergency develops, you're only a short distance from a runway.

In performing basic fighter maneuvers, there are two types of minimums that should *never be cheated on,* no matter what the circumstances. These are weather minimums and maneuver minimums. The latter are really the basis for establishing the former. Before you attempt any of these maneuvers, an absolute floor to the area should be determined. This floor should be high enough to allow a safe recovery from any of the maneuvers you plan to execute; it can be estimated from the amount of altitude the bird with the highest wing loading requires to pull out of a split S. Be sure to compute this floor above the highest terrain obstacle in the area, and it may be a good idea to add a couple of thousand feet as a cushion. Once set, this minimum altitude should be rigorously adhered to by all participants— don't let yourself be suckered into a treetop chase just to prove you can hang in there. One wrong move in this situation could be hazardous to your health.

After you've decided on this base altitude, you can determine what weather ceiling is required for any given mission involving fighter tactics. During the early phases of your training, a working area at least 5,000 feet deep should suffice. However, as you get into the more involved overhead maneuvers, and extended engagements, you'll probably find that you will need at least 8,000 to 10,000 feet, service ceilings, airspace restrictions, and terrain permitting.

Weather in the area is another factor to consider. A scattered to broken deck of fair-weather cumulus moving through your working area can restrict air-to-air and air-to-ground visibilities to the point where the mission is hardly worth the effort. Such a situation offers too many opportunities for loss of visual contact with other birds, which may inadvertently pop in and out of clouds when your attention is diverted during a hassle. It takes a lot of vertical and horizontal airspace to practice fighter maneuvers or simulate an engagement; it's no fun to have to keep breaking off because of clouds.

A low deck of clouds or a fogbank obscuring the landscape can also cause problems. Prominent boundary landmarks and rendezvous points should always be visible, for safety considerations and to expedite different phases of the mission. Excessive haze is another condition that should be avoided, particularly on bright days when the sun is close to the horizon. In-flight visibility should be at least five miles in order to properly clear the area for other traffic, and to avoid situations where high closing rates and late visuals could be hazardous.

Disengagement Criteria and Emergency Procedures

Before going out to practice these maneuvers, everyone should have firmly set in his mind the criteria for disengagement. Continuing an engagement or a maneuver beyond these conditions is foolish, wastes gas and time, and could result in a dangerous situation.

Some of the more common reasons for discontinuing a maneuver or an engagement are: an airplane exceeds the airspace boundaries or goes below the minimum altitude; someone reaches bingo fuel (enough to get you home and then divert to an alternate); someone has a radio out, or there is any other type of problem with the aircraft or the pilot; one bird obtains a definite position of advantage; a specific maneuver has been demonstrated and/or practiced. Whenever a pilot wants to break it off for any reason, he should call "Disengage" over the radio, and smoothly bring his bird to a wings-level, unaccelerated attitude.

It can be seen here that absolute radio discipline is a must during basic fighter maneuvers. Keep the mission channel as free from chatter as possible. If anyone calls "Disengage," all tactical action should cease until the reason for breaking it off can be acted upon and corrected. NEVER cry wolf and use the "Disengage" call as a ploy to gain the advantage.

If a pilot calls it off for aircraft problems, real or imagined, he should immediately take up a heading for home plate. Other birds should rejoin with the afflicted aircraft as quickly as possible and help out in any way they can. This assistance could take the form of a visual inspection of the other bird, help with navigation, or general moral support. *Since emergencies have a way of compounding, and since basic fighter maneuvers are really modified acrobatics, make certain that all participants comply with the regulations concerning the wearing of parachutes.* This precaution goes double on missions early in the game, when you are feeling out your bird under high G loads and in unusual attitudes.

An item almost too obvious to mention is a completely thorough understanding of all the emergency procedures applicable to your airplane. The corrective action for major and minor in-flight problems should be memorized, and also written down on a checklist to be carried on each flight. Some good insurance in this respect is to have someone give you a blindfold cockpit check to make sure you know where each switch and control is located, and which way it should be moved for a given emergency procedure. If things start coming unglued in the air, you may not have enough time to sit and think through the required corrective action. Be prepared to react instinctively and properly to each potential problem.

Commonsense Precautions

One of the best ways to avoid emergency situations is to plan ahead, and there is no area in which this is more critical than that of fuel management. Your checklist should contain actual fuel consumption figures for two or three power settings for your bird. It's a good idea to note on a map the headings and distances from key checkpoints in the acrobatics area to home plate; it would be handy to have no-wind times and fuel figures alongside these. A little planning here sure saves a lot of E6B time in the air, when you'll have more important things on your mind. If anticipated traffic or forecast weather conditions indicate possible problems and/or delays at your proposed landing time, be sure to adjust your bingo fuel to compensate for this. A little extra fuel over home plate is always like money in the bank in case of delays. On fields where only one runway is available, a hip-pocket alternate should always be considered in case the guy landing in front of you blows a tire and closes the field.

Although one of your chief aims in basic fighter maneuvers is to remain undetected by your opponent until you are at his six and waxing his tail, the name of the game with respect to other aircraft in the area is, "See and be seen." Everyone in the flight should constantly keep his head on a swivel, not just to keep track of his opponent(s), but to locate any other birds that might be using the area. Call out "Stranger" information by means of the clock code to other guys in the flight, to insure that each of you is aware of the stranger's position with respect to your intended maneuvers. It's a good idea to check at the operations desk of your local air patch to see if they know of anyone who might be using the area at the same time you plan to. Also let the operations know when you will be there, and what you are planning to do, so that other people can be advised accordingly.

Whenever you pull up into the sun in an effort to lose an opponent, you must assume that the pilot chasing you has lost his visual on you. Therefore, *you* have the responsibility for maintaining adequate separation between the two birds. All the maxims of safety are probably covered best by the use of common sense, and being prepared—both for the mission and the unexpected. Always keep in mind that it's just a game, and there is never an excuse for exceeding your skill level or the aircraft's capabilities just to secure an advantage or to shake off a pursuer. If somebody's had you, bite the bullet and admit it rather than trying something foolish and/or dangerous. Play it so you can stick around to fight another day.

Briefing

Any mission involving basic fighter maneuvers should be thoroughly briefed. These are definitely not "kick the tire, light the fire, first one off is leader and we'll brief in the air" missions. Time in the air is too short, and too many questions remain unanswered in whole or in part if you try to take an off-the-cuff approach to what you want to accomplish when you're airborne. No one should leave the ground with any doubts about what he is going to do, when it should be done and how, and what he should be looking for in the way of learning experiences. The surest and safest way to accomplish all these ends is to have available a *written* briefing guide for each mission—covering both the general and the specific. *The items common to every mission, such as weather, safety procedures and local operations requirements, should be repeated each time* so that they become second nature to everyone involved, and should be the first topics covered in the briefing. Once these have been gone over, with special attention to any exceptions to the normal routine, the more detailed descriptions of the maneuvers to be performed may begin.

The briefing guide can be as long or as short as your particular program demands. However, as a minimum, it should address these topics:

(1) *Hand signals* for both normal and emergency situations. At the very least, signals should be developed for transmitter and/or receiver out; fuel checks; flight lead changes; aircraft emergency—must land as soon as possible; and radio channel changes. Be sure that whatever signals you come up with are distinctive enough that they won't be confused with any other hand motions.

(2) *Emergency data for the area,* such as minimum altitudes, high-terrain obstacles, emergency headings to the nearest airfields, known traffic in the area, and temporary restrictions that change the boundaries of the area.

(3) *Emergency procedures review.* Ask each other about a few aircraft emergencies to see if the remedies can be recited verbatim according to the checklist.

(4) *Rendezvous points to be used* and the altitudes at each. Be sure to state whether the rendezvous will be made using circles to the right or to the left, so as to minimize the chances of a head-on pass.

(5) *Radio channels* to be used during the flight. Include en route frequencies; tactical or discreet frequencies to be used in the acrobatics area to minimize inter-

ference with the mission by a lot of chatter from other pilots; and, of course, an emergency channel. It may be a good idea to assign single-digit numbers to the frequencies chosen, since they lend themselves to hand signals better than the megahertz for each channel.

(6) *Routes to be flown* and the type of formation to be used going to and from the acrobatics area.

(7) *Bingo fuel.* Be sure to compute this from the *farthest* point in the acrobatics area to the field where you intend to land. If head winds are strong enough to be a significant factor, add a little extra to compensate for them. When the weather at home plate is uncertain, be sure to set your bingo high enough so that you can make it to a usable alternate field if things go sour. (A good practice to follow is to make a fuel check after each engagement or set of maneuvers, so that further activity for the flight can be planned accordingly.)

(8) *Call signs.* Assign these for use in the acrobatics area to minimize confusion; it's always possible that you'll pick up radio calls by other aircraft whose tail numbers are similar to yours. Choose call signs that are short, simple, and distinctive. This will insure that they are clearly understood on a crowded radio channel, or when a dangerous situation is developing and must be brought to another pilot's attention *immediately.* Cute, lengthy, or hard-to-pronounce call signs will only serve to complicate matters by confusing everyone concerned.

Appendix C of this book contains a Briefing Guide and Form that meets these requirements, and more. For safety's sake, use it.

A final word on briefings—don't cheat yourself by cutting them short. Allow sufficient time before your planned takeoff to permit a thorough discussion of the maneuvers, including a demonstration with models. Encourage note-taking with respect to the sequence of events, radio frequencies, rendezvous points and altitudes, bingo fuel, and so forth. A few key items jotted down here will save a lot of head scratching once you're airborne.

CHAPTER 6
DISCIPLINE AND TECHNIQUE

Simulated air combat is an exciting facet of flying, and if it's properly approached it can provide as much fun and excitement as any competitive sport—probably more. However, like all sports involving a combination of people, machines, and high speeds, its proper enjoyment demands certain things of each participant. Paramount among these is absolute self-discipline—discipline to take the time and effort necessary to learn all there is to know about your airplane, fighter maneuvers, and yourself. It may seem strange to talk about discipline to pilots, who by the very nature of their craft are supposed to be a thinking, disciplined group. My intent is merely to emphasize that a simulated air combat situation offers a host of temptations that are very hard to resist, but which, if yielded to, could lead to physical and/or financial disaster. Among these temptations would be to *half* learn or understand a maneuver or tactic before proceeding to something more complex; to continue an engagement that has exceeded airspace boundaries; or to bounce some unsuspecting pigeon who is not a part of the mission, just to shine your own posterior. These and myriad others may seem like great ideas at the time, but if pursued they can, and probably will, eventually cause you problems.

Obviously, it's best to know your mission and to fly it as briefed—then you'll be around with the other old, bold pilots as they swap hairy war stories over a couple of cold beers. In reality, cultivating the self-discipline I am speaking of is not the harsh unpleasant drudgery you might envision, but should be a labor of love for anyone who has even a little bit of fighter pilot in him. If it becomes too much of a chore to properly prepare yourself to press on after hearing "Tally Ho!", then maybe the fighter jock's game isn't your bag. However, I sincerely hope it is, because even if the learning process takes time and patience, the exhilaration of a five-minute engagement is worth it. Just as earth people will never know the freedom of flight, never will the straight and level pilot know the thrill and satisfaction of an evenly matched dogfight.

I can't say too often that you shouldn't expect to become the Red Baron overnight. Take the time to become thoroughly proficient in basic acrobatics, especially overhead maneuvers—loops, Cuban eights, Immelmanns, cloverleafs. In other words, be at home on your back, and know how your bird flies and feels in the unusual positions that are part of these maneuvers. The tactics I discuss in Part 3 of this book will not make you the scourge of the airways, whose skill and cunning inevitably triumph over the superstition and ignorance of all comers. They are *only the basics*—the school solutions to canned situations, which in reality you'll see very infrequently during actual dogfights. However, they are essential building blocks on which to base your plans as you evaluate each tactical situation. Remember: All maneuvering must be done in relation to your opponent, and during an engagement there will often be times when a variant of a given maneuver can be used to advantage—perhaps only half of a specific maneuver, or a drastically modified one, will best fit the particular situation. Before you can proceed to these ad hoc tactics, you must have a thorough understanding of what basic move you are modifying, what you want to accomplish by using this modification, and what the consequences will be with respect to speeds, G loads, and recovery minimums. Familiarity with the basics is essential because, in a hassle, you'll have just seconds to recognize the applicability of a specific maneuver, and to execute it. You must be ready to capitalize on these fleeting chances at every moment.

Because the air-to-air situation is fluid, and it is impractical to try to discuss every possible maneuver the attacker and defender may try, in this book I will cover only an opponent's most probable reactions to a given move. Where appropriate, I will discuss the counters to these maneuvers so that you can utilize these actions as the need arises.

As you read through the maneuvers in the next part of this book, you may find that it gets a little difficult to visualize the spatial relationship of the two birds, particularly if you have various options at some specific point in the maneuver. A proven solution to this problem is to work through each maneuver using your hands as airplanes in order to set in your mind's eye just how things look with both aircraft moving. An even better technique is to use small plastic models of fighters painted different colors, with dowels glued in the tail pipes. You will find that the models are far superior to your hands unless you've got 360-degree ball joints in your wrists. As you move the models through each maneuver, stop at the key points to study how the situation would look from each cockpit and just what control actions would be required to get your bird where you want it to go next. A little time spent studying each tactic in this manner will save you a lot of valuable time in the air.

Finally, a word on your attitude toward the game. Although the term "defensive maneuver" is used in this book, these moves should more properly be thought of as "counteroffensive." The mission of the fighter pilot is offensive in nature, and is neatly summed up by a quote from *No Guts, No Glory,* a book by Korean War ace Major General Frederick Blesse: "If your primary concern is defense, don't go on the mission." Until your opponent is parked in your deep six and is eating your socks, always work to regain and keep the offensive. If an opponent with an initial edge expects you to break for home plate because of his advantage, he will probably be caught unawares and be more likely to make a mistake if he sees you pull up into the attack. Always play the game to win—but if you're having one of those days where nothing seems to be working for you, pick an opportune moment and disengage. Debrief your flight thoroughly to find out what mistakes you made, and have a go at it tomorrow.

This next section will be a potpourri of a lot of things that apply to all phases of basic fighter maneuvers—techniques, do's, don'ts, and things to be aware of and to beware of. These items will be loosely grouped in three categories: aircraft maneuvering, aircraft energy level, and keeping an eyeball on the enemy.

Aircraft Maneuvering

Please keep in mind that we are here discussing *all* combat—mock and real. Not all the conditions described will pertain to light plane mock combat. Again, as you read, use common sense. The time to start thinking about aircraft maneuvering is well before you're in the area where an engagement is planned or is possible. If you are bounced unexpectedly, your planning time is considerably shortened. Whether you decide to stay and play or cut for home, you'll have to assess the situation rapidly at the initial contact. Before starting an engagement, consider your distance from home plate, available fuel, altitude, and the relative position of both birds. Also look around for the bogey's wingman. If they seem to have you boxed in, the best tactic may be to counter the initial pass and head for home at the first opportunity. A wise decision to disengage at this point may keep you from getting into a position that you'll regret after it's too late.

If you decide to mix it up, the whole idea from then on is to plan your maneuvering so as to place yourself within the 60-degree vulnerable cone behind your opponent's tail—and, naturally, to keep him from getting into this position behind you. You must not only get into the defender's vulnerable cone; you must be able to stabilize your position there long enough to give him a good hosing. This means keeping the pipper on the target for three to five seconds.

Never underestimate your opponent. Let him prove different. Until then, fly as if you were pitted against the Red Baron himself, who can be expected to counter your every move with superior skill and cunning.

The maneuvers I discuss in the following chapters will generally be described with reference to the horizontal plane; however, any of them can be executed in any plane. A word of caution here—as you approach the vertical plane, you should be prepared for higher diving airspeeds, deeper pullouts, more unusual attitudes, and greater possibility of momentary disorientation.

I've made the assumption that all airplanes executing the maneuvers I describe are essentially equal in capability. As your skill increases you can adopt tactics that emphasize your aircraft's better qualities—e.g., superior airspeed or turn rate—and take advantage of known shortcomings in other types of aircraft, such as limited visibility in certain quarters.

Let's pause here for a moment to go over some of the factors that affect the appropriateness of these maneuvers for light aircraft. As I mentioned earlier, these tactics were designed for high-performance aircraft whose ability to accelerate and decelerate as the tactical situation demands is considerably enhanced by afterburners and speed brakes.

The difference between cruise and combat speed is much greater for a jet fighter than it is for a light plane. In planning his actions, the light plane jock must keep in mind that the differences between his normal cruise, max cruise, and red line speeds are not too great. Conserving energy, which will be explained shortly, is critical in light plane maneuvering, because there is so little energy to lose before a tactic must be modified or terminated. But if your airplane can handle acrobatics speed- and stress-wise, it should be able to perform basic fighter maneuvers if you adjust your techniques slightly.

Since these maneuvers are, in reality, only basic aerobatics adapted to the combat situation, the major adjustment the would-be fighter pilot has to make is to be absolutely certain that he has at least the minimum entry airspeed before trying a given maneuver. In fact, if the situation permits, it would be best for him to have all the airspeed he can get, as cushion. Fighter maneuvers are usually performed with more Gs on the bird than comparable acrobatic maneuvers. This G load will dissipate your airspeed and energy level more rapidly than you are accustomed to, and might cause you to fall out of a maneuver halfway through.

It is also essential that you glance at your airspeed indicator occasionally during a maneuver so that you don't end up in a hairy situation without the airspeed to execute a safe recovery. The Gs, turning rates, and desirable positions specified for fighter tactics in later chapters must all be continually played by ear, and fitted to the maneuvering potential you have at any given moment. The lack of maneuvering potential, or its rapid loss, may preclude a continued use of the vertical plane in your attack. It is very possible that you will have to go rapidly from the overhead vertical, through the horizontal, to the diving vertical, in order to keep your airspeed high enough to accomplish the high-G turns you need to win out over an opponent.

Deciding what tactic is most appropriate for a given situation boils down to doing the best with what you've got. If your energy level is such that you know you can hack only one overhead maneuver before you have to dive to get up a head of steam, give it a whirl. One gyration in the vertical may be all you need to obtain a position of advantage, and that's the name of the game.

Light planes and jet fighters also differ in the amount of Gs and in turning radius, and, consequently, in the amount of space necessary for performing combat maneuvers. So it isn't necessary to put a max G load on your aircraft every time Gs are called for, especially during the initial phases of learning each tactic. Work up to the higher G loadings once you've got the basic pattern mastered. In the case of overhead maneuvers, the minimum number of Gs necessary to get the bird over the top may suffice; however, if the other guy is pulling just a little harder than you in his maneuvers, he'll be in your six in no time. Again, do the best with what you've got, and use only the amount required to do the job.

A light plane's shorter turn radius and slower speed allows it to perform these tactics in a much smaller chunk of airspace than a jet fighter. This means you will be working in close proximity to the other aircraft once you start to tangle with him, and should count on the decision points of these maneuvers coming more rapidly. Of course, if everybody is playing it loose, and no one is honking his bird around, your maneuvers will cover more ground, and the timing at decision points will not be so critical.

A term that you will come across in my descriptions of some combat maneuvers is "flying in the pebbles, rocks, and boulders." This term attempts to describe the physical sensations of flying at various G loads. "Flying in the pebbles" denotes a light G load; the burble is just starting to nibble at the wings, producing a light airframe vibration. (Driving your car over a gravel road gives the same sensation.) If the G load is increased, the burble becomes more pronounced as the vibrations increase in both frequency and amplitude. (Your car is now driving over a road covered with large rocks.) At maximum G load the whole aircraft is bucking constantly as you approach the fully stalled condition. You are flying at maximum performance, and any further increase in Gs will cause a stall and/or an out-of-control situation. (This is akin to attempting to drive over boulders.)

The relative areas of pebbles, rocks, and boulders are just that—relative areas. No specific G load can be identified with each except in a generalized sense. Atmospheric conditions, gross weight, and altitude will all affect the G loading at which each of these sensations occurs. Also, some aircraft have flight characteristics that take you from an area of small pebbles to one of large boulders almost instantaneously. If you've got a bird that gives you little or no warning before a complete stall, it will be important to know beforehand the airspeeds at which various stalls occur. Then, as you go through these gyrations, keep an eyeball on the airspeed so that you don't inadvertently stall out just when you're ready to move into an opponent's six.

As you practice these maneuvers, you will discover that once an engagement starts, nearly all your flying is done by feel. Your attention will be focused primarily on the bogey, and your maneuvering will be in response to his actions. Therefore, it is imperative that you know what your bird sounds like at or near red-line speed. Airframe and/or engine noise, vibrations, and control pressures all provide clues to approaching airspeed limits, and you should stay tuned in to them *at all times* so that throttle adjustments can be made automatically during maneuvering flight. (With experience, this becomes instinctive.) Furthermore, you should be familiar with the high- and low-speed stalling characteristics of your aircraft so that you'll know when one of these stalls is approaching, and just how much farther you can go.

During a hassle, a lot of situations crop up that require a ham-fisted approach to get the bird to go where you want it to go at the proper time. Crossed controls, negative Gs, and skidding all may be required at one time or another; therefore, your bird's response to these control inputs should be known in advance. Try these things when you're off by yourself one day when you have the time to study how your bird reacts, and avoid an unexpected hairy experience at some later date.

Naturally, smooth control techniques are preferable whenever possible, especially under high-G conditions. You'll find that once you get behind your opponent and you're closing to firing range, a light touch on the stick is absolutely essential to keep the pipper on the target. Then, too, small corrections work better when you're in someone's six and he's working to throw you out of position. When you're behind a bogey and have him pretty well wired except for closing to firing range, you can expect him to try all sorts of gyrations to ruin your tracking solution; he'll want to throw you out far enough that he can try a scissors maneuver (see Chapter 7) and regain the advantage. In this situation, *don't* match your angle of bank with his, because you will always be just a little bit behind, and probably will get thrown out eventually. Instead, turn just enough to keep the advantage and stay in his blind spot, using only enough Gs to stay in the cone of attack. If he's making a run for it, you can expect that he will jink in random directions in an attempt to keep you from having an easy target. Just average out his turns as you close to gun range, and save your energy until you're ready to nail him and will have to match his every move.

A technique that I will be mentioning quite frequently is zero-G acceleration, or unloading the aircraft. Its primary function is to allow you to increase your airspeed/energy level as quickly as possible. The zero-G maneuver is accomplished by flying the aircraft along a ballistic curve, which allows all the available power from the engine to be used for increasing airspeed, with none wasted to provide lift or to compensate for gravity.

In order to gain maximum effectiveness from zero-G acceleration, you should have a G meter in your cockpit; however, you can closely approximate zero-G conditions by applying forward pressure on the stick just to the point where you start to rise out of your seat against the safety belt. Another good indication that you are at zero G is that loose items in the cockpit, including dirt and other crud on the floor and under the seat, start to float around. (The chances of getting something in your eye during zero-G acceleration are very good unless you vacuum the cockpit regularly, and keep all loose items tied down.) If a G meter is available, just push forward on the stick until the meter reads zero, and hold it there until you've picked up the desired airspeed.

The length of time you keep the aircraft unloaded will depend on the tactical situation—on whether you are trying to achieve separation or generate a closing rate. In the latter case you don't want to stay in the dive too long, because you'd have to to use too much energy to climb back to your opponent's altitude; and a long dive might also give him a chance to take the advantage.

Zero-G acceleration can be started with the aircraft in any attitude, and increased angles of bank only mean that less forward stick will be required to achieve the ballistic curve. A word of caution about maneuvering at zero G—don't snatch the aircraft from an unloaded condition to one of high G loading. If you rapidly apply back pressure while you're at zero G, to an extent that would normally not exceed the bird's G limitations, you will be surprised at the number of Gs recorded on the meter.

The best way to avoid exceeding your G limits is to ease off the forward pressure, and then to smoothly feed in back pressure to the desired G loading. Try to be particularly aware of this if you are chasing some guy through an overhead maneuver. In order to stay in position you may have to add a little forward stick while you're floating over the top, only to find that while you're in this more or less zero-G condition, your bogey tightens up his turn. The time it takes you to make a smooth transition to a loaded condition shouldn't cost you that much of your advantage. But even if it does, it's better to lose the fight than to bring home a bent or broken bird.

Other things to keep in mind when unloading the aircraft are engine limitations on positive oil flow, and the possibility of the engine's stopping momentarily due to interrupted fuel flow. The latter situation should be checked out for your particular aircraft within gliding distance of a runway, so that you'll have a pretty good idea of just how long your mill can run under zero-G conditions. Keep an eye on the G meter during these trials to find out exactly how far you can go toward zero G before the problem crops up. Know what the aircraft feels like in this best partial-G condition, and note any preliminary symptoms that indicate that you've gone too far. It certainly won't do you much good to accelerate with the zero-G maneuver, only to find out suddenly that you've temporarily got a glider on your hands. If the engine does cause you problems when the aircraft is unloaded, you may have to modify the zero-G maneuver to a shallow dive to keep some small G forces on the bird. In this case, obviously, your rate of acceleration will be somewhat slower than what would be possible if the bird could be totally unloaded.

Adverse yaw is a condition of flight that you probably won't encounter, but its effects are hairy enough to warrant a short blurb on what it is, what it can do, and how to prevent or correct it. Adverse yaw can occur when an aircraft is in a hard turn and is really pulling Gs—that is, flying in the area of the rocks and boulders. For simplicity's sake we'll only consider a horizontal turn, although adverse yaw can occur in a highly loaded turn in any plane.

Let's assume you've entered a hard turn to the right and have established a bank angle of approximately 90 degrees, and you've started to apply the G load to the aircraft. Let's also assume that as the G load gets fairly high, you still have a tad of right aileron pressure applied. Now, consider the condition of the airflow over the top and bottom surfaces of the wings. Since you are pulling a relatively high G load, your wings will be at a high angle of attack. In this situation, the airflow separates from the top surface of the wing and becomes highly disturbed, particularly aft of the wing centerline. At the same time, the airflow along the bottom surface of the wing remains smooth and undisturbed, so the energy of the airflow stays constant. On the top of the wing the disturbed airflow is losing energy.

Now back to our turn. Remember that you have inadvertently left a little right stick still applied. The right aileron is thus deflected up into the low-energy airflow over the top aft surface of the right wing. Conversely, the left aileron is deflected downward into the high-energy airflow over the bottom surface of the left wing. The resulting imbalance of pressure on the ailerons causes the left control surface to act somewhat like a speed brake. The drag created on the high wing by this imbalance causes the nose of the aircraft to yaw to the left, or up in this case. The tendency for the nose to rise and the drag on the left wing make the aircraft want to roll out of the hard turn.

To the jock, who is most likely flying by feel with his attention concentrated on the bogey, it feels as if the bird is not turning as tightly as it should be. The natural reaction is to apply *more* aileron and back pressure, which only aggravates the situation. If control pressures are continued or increased further, there is an excellent possibility that the effects of adverse yaw will cause the airplane to depart its controllability envelope. This is a really grim situation, and it gets your attention in a hurry. The aircraft will seem to have a mind of its own—not responding to your control inputs, while at the same time going through a series of wild oscillations and gyrations about all three axes. You are, in essence, out of control. The abruptness with which the situation hits, coupled with the random, unpredictable movements of the aircraft, all help to generate considerable confusion about what is happening. The engine is roaring like mad, yet you are probably registering zero airspeed, and the controls seem to have no effect at all.

Recovery procedures vary with each aircraft; there is no standard, universally most effective technique. The main idea is to try to relieve the stalled condition and to regain flying speed and, with it, controllability. The best corrective action is, of course, avoidance. Therefore, if you feel the bird trying to go against your control inputs, look down and make absolutely sure that your ailerons are neutral. Remember to use rudder to control bank angle in a high-G condition. If the aircraft starts to depart the controllability envelope, release all control pressures and try to hold the stick in a neutral position. It may sometimes be helpful to put in a little forward stick to assist in bringing the nose down.

It takes quite a bit of concentration to insure that nothing is done to aggravate the stalled condition as you try to regain control. Probably your first impulse will be to say, "See you on the gro-o-o-u-u-u-n-n-n-d-d-d !!" as you institute your nylon letdown procedures. It is of vital importance to keep an eye on the altimeter, because you don't want to go below your minimum bailout altitude in vain attempts to save the bird.

When setting your minimum bailout altitude, be sure to consider the altitude necessary to regain airspeed and recover from the out-of-control condition. It's a good bet that the first semblance of recovery and control will occur in a steep diving attitude. Therefore, when figuring your minimum bailout altitude you must allow for sufficient altitude to pull out of a vertical dive. Again, a good estimate of this is the altitude your bird requires to regain level flight following a split S.

Adverse yaw, like thunderstorms, should be avoided like the plague. From the very outset of your training in basic fighter maneuvers, remember to use ailerons *only* to establish your initial bank angle; as soon as a G load is applied, make sure the stick is centered, and accomplish additional roll with rudder. If you feel adverse yaw starting to affect your aircraft, decrease the G load immediately. And by all means break off the engagement until you are sure everything is under control.

Aircraft Energy Level

Frequently during the discussion of each of these maneuvers you will come across the term "energy," or "energy level." This term has evolved as the best description of the maneuvering capability, or potential, of an aircraft at any given time. Although its meaning is nearly synonymous with airspeed, it probably describes the physics of the situation a little more completely.

Of course, a high energy level is desirable in nearly every phase of an engagement, except perhaps when it may lead to overshooting your target. A high energy state can be achieved by adding power and/or diving, and in most instances during a hassle, diving is the only option you will have.

At the beginning of an engagement, being at a higher altitude than your opponent is always like having money in the bank. This allows you to convert this altitude into maneuvering potential almost instantly with a dive, without sacrificing your positional advantage.

If you are bounced in a situation where your airspeed is low and you don't have an altitude advantage, probably your best move is to counter the initial pass, and then dive to increase your energy level to a point where you can stay in the game and maneuver effectively. Energy is lost very rapidly in high-G maneuvers, and some of them are used for just that reason, to force an opponent into an overshoot. Ham-fisted control techniques that result in a lot of uncoordinated flight (skidding, slipping, yawing) also decrease your bird's energy level. There are times when this type of flying is necessary in order to keep control of a situation; however, it is usually advisable to use smooth control techniques and apply only the Gs that are required so that your energy level stays as high as possible.

Here's an example that shows the importance of a high energy level at the beginning of an engagement: Your first sighting of the other guy indicates that you're on a head-on approach to each other at approximately the same altitude. You know you're going to have to make a 180-degree turn, and, if you want to keep the bogey in sight, it will have to be a fairly tight turn that must be started as soon as you pass each other. In this situation, you don't want to start your turn before you pass the other guy, because if the bogey knows which way you are going to turn, and he hasn't indicated which way *he* is going to go, he's got a leg up on you from the start.

A bit of strategy that may be used here is to fake a turn in one direction when you are fairly close together, and then to reverse to the other direction after you pass. If the visibility is good and you can see each other while you're still some distance apart, you might try a couple of fakes in each direction to really confuse the issue. These fakes need be nothing more than a few degrees of roll in either direction—sort of a continual snaking motion as you approach the bogey.

Getting back to our 180-degree turn: this maneuver is going to cost you energy no matter how you slice it; therefore, your best bet may be to do a climbing turn instead of a level one. The big advantage a climbing turn offers is an increase in altitude, and the chance to quickly convert altitude back into airspeed. If your opponent does not climb in his turn, there are two small disadvantages to a chandelle. First, you will be silhouetted against the sky in your climb and thus will be easy to spot. Secondly, your opponent will be a little more difficult to pick up, because he will be flying against the changing patterns of a landscape background. In most instances, the advantages of altitude will outweigh the problems of getting an eyeball on the bogey.

A variant of this climbing turn that has been found to offer advantageous options is the Immelmann turn. Although it would take more energy to do an Immelmann than a chandelle, you will be in a better position tactically once the Immelmann is completed. As you approach the top of the loop, and before you roll right side up, you can try to determine which way the bogey has turned, and then adjust your rollout to end up in a turn toward his six. If you can't pick up the bogey immediately, complete the Immelmann, and most likely you'll still have an altitude advantage over your opponent when you do spot him, since your Immelmann may well have carried you higher than his climbing turn. The Immelmann may delay your reacquiring a visual on the bogey a little longer than a chandelle, but this difficulty is more than compensated for by the positional and energy advantages the Immelmann turn offers.

One of the basic rules of air combat is to establish and maintain as high an energy level as possible. This means that as soon as you enter the maneuvering area, or discover that you are being bounced, your power should be set at max continuous. Naturally, without a constant-speed prop, you will have to continually adjust the throttle during an engagement to prevent an overspeed. The idea is to keep the mill turning at the rpm that gives you the best performance, without putting an excessive strain on the engine.

Keeping your energy level high is of the utmost importance during a sustained engagement, because the pilot who is able to accomplish this will retain the maneuvering advantage. Further, the jock with the more comprehensive knowledge of the forces acting on his bird, and a thorough understanding of the specific maneuvers demanded by the particular spatial relationship of two birds at any moment during a hassle, should be the one who does the victory roll over home plate.

One way to keep your energy level high while gaining an edge in relative maneuvering advantage is to make use of the vertical plane. The primary advantage that maneuvering in the vertical plane offers is the availability of vertical, or radial, Gs. Any time you're on your back during an engagement, you have one extra G working for you. In other words, if you are executing an overhead maneuver in a loaded-up condition, you have the normal pull of gravity helping you to complete the maneuver. This allows you to turn more tightly than would be possible under similar airspeed, power, and G conditions in the horizontal plane. If your opponent tends to work basically in the horizontal plane, and you are able to utilize the vertical, your ability to turn more tightly coming over the top should put you in his six in no time.

Because of the higher airspeeds, increased Gs, and unusual attitudes involved in working the vertical, a lot of people are reluctant to try vertical maneuvers during a dogfight. This gives you the added psychological advantage of doing the unexpected, and, if you're up against a bird that can out-turn yours, working the vertical is just about the only way you can stay in the game. Another advantage in working the vertical is that you can make better use of the sun. Not only will this make it more difficult for your opponent to keep an eye on you while you are above him; if he's on your tail, he may be a little hesitant about following you in a steep climb straight up into the sun.

Visual Acquisition of Targets

As I will mention many times in the following chapters, the one absolutely basic rule of all air combat is to keep visual track of the opponent. This is particularly true at long range, where it is very easy to lose contact with an airplane because of clouds, terrain background, the sun, aircraft structure, and so forth. Your first sighting of the bogey may be only a momentary glimpse when you catch the sun flashing off his wings or canopy. At this point, *don't* take your eyes off the bird or the area where you spotted it just to make a power setting or to check something in the cockpit. You should know the approximate position of the throttle at the max continuous setting by feel, and keep your eyes glued to the area where you think the bogey is. If you shift your gaze into the cockpit and focus on the instruments, say to make a power adjustment, your vision becomes maximized at the distance to the instrument panel. When you re-shift your gaze back to where you spotted the bogey, for a little while your eyes remain focused for objects only a foot or so in front of your face. This is particularly true if you are looking into a cloudless sky.

A good rule of thumb to follow any time you are making a long-range scan around your aircraft is: if you must check something inside the cockpit, refocus your eyes on infinity when you return to scanning outside the cockpit. Do this by looking at some definite object in the distance, such as a cloud or the ground, before returning to your scan. After you consciously practice this technique a few times, it should become automatic any time you're checking the area around your bird for bogeys or any other type of traffic.

When you must check the gauges in the cockpit, do it as rapidly as possible. Check only the key instruments relating to the performance information you need, and know the range on each dial that the pointer should be in. If switch actions are required, make as many as possible by feel. Spending too much time looking around the cockpit will give a maneuvering bogey ample time to be long gone from the last place you saw him, and the next time you spot him he may be at 1,000 feet in your 5 or 7 o'clock position.

A more or less obvious but often overlooked factor that directly affects your ability to pick up bogeys at long range is a clean windshield and canopy. Attention to this detail is a definite necessity. A smeared or crazed canopy will create a blind spot when hit by the sun at the right angle. It's also a little embarrassing to call a "Tally Ho!" and then find you've been chasing a flyspeck on your windshield. And I'd recommend using a tinted visor rather than sunglasses, unless they are held on tight by an elastic band so they won't slide down your nose or fall off during abrupt or high-G maneuvers.

Know the blind spots on your opponent's aircraft. A little extra time spent in working your attack plan so you'll arrive in one of these areas is well worth the additional effort. Countering a visible attacker's moves is one thing, but the uncertainty and confusion that exist when you can't see your adversary and are unable to decide what counter is required put you in an untenable position. In this situation, the psychological edge is always with the attacker; and if the defender knows he's been spotted, but can't regain a visual on the bogey, his best bet may be to disengage and break for home plate.

Everybody has a blind spot at the six o'clock low position, and if you're going up against a guy with a full bubble canopy, this may be the only area from which you can approach undetected. However, if the bird you are working against has a turtle deck behind the canopy, the space you can work in is just about doubled.

Once you're in the area where getting bounced is a definite possibility, don't let your own blind spots work to your disadvantage. Every so often, roll up on each wing to clear the area blocked by the nose and your wings. This maneuver should be combined with a gentle S turn so you can also clear your 6 o'clock position from both sides. A handy gadget that may keep you from being surprised from behind is a slightly convex rearview mirror mounted on the top of your windshield or canopy bow. The wide-angle view that this mirror affords may help you spot someone in your deep six position, and is also useful for ground operation.

One of the requirements of basic fighter maneuvers that a pilot must master early in the game is the ability to accurately estimate the range of the bogey, particularly at or near the firing point. A good way to find out just what another aircraft looks like at 1,000, 2,000, and 3,000 feet is to utilize runway distance markers, if your local air patch has them. Using a taxiway, or a portion of the ramp parallel to the runway, have your wingman park opposite a given marker. Then taxi down to the next three markers, pausing at each one to study the relative size of the other bird at each distance. Note how much of your windshield or canopy he fills up, and what details and markings on his bird are distinguishable. After you are both airborne, have one guy act as target, and set yourself up at these same three distances in the target's 4 or 8 o'clock position. Then switch off and repeat the procedure. These exercises should be done on your first basic fighter maneuvers mission, and will give you both an opportunity for an unhurried, systematic study of these critical distances from offensive and defensive positions. Of particular importance is knowing what the 1,000-foot firing position looks like from both sides of the guns.

PART 3

Basic Fighter Maneuvers and Formation Flying

CHAPTER 7
BASIC DEFENSE

Now that we have gone over most of the generalities pertaining to basic fighter maneuvers, it's time to get down to the nitty-gritty of the maneuvers themselves. Since you must be able to survive in a hostile environment before you can take the offense, the first maneuvers to be discussed will be defensive, or counteroffensive, in nature. Those to be considered are the defensive turn, the break, the scissors maneuver, and the high-G barrel roll. These counteroffensive actions are taken mainly when you have little or no choice in the matter, as would be the case if you were caught by a surprise bounce, or if things didn't work out the way you planned in a hassle, and your opponent worked into your rear hemisphere. Since you can't shoot while you're on the defensive, these maneuvers will not win the engagement by themselves; however, if executed properly, they will allow you to stay in the game until an opportunity arises for you to take the offensive, or cut for home, as the situation dictates.

The Defensive Turn

A defensive turn is just what the name implies—a turn that is used to spoil an adversary's offensive setup or tracking solution. Normally, the defensive turn is only used after sighting a bogey who is already on the attack, and therefore is at relatively short range. "Relatively short range" means that your opponent is beyond firing range, but too close in for you to turn to meet his attack and negate his advantage.

Of course, your first reaction after sighting the bogey will be to get the power up to max continuous, to get as high an energy level as possible. Let's say that you spot this guy starting in for his pass when he is at your 4 o'clock high position. The first maneuvering action you should take is to start a gentle turn toward him— just enough to keep his angle off higher than he would like, and to help you keep a visual. This turn "toward" the attacker should perhaps be described more as a turn *right at* the attacker. In other words, you should be turning into the plane of the attack.

As your opponent closes in on you, it is strictly a judgment call based on your relative positions and his closing rate and angle off as to when you should start the defensive turn; the same goes for the rate of turn you initially apply. If the attacker has a relatively low angle off—that is, if he's more toward your stern than your beam—you must turn hard from the outset in order to rotate your vulnerable cone away from the attacker as quickly as possible. The timing and execution of this turn are fairly critical, and for maximum effectiveness it should be initiated just before the enemy reaches firing range. If you start turning too early, before he is really committed to the pass, he can counter without too much difficulty. If you're too late, he can probably match your turn well enough to avoid the overshoot you are trying to create.

Once you decide it's time to go, roll into the turn hard, using both ailerons and rudder. At the same time, feed in back pressure until you get a good G load on the bird—you should be "flying in the rocks" for a good defensive turn. Stabilize your bank at or near the 90-degree point and keep the Gs on, but most important of all, keep the bad guy in sight as long as possible. This is a fairly uncomfortable situation—loaded up to about four Gs and trying to look back over your shoulder and up at the same time. However, you must keep an eye on the enemy to see if your defensive turn has worked, or if he caught it in time and has successfully countered. If the maneuver is done properly, his higher energy level will not allow him to match your rate of turn, and he will be forced to overshoot your flight path. This will give you a chance to use the scissors maneuver, described on page 129, or to head for home if things don't look too shiny.

If the bogey is not expecting you to take defensive action, the abruptness of your turn, coupled with the high rate of turn you establish, may cause a moment's indecision on his part that may give you the beginning of an edge. A word of advice at this point: before you start the defensive turn, have a definite idea of what you want to do next. Your options usually boil down to two: if you don't want to stay in the game, you can tighten up your turn and roll to the best heading to achieve separation; if you want to tangle with him, you probably should plan on using the scissors. Above all, don't stay in the defensive turn too long, especially after the overshoot has occurred. In this situation, the defensive turn starts to work in favor of the attacker, who will be able to stabilize his position outside your turning flight path, and then move in for the kill.

The Break

The break is used only in an emergency, when you are caught completely unawares and find a bogey on your tail who is at, or close to, firing range. There is no time for planning, and immediate action is essential to keep you from becoming a statistic—or, worse, having to buy the beer at the debriefing for having been tagged so easily.

The break is a maximum performance turn into the attack. The instant you recognize the threat, your power should go to maximum while you simultaneously roll in with a hard application of aileron and rudder. (The rudder is used here to increase your rate of roll, and to keep your nose from rising too high.) At the same time, increase the Gs until you are in the boulders, but *don't* over-G the bird or get into a high-speed stall, for this will cause you to lose all your energy and will leave you nothing with which to achieve separation or to counter.

The maximum rate of turn you are trying to generate is realized in the region of moderate to heavy airframe buffet. In most situations—that is, when the threat is lower than 30 degrees above the horizon—it is advisable to continue your roll until your nose is well below the horizon; you can utilize the resulting dive to keep your energy level up. Although it is uncomfortable, you must twist around in the seat to keep an eye on the attacker at all times. Do not let the added Gs and the rapid transition to an unusual attitude distract you from keeping him in sight and knowing his relative position and the distance between the two of you. You must also stay aware of your attitude with respect to the horizon. Above all, be sure not to overreact and get yourself into a vertically descending corkscrew.

If you are forced into a break situation, your first reaction must be to keep the bogey from achieving the firing position; therefore, you have little or no time to assess the total threat and decide on an effective strategy. If your break was hard enough to destroy the enemy's tracking solution for the moment, you probably have used up too much energy to effectively counter with a reversal. Here a possible tactic might be to maintain or steepen your dive and ease off the back pressure in order to pick up some airspeed and increase your nose-tail separation. If your break forced an overshoot and some lateral separation has developed, you might be able to fake the bogey out momentarily with this move. Your turning flight path won't appear to change drastically, so the bad guy will probably hang in there trying to match your turn, and will be dissipating his own energy in the attempt. It's pretty much a matter of judgment in each situation as to how much you can ease off your turn in an effort to widen the range. However, this time will give you a few moments to decide whether to try a counter when you feel the time is right, or to pick a likely escape route to home plate.

The Scissors

The classic scissors maneuver is a series of turn reversals performed by two aircraft, each working toward the other's 6 o'clock position. Because of the large amount of energy required to execute the scissors, especially after the second reversal, the maneuver usually degenerates into a low-speed flying contest that is won by the aircraft with the lower wing loading—that is, the one with the ability to pull more Gs at lower airspeeds. The scissors maneuver is mostly used when you are aware of an impending attack and can plan your strategy. "Awareness" in this instance consists mainly of knowing that bogies are in the area and that they will probably attack. This situation requires that you be at a high energy level from the outset. Before entering the hostile area, have your power set at maximum continuous. Then, if bandits appear at your altitude, you are at least matched evenly; if they are below you, the added advantage of altitude is yours. If you spot the bogies above you, your high energy level may allow you to convert this initial disadvantage into an even shot by enabling you to maneuver into a more favorable position—particularly if your attacker hasn't spotted you.

Let's assume that this guy has started his run on you from above and behind, and at the proper time you execute your defensive turn. If your plan is to continue the engagement, the whole idea at this point is to set up a situation in which the bad guy can't match your rate of turn because of the higher airspeed resulting from his dive. Your objective is to force him to overshoot your turning flight path and pass behind you while he is still attempting to match your turn rate.

Once you start the defensive turn, don't take your eyes off the enemy, because the timing of the scissors maneuver is critical—if you start it too early, he will have time to reverse with you and stay in your 6 o'clock position; too late, and he may have time to match your turn and maintain his advantage.

A good rule of thumb to help you decide on when to start the scissors is: with a rapid overshoot, reverse early; with a slow overshoot, reverse late. Fly the bird by feel, staying in the range of a good burble, but not to the point where you are losing a lot of energy with a too-tight turn. Once the bogey starts to slide out of sight behind you (position 1 in the accompanying sketch), start an immediate hard roll in the opposite direction while maintaining back pressure on the stick.

The use of rudder during this maneuver is extremely important, to keep your nose from rising too far above the horizon as you roll through the level flight position. Keep in mind that under high-G conditions, your rudder is the most effective means of establishing and controlling your rate of roll.

After completing approximately 180 degrees of roll, and still keeping in the back pressure, you should be able to see your bogey through the top of your canopy, in a position nearly abreast of you laterally. It is essential to get your head cranked around so you can pick him up as early as possible during your reversal—primarily to see if he has countered, but also to see how effective your reversal has been. At this point, both aircraft should be approximately canopy-to-canopy (position 2) if the bad guy has not countered, and they should be turning toward each other. It may be necessary for you to ease in a tad of top or bottom rudder to swing your nose up or down to insure adequate vertical clearance when you cross.

At this point in the maneuver, your energy level should be quite a bit lower than your opponent's, allowing you to maintain a tighter turn. As you close toward each other, his higher airspeed and lesser rate of turn will force him ahead of your beam position and allow you to pass behind him as your flight paths recross.

The advantage has now swung in your favor. As soon as you can see that the bogey is definitely ahead of you, reverse your turn again, using back pressure and rudder as described above. If possible, start this second reversal before your flight paths recross, but not before you know you are definitely behind his beam. After completing the second reversal you should be within a 45- to 60-degree cone on either side of his tail (position 3), and you should be able to maneuver relatively easily into the firing position.

A word of caution here: after the second reversal you will have dissipated nearly

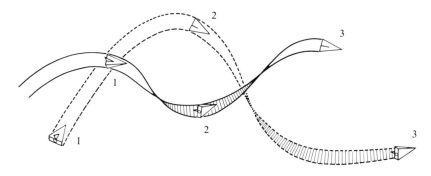

The scissors maneuver

all your energy, and will probably not be able to close to gun range immediately. However, your opponent has also lost a lot of his energy, and thus will have restricted options in his efforts to counter or run away. Since your aim is to keep him from gaining too much separation, fly your bird with a light touch, maneuvering only enough to stay behind him, preferably in a blind spot, until you can close in for the kill.

If your scissors maneuver caught your boy unawares, you have gained a psychological advantage—the original attacker now finds himself the attackee. To add to his woes, he also finds himself at a relatively low airspeed with somebody in his 6 o'clock position. Since hard turns are pretty much out of the question because of his low energy level, he will probably try to increase separation with a diving turn. Therefore, after completing 90 to 120 degrees of roll during your second reversal, watch for any increase in your nose-tail separation, and be ready to release your back pressure and try a zero-G maneuver or a low-speed yo-yo (which we'll discuss in Chapter 8) to keep him in range. If, after the second reversal, your boy still hasn't seen the writing on the wall and indicates that he still wants to mix it up by trying a turn into you, keep control of the situation with easy, low-G, rolling maneuvers to keep him ahead of you.

It is not of paramount importance to stay in your opponent's 5 to 7 o'clock position, though this is certainly desirable if you can swing it. Just work to stay behind his beam until he runs out of airspeed and ideas, and then slide into the 30-degree cone behind his tail and hammer him. After you complete your second reversal, your bogey's altitude will pretty much determine what your options are. The worst situation, of course, would be if he ended up higher than you before starting his turn back to meet your threat. In this case, remember that your opponent will have to play it close to the vest, because he shouldn't have enough energy left to do a lot of maneuvering. Because he does have that touch of advantage by virtue of his altitude, he will most likely be doing a wingover to come back toward you. Your best bet here would be to use a gentle bank and rudder to swing toward the outside of his turn; as he passes your beam in a dive, do your own wingover, or a split S if required, to stay behind him.

If, after your second reversal in the scissors, you end up at a higher altitude than the bogey and he still turns back into you, it's a good bet that he has more guts than brains, and should be a fairly easy mark. Once you determine that he is definitely turning into you and not just weaving in an attempt to keep you in sight as he dives away, start an easy barrel roll in the direction that allows you to keep an eyeball on him—that is, if he's coming from your 10 or 11 o'clock position, your barrel roll should be counterclockwise with respect to the horizon. As you pull up to the inverted position, relax the control pressures for a moment to see what he is going to do. He should be roughly below you and heading in the opposite direction, and will most likely be fairly low on airspeed. In this situation he will probably have insufficient energy to do the climbing necessary to spoil your attack. The trick here, as you float over the top of your barrel roll, is to see which way he is turning; then either complete your barrel roll to stay behind him, or, as you are starting down the other side of the roll, use bottom rudder to pull your nose down through the horizon while keeping your roll going to maintain a visual. A note of caution here: utilizing this latter technique will put you in a near vertical dive at a high power setting. Therefore, be sure you have sufficient altitude to recover, and start applying back pressure as soon as possible without generating a high-speed stall. Also keep in mind that you don't want to build up too much airspeed in this dive, because that might cause you to squirt out in front of your opponent, and the roles would be reversed again.

The whole idea of the maneuvers I've just outlined is to maintain the advantage you gained with the scissors, and to stay in your opponent's rear hemisphere while maneuvering into gun range. If during any of these gyrations you find that you don't have the airspeed and/or the position to stay in the hassle on your terms, pick an opportune moment and press for home in a direction that will provide the most separation from your opponent.

In general, only the defender has anything to gain from the scissors, and this gain will occur only if he is flying a "like" aircraft, or one with a lower wing loading than his opponent's. If this situation does not exist, it is better for the defender to try to achieve maximum separation after the attacker overshoots. As an attacker, you should always avoid the scissors. As soon as you realize that an overshoot is going to occur, counter the bad guy's defensive turn with a high-speed yo-yo or the quarter plane maneuver (see next chapter). If you have already overshot the defender and he reverses in an attempt to scissor you, your counter should be to relax Gs and zoom above your opponent in a loose quarter plane maneuver.

The High-G Barrel Roll

The high-G barrel roll is used when you want to decrease your velocity along the longitudinal axis of your aircraft. Its primary value is in countering an attacker who is already fairly close in at your 5 to 7 o'clock position, *and* has a high closing rate. This last item is quite important, because if he doesn't have a high rate of closure, he will be able to match your maneuver while staying behind you. In this case, all you will succeed in doing with a high-G barrel roll is lowering your own energy level and momentarily spoiling his tracking solution.

The best time to use the high-G barrel roll is when you spot someone making a diving attack on you from behind, at such a shallow angle off your tail that the defensive turn would not be very effective. Because the bogey is approaching from a more or less blind area, you probably won't know he's there until he is pretty close. In fact, for you to be able to spot him at all he will have to be above you and still diving for the firing position.

Normally your attacker will be running at full blower and really have a head of steam built up by the time you get a visual on him. However, his high airspeed and closing rate can be used against him if you catch him still in his dive. As with the defensive turn, your objective with the high-G barrel roll is to cause an overshoot, but in this case you are trying to cause an overshoot along the longitudinal axis, or projected flight path, of your bird. This maneuver is thus somewhat different from the defensive turn, where the overshoot is caused by the enemy's inability to match your rate of turn.

The high-G barrel roll is very similar to the normal barrel roll done in acrobatics training, with the addition of a high G load throughout the maneuver. As I said before, you probably won't see the threat until he is fairly close; therefore, the best time to try the high-G barrel roll is as soon as you know he's back there—preferably just before he reaches firing range. Don't perform this counter when the attacker is still some distance away and can maneuver without losing the advantage. If you do, the high-G barrel roll will only work to the attacker's advantage by bringing him closer to your six, because it rapidly reduces your velocity. If you're the beady-eyed type who can spot a bogey a long way out, and you're lucky enough to catch a glimpse of him at long range, an immediate defensive turn up into the attack will gain you more time than the high-G barrel roll.

Let's assume that you're like the rest of us near mortals (earth people being all mortal), and you don't pick up the enemy until he's just about ready to eat your socks. Smoothly but smartly feed in back pressure and ailerons to start you into a rolling climb in either direction. Keep the G load on the bird and continue the roll as you would in a normal barrel roll, though in this case you'll be using a lot more rudder (in lieu of ailerons) to keep the roll going. Remember, you want to avoid the adverse yaw, which will prevent you from completing the roll under high-G conditions.

As you pass through the 270-degree point of the roll, check for your bogey below or level with you; most likely he'll be a little ahead of your beam position. His high energy level, caused by his dive, coupled with your decreased velocity due to the high-G barrel roll, will cause him to squirt out in front of you, and thus swing the relative advantage to you. The final 90 degrees of your roll can be adjusted by using rudders to either increase your rate of roll, or to dish out of the maneuver so as to better position yourself in his six. When you see that the bogey is definitely ahead of your bird, release the extra back pressure, for now the idea is to increase your energy level as much as possible in order to capitalize on your newly gained advantage.

When you find yourself behind the bogey as a result of your barrel roll, you will be in a somewhat better position than if you had used the scissors maneuver to get behind him. This is because the high-G barrel roll uses up less energy than the hard turn and reversals required for the scissors. So, once he's out in front of you, a zero-G maneuver and/or a low-speed yo-yo (see next chapter) will generate a positive closing rate on your target.

Possibly it may help to visualize the high-G barrel roll as a rapid, tight version of the normal acrobatic barrel roll. The latter is a loose, easy, one-G, floating type of maneuver that describes a large circle on the horizon; the former is done more quickly, with a higher G load until at least the 270-degree point, and it describes a fairly small circle on the horizon.

Going back to the 270-degree point in the roll, let's suppose that when you check for the bogey's position, you find him more or less level with your bird, but still in your rear hemisphere. What has happened here is that the attacker has countered your counter by doing a high-G barrel roll of his own, in the opposite direction. In this situation, don't complete the roll, because the bogey has successfully negated your counter by staying behind you. Instead, start an immediate level turn toward the attacker, which will cause him to overshoot. Once this overshoot is assured, your best bet is to unload and dive for separation.

Another counter the attacker could use against your high-G barrel roll is a quarter plane maneuver (see next chapter). In this case, when you check for his position at the 270-degree point of your roll, he will still be in your rear hemisphere, and will also be high with respect to your bird. This means that you'll pick him up close to the rear corner of the canopy on the high side of the roll; that is, if your roll was to the left initially, he should be high over your left shoulder at this point. Your best best in this situation is to continue the roll and use top rudder to keep your nose high. This should force the bogey into an overshoot below and ahead of your position. Your energy level will be fairly low by this time; if you can't jump right on his tail after the overshoot, you should start a dive for separation, preferably on a heading 180 degrees away from the bogey.

During a mock engagement against F-104s in 1968, our group's mission was to defend a strike force against F-104 "aggressors," who dove in from above and behind us at a very high Mach number. We were in the Six Pac formation (to be discussed in Chapter 10) when my wingman called a bogey at my 6 o'clock high and closing fast. I immediately wracked my F-106 into a high-G barrel roll. Just as advertised in the textbook, the 104 squirted out in front of me, and as I rolled wings level, he was in my 12:30 low position at about a half mile.

Figuring that this guy was going to be a piece of cake, I lit the burner and zero-G'd the bird to pick up some speed so I could close the short distance enough to satisfy my missile parameters. As soon as he saw me back there, he also lit his afterburner and started to accelerate. Since he already had a head of steam built up, I was unable to close to missile range quickly, although deep in my heart I knew that I would have this turkey shortly.

Wrong! By now we were both doing Mach 1 or better, and he pulled the Starfighter into a vertical climb. I foolishly followed, still thinking I'd be within firing distance any second. As we climbed straight up, the higher energy potential of his lighter aircraft started to pay off. My airspeed was bleeding off rapidly as he continued his climb, and he finally pulled it through the top half of a loop and sort of floated there upside down watching me. Glancing down at my instruments, I noticed my airspeed going down through 115 mph, so I started a vertical recovery, and at once the horrible realization struck me—I'd been had!

As my bird rotated out of the vertical, I could see the bogey starting down from his inverted position to follow me, and I knew it would just be a matter of time before his faster bird had him eating my socks. As I was vainly trying to coax a little more airspeed out of my bird so that I could at least start a turn, someone fortunately called the engagement off for fuel, and I was spared the final humiliation of seeing the whole mess replayed on his gun-camera film at debriefing.

The moral of the story is: "Don't get suckered into fighting the other guy's kind of fight." Instead of trying to follow the 104 in his climb, I should have swung in a wide, fairly level circle around his climbing flight path, keeping him in sight while conserving my energy. By doing this I would have made him come back down to my level where I had the maneuverability advantage.

CHAPTER 8
BASIC OFFENSE

Now that we have covered the basic defensive maneuvers, it's time to consider the offense, and what you can do to counter your opponent's defensive actions. The basic offensive maneuvers are the high side pass, the high-speed yo-yo, the quarter plane maneuver, the low-speed yo-yo, and the barrel roll attack. The first thing to master is the proper execution of the classic gunnery pass—also called the high side pass. Though nearly all air-to-air hassles develop from situations that prevent you from using this canned, textbook maneuver, it is essential in setting up your practice of nearly all the rest of the tactics discussed in this book. And if you happen to luck out during an engagement and find yourself in a position to use the high side pass, you'll know just how to capitalize on this one chance in a million.

The High Side Pass

The high side pass starts with both aircraft heading in approximately the same direction, with the attacker positioned about 3,000 feet out from and 3,000 to 4,000 feet higher than the defender (position 1 in the accompanying sketch). This is known as the perch position. The ideal position would be slightly ahead of the target's beam or, at a minimum, even with him. Although gunnery passes can be initiated from nearly any position from which you can see the target, the farther you deviate from this ideal spot, the more critical the judgment factors become, which in turn makes it more difficult to achieve the correct firing position.

If you perch too far forward, you stand a good chance of losing sight of the target beneath your nose as you turn to get behind his beam. If you choose to maintain a bank angle that allows you to keep a visual, you probably won't get into firing position, because your crossing angle will be too great. Instead of sliding into a 15 to 20-degree cone off the bad guy's tail, you'll arrive at firing range while you're

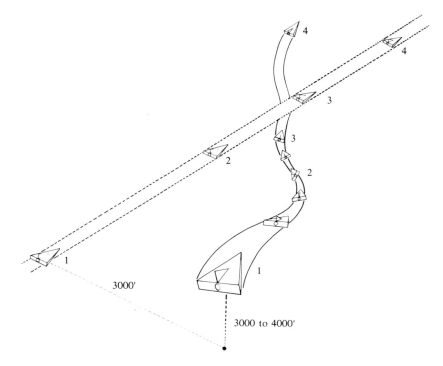

3000'

3000 to 4000'

The high side pass

still at an angle off of 30 to 40 degrees. This high crossing angle almost guarantees an overshoot on your part, especially if you've picked up a lot of airspeed in your dive. If you overshoot, all your bogey has to do is lay a scissors maneuver on you.

On the other hand, if you're too far aft of the target's beam, you will roll out of your pass outside firing range at a shallow angle off, and the resulting tail chase may give the bogey time to counter or escape. If you are too low, you will be unable to build up enough airspeed in your dive to generate an adequate closing rate. The opposite is true if you're too high. The excessive airspeed that results from your dive could force an overshoot; or, if you do get the pipper on him, you'll have less tracking time.

Let's assume that you're in the ideal position. The entry into the high side pass is an easy, rolling dive in the direction of the target, and normally a 90-degree bank is the maximum needed. Avoid applying a lot of Gs at this stage of the game, because the whole idea now is to build up your airspeed. Continue the turn until the target passes your 12 o'clock (position 2), and then smoothly roll in the opposite direction and establish a turn that points your aircraft slightly ahead of the target. Keep adjusting your dive and bank angle to settle into the groove as you approach firing range (position 3). Use smooth, small corrections to keep the pipper on the target.

At minimum range (about 700 feet), break off the attack with a sharp bank away from the target so that you will pass behind him. When you are clear, start a climb back up to a new perch position on the opposite side of the target (position 4). Practice the high side pass using roll-ins from the right and from the left so that you will feel comfortable with the maneuver no matter what side the target appears on.

As a defender, your counter to the high side pass is a defensive turn into the attack.

The High-Speed Yo-yo

The high-speed yo-yo is a maneuver designed to counter the defensive turn, and its objective is to keep you from overshooting and to help you stay behind your target, even though you can't match his rate of turn. It should be used only when the angle off from your opponent's tail is relatively low—say, less than 45 degrees. If your angle off is greater than this, the high-speed yo-yo is not your most effective counter, and the quarter plane maneuver should be used (see page 141).

Let's assume that you're pressing home an attack and you're still outside firing range (position 1 in the accompanying sketch), when just at the right time the target executes a defensive turn. Naturally you apply back pressure in an attempt to match his turn, but the guy you're chasing has read Chapter 7 of this book and has caught you perfectly with his turn; you realize that an overshoot is inevitable. As soon as you see that you can't avoid an overshoot, start the high-speed yo-yo (position 2). Keep the back pressure in to maintain the high G load on the bird, and then add top rudder to start the nose of the aircraft up. Adjust your angle of bank as necessary to keep the bogey in sight. The purpose of this climb is to convert your high energy level, caused by the dive, into altitude (position 3). Keep the climb going only long enough to let your energy level bleed down close to his. As soon as you see that you're not going to overshoot and you're starting to match his turn, apply bottom rudder (position 4), still keeping in the back pressure, to swing the nose of the aircraft below the horizon and back into his 6 o'clock (position 5). The altitude gained by the yo-yo can be traded off for airspeed to generate a high closing rate as you dive for the firing position.

At the top of the high-speed yo-yo you may be partially inverted; however, this is the only way you'll be able to keep an eye on the bogey and tell when you've got his turn hacked and you can start back down. The purpose of this hump in the attacker's flight path as he performs the high-speed yo-yo is to regain nose tail separation while controlling the overtake and maintaining an airspeed advantage.

Even as the high-speed yo-yo is a counter to the defensive turn, it, like every offensive maneuver, can be countered. From the defender's cockpit, the situation illustrates the need for keeping an eye on the attacker during the defensive turn. Suppose that you've started your defensive turn and, looking back, you see the attacker starting to go high, rather than overshooting as you planned. Realizing that his high-speed yo-yo will negate your defensive turn, you change tactics; when you see his nose definitely established in a climbing attitude, you relax the back pressure that was keeping you in the turn and start a zero-G dive away from him *while maintaining your angle of bank.* Keeping your angle of bank the same as it was in your turn will make less apparent what you are actually doing—it momentarily gives the impression that you are staying in your turn.

The object of this counter is to increase the separation between the two aircraft and give you a moment or two to plan your next move. This gain in space and time is possible because it will take the attacker a second or so to realize what you are doing, and then he must rotate his aircraft, whose energy level now approximates yours, out of its climb and into a dive. Once you have gained separation and airspeed from the dive, you can use this higher energy level to head for home, or to start a turn back up into the attack. If you can complete such a turn and meet the attacker head on, you have evened the odds and set up a whole new ball game.

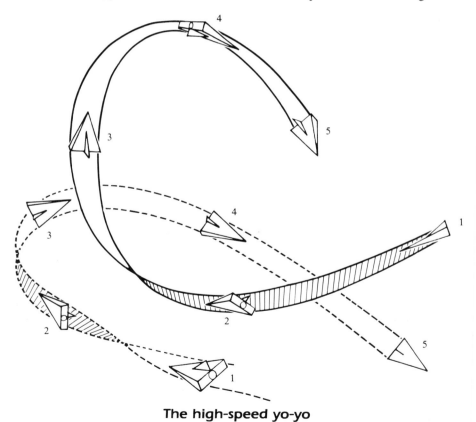

The high-speed yo-yo

Some of the more common errors in performing the high-speed yo-yo are:

(1) Being too conservative in your attack by starting the yo-yo too early, or going too high in your climb above the target's turning flight path. Either of these miscalculations will allow the defender to unload from his defensive turn and gain separation.

(2) Starting the yo-yo too late, or not going high enough in your climb. In either of these cases you will still overshoot the defender and lose nose-tail separation. This overshoot will allow the defender to take the advantage by means of a reversal and/or the scissors maneuver.

(3) Relaxing Gs during the pull-up above the plane of the defender's turn. This will cause you to zoom outside the defender's flight path in an overshoot, which will allow him to counter with a reversal or a dive for separation.

Once the basic techniques of the high-speed yo-yo have been mastered, a slight variation of this maneuver may prove valuable, since it is very difficult to defend against. This would be used in a situation where the attacker sees early in his pass that an overshoot will occur. In order to correct this condition, the attacker performs a series of small yo-yos as he closes in on the target. Here he would use top rudder to bring his nose up, and bottom rudder to bring it back down, while keeping his wings nearly matched to the defender's bank angle. The idea here is the same as with the basic maneuver—to prevent the overshoot while maintaining a controllable overtake as you work toward the bogey's vulnerable cone.

The Quarter Plane Maneuver

The quarter plane maneuver is a "last-ditch" offensive tactic that may be used by the attacker to maintain a positional advantage and nose-tail separation with the bogey. The objective of the quarter plane maneuver is not to place the attacker in the firing position on the defender's tail; rather, it is to keep the initiative with the attacker so that he can later maneuver in for the kill.

The situation to which the quarter plane maneuver is best suited is one of excessive overtake where the angle off is too great to use a high-speed yo-yo (position 1 in the accompanying sketch). Selection of this tactic also presupposes that you are too close for an effective barrel roll attack (see page 146). You're most likely to find yourself in this position when you're pressing home an attack and the defender lays a really hard defensive turn on you, and/or starts the turn just a tad early. In either case you suddenly find yourself with an angle off of 50 to 60 degrees, guaranteeing an overshoot.

Your main concern at this point is to maintain your advantage position-wise, and to keep your energy level as high as possible. This is accomplished by rolling out of your bank a sufficient number of degrees to cause your projected flight path to cross the bogey's at a right angle (position 2). This quarter roll away from the bogey's flight path maintains the desired nose-tail separation. As you roll out, you also want to stay in your dive so as to pass *under* the bogey's flight path while increasing your energy level.

In this situation, with the target still turning hard, the angle off between you and the bogey will increase very abruptly—in essence, you are both momentarily turning away from each other. Therefore, by the time you complete your quarter roll away from the defender's flight path, it will be time to start your pull-up (position 3).

Smoothly apply back pressure so as to execute the first half of a loop around the bogey's flight path, while at the same time adjusting your angle of bank to maintain your visual. (Keeping an eyeball on the target at this point may require some vigorous head turning.) Keep the Gs on as you come over the top of the loop; as you start down the back side (position 4), check to see if you have gained sufficient nose-tail separation. If your advantage has been maintained, start a reverse roll (position 5) and feed in enough back pressure to pull in behind the defender (position 6).

Because the quarter plane maneuver is designed only to maintain positional advantage, you will probably not be very close to firing range at this point. Depending on the relative positions of the two aircraft, their rates of turn, and their airspeeds, another maneuver (such as a cutoff turn, zero-G maneuver, or low-speed yo-yo) will probably be required to get you into firing position (position 7).

Some of the more common errors that can accompany the quarter plane maneuver are:

(1) Not realizing that it can, and should, be used in all planes of maneuvering—not just the horizontal.

(2) Not loading up the aircraft with sufficient Gs during the pull-up. This mistake will cause you to zoom too high, and, if the defender has enough energy available, he will be able to reverse back up into you. If the attacker does find himself in this untenable position, he will soon become the defender, and will have no choice but to pull hard into his opponent and try to gain separation on a heading 180 degrees away from that of the attacking bird. However, suppose you do start your pull-up with less than the optimum G load and your opponent reverses his turn—what can be done to correct the situation? It is probably too late to add more Gs at this time and anyway the other guy's reversal will swing him behind your beam if you continue with the quarter plane maneuver. The correct counter to his reversal is to relax the Gs and zoom up at a steep angle, all the while adjusting your bank to keep him in sight. Since the defender's reversal will lower his energy level quite rapidly, he will not be able to match your climb. Therefore, you will end up at a higher altitude and will only have to roll off into his 6 o'clock position.

(3) Quarter planing too long before starting the pull-up, which will give the defender a chance to execute a zero-G maneuver and gain separation.

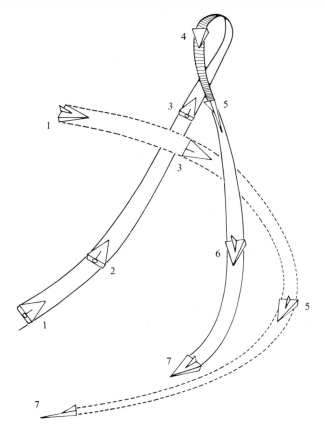

The quarter plane maneuver

The Low-Speed Yo-Yo

The low-speed yo-yo is a useful maneuver when you find yourself in a tail chase with a bogey who manages to stay just out of range. In this situation both aircraft will be at maximum power and their airspeeds nearly equal. Your problem will be to increase your airspeed and generate a closing rate while still staying behind the bogey and controlling the situation. Your answer will be the low-speed yo-yo, whose objective is to increase your energy level by trading off a little altitude for a gain in airspeed.

Normally, the low-speed yo-yo is executed in a relatively non-turning phase of the engagement, with both aircraft in a more or less wings-level attitude. This may occur if your bogey is making a run for home or trying to gain sufficient separation to turn back into your attack. However, if the situation dictates that you must turn and accelerate in order to close on your opponent, you should increase your airspeed first. Even if the aircraft is in a bank, unload it to a zero-G condition; while accelerating, the bank angle can be changed to establish the desired direction.

Before starting the maneuver, try to swing into the bogey's blind spot dead astern, and then start an unloaded shallow dive to pick up airspeed. The length of your dive will be a matter of judgment based on the distance you are behind the bad guy and directly proportional to the airspeed you must generate to close to gun range. Don't expect this maneuver to put you in range immediately—it produces only moderate increases in airspeed, and may have to be repeated a few times before you get close enough to nail him.

Let's assume that you've picked up enough airspeed and have closed to gun range. However, your position is now below and slightly behind the bogey; you have a small speed advantage. You can convert this airspeed into altitude with a climb that allows you to bring your guns to bear on the target. Gently ease back on the stick so as not to kill off your energy too quickly, and aim a little ahead of the bogey from the smallest angle off you can achieve. The climb will naturally slow you down, but as you continue up, the bad guy will fly right into your sights, where you can hose him.

Staying in the bogey's blind area is especially important to the success of the low-speed yo-yo, because this maneuver is probably the easiest of all the offensive maneuvers to counter. If you are on the defensive and notice that your opponent is trying a low-speed yo-yo, all you have to do is start one of your own, and the odds are immediately evened.

Staying out of sight also works to your psychological advantage, because once the bogey loses his visual and you don't reappear when he thinks you should, he starts to get a little worried about what you are up to. If this works on him long enough, he may start a turn to check his deep six, and this is exactly what you want. From your position directly behind him, and with airspeed about equal to his, you can match almost any turn he can make and thus keep a handle on the situation. Additionally, if he turns hard enough to get a good look behind him, his turn will cost him energy and airspeed, which will allow you to build up a closing rate.

If you are on the attack, remember not to let the difference in altitude between you and the bogey become too great on your initial dive. There are a couple of good reasons for this. First, even though a long dive will probably close the nose-tail gap between you and the other aircraft, you will probably end up almost directly beneath the bogey. If this happens, and the bogey starts to get curious about where you are, he may roll over far enough to spot you beneath him. At this point, since he is already partially inverted, all he has to do is cut his power a tad and complete the second half of a barrel roll, and he'll slide right into your six. Secondly, a large vertical separation increases your chances of losing your visual, particularly if the sun or clouds are a factor. Besides, a long dive probably won't increase your airspeed sufficiently for you to climb all the way back up to the bogey's altitude and still arrive within gun range. So, obviously, in most situations the best course of action is a series of low-speed yo-yos, rather than one enormous yo-yo that could put you in a weak position.

Should the bogey start rapid turns from side to side while you are below and behind him trying to build up airspeed, *don't* try to match him maneuver for maneuver. Use gentle turns to average out his gyrations so as to stay behind him, preferably in a blind spot, while keeping your energy level up to allow you to close to shooting distance.

Another time when the low-speed yo-yo might come in handy is when your opponent works you into a Lufbery and doesn't show any signs of wanting to break out of it. The situation here is about the same as the one described above—you are in a tail chase and cannot close because both aircraft are maxed out at about the same airspeed. The only difference is that in a Lufbery both birds are constantly in steep turns. Your problem and objective are still the same—only the solution requires some modification.

Most Lufberys develop in a horizontal plane with the aircraft at opposite sides of the circle (position 1 in the accompanying sketch). Here again, a shallow dive on your part is the answer, and since you're already in a steep turn, all that is required is a little bottom rudder. Allow your nose to go down 20 to 30 degrees (position 2), and then stabilize the dive (position 3) while keeping your rate of turn the same as it was. The resulting increase in airspeed will allow you to close the gap a little before you start back up to the bogey's altitude by applying top rudder (position 4). The shallow dive and climb are repeated as many times as necessary until you reach a position where you can get him into your sights as you pull back up to his level (position 5).

Naturally, the low-speed yo-yo in a Lufbery situation will require a light hand and foot on the controls, because the steep turn and G load will mean you'll be flying the aircraft close to its maximum performance level.

If the Lufbery should develop in a plane angled to the horizon, say at 45 degrees, there are two additional points to remember. The first is: as you pass through the high side of the circle, remember to take advantage of vertical Gs to tighten your turn up a bit. The other is: wait until you begin the down side of the circle to execute the low-speed yo-yo, which will mean that your dive angle will be somewhat greater than your opponent's. The combination of these two factors should enable you to close more rapidly than in a horizontal Lufbery, particularly if you can couple them just after passing the high side of the circle.

The counter for the low-speed yo-yo in a Lufbery is the same as that described for a tail chase situation: if your opponent gets the jump on you by starting a low-speed yo-yo, counter immediately with one of your own.

Errors that are commonly found in performing the low-speed yo-yo are:

(1) Trying to accelerate and turn at the same time, so neither is done very well. Remember to build up your airspeed first with a zero-G maneuver; *then* initiate your turn.

(2) Letting the aircraft get into too steep a dive on the initial zero-G maneuver. As I mentioned above, this could give the defender an opportunity to assume the advantage.

Up till now, we've only considered ·tactics utilized when the attack is initiated from somewhere behind the opponent's beam position. In reality, these situations are somewhat rare, and mostly occur when you catch a bogey by surprise and can work around to his rear hemisphere unobserved. More often than not, your first visual contact with the target will be when you are ahead of his beam, or, more properly, at a high angle off his tail, say 120 to 150 degrees. If you are fortunate enough to spot your target while he is still at long range under these conditions, the barrel roll attack is just what the doctor ordered.

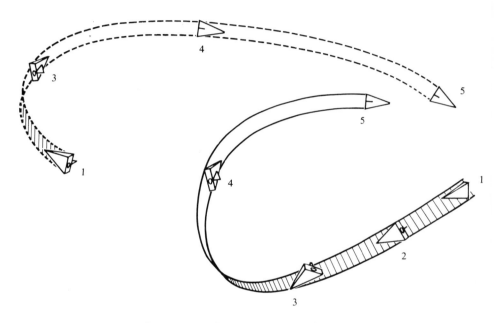

Low-speed yo-yo in a Lufbery

The Barrel Roll Attack

The objective of the barrel roll attack is to convert a high-angle-off *and* long-range position into one of advantage (position 1 in the accompanying sketch). The barrel roll attack does this by changing both your position and velocity with respect to the defender, while preserving your airspeed and maneuvering potential.

When you begin the barrel roll attack, you should be at approximately the same altitude as, or a little higher than, your opponent. If you are quite a bit higher or lower than the bogey, the barrel roll attack is not too effective or appropriate, and other tactics would be more suitable. Maintaining a visual would also pose some difficulty if you were lower than the bogey.

If executed properly, the barrel roll attack is one of the most beautiful, effective, and slick ways of changing an almost neutral situation into one where you can pick up all the marbles just about any time you wish. The long range at which you start this maneuver makes the defender uncertain of just what you are up to; when he sees your diving turn more or less away from him, he may even think he hasn't been spotted, and you're going for someone else. If he can be faked out for just a few moments until you start your climb, you've pretty near got the program wired, because there isn't much he can do at that point except split S for home. From the attacker's perspective, this maneuver offers quite a few options; if these are exercised at the proper time, they can negate almost any move the bogey can make, short of an immediate counter when you start the pull-up.

To enter this maneuver, start a diving turn in the direction of the bogey (position 2) so as to roll out on a heading approximately parallel to his (position 3). The tightness of the turn will depend on your angle off—if it is fairly high, say 150 degrees or better, you'll really have to honk it around to stay on the same side of the bogey. Keeping on the initial attack side is important, because it will preclude your losing a visual on the bad guy by crossing his flight path. Furthermore, a loose turn that takes you across his flight path will momentarily give an alert adversary the advantage. This, coupled with your loss of visual contact, will probably nullify the effectiveness of the entire maneuver.

The diving portion of the entry serves two purposes—it generates the airspeed you'll need to complete the attack, and it keeps the nose of your bird from blocking your line of sight to the bogey. A well-executed entry into this maneuver is critical, and, as I said, your aim is to end up on a heading roughly parallel to the target's; at this point you should be ahead of him but off to one side (10 to 20 degrees), and slightly below his altitude and you should have enough airspeed to complete the overhead portion of the attack (position 4). A word on this last item—if the recommended airspeed for a good loop in your bird is 150 knots, this is the speed you should shoot for during your entry into the maneuver.

You should still be a good distance from the target, but of course this will depend on when you first saw him, and how tight you made the entry turn. From position 4, start a moderately steep climb, just as you would if you were going to an acrobatic barrel roll (position 5). The difference here is that your rate of roll will be quite a bit less than in the standard barrel roll; consequently, the arc you describe on the horizon will be considerably larger. Keep the back pressure in and the gentle roll going as you climb well above the target's altitude (position 6).

As you approach the inverted position, ease off on the back pressure and roll rate. Then, with the controls almost neutral, you will just float, in an inverted position, over the path of the target, which should be just about beneath you or slightly ahead of your nose (position 7). During this time, keep just enough positive Gs on the bird to keep you barely in the seat. (Much more than one G here will cause you to start down the back side of your roll too quickly.)

If the bogey hasn't taken any action to counter your attack by this time, the ball game is just about over for him. You have achieved a positional and energy advantage that gives you nearly complete control of the situation. At this point you can effectively negate almost anything he can try, short of pulling straight up and exploding, or bailing out.

If you do your barrel roll in a counterclockwise direction and the bogey starts a level or diving turn to his right, just continue the barrel roll, adjusting your roll rate and playing bottom rudder as necessary to keep him in sight. Your objective here is to stay in your rolling dive until you end up in the target's deep 6 o'clock position. If he stays in his turn, this may involve continuing your roll past the point where the normal barrel roll maneuver would terminate. As I mentioned before, the main idea is to do whatever you have to to get behind your opponent and stay there. Try to get a little below his flight path and directly behind him to take advantage of his blind spot.

During the latter half of your attack you've been in a dive with no appreciable G load on the airplane, so your altitude advantage has been converting to airspeed, and you should be able to close to firing range fairly easily. A note of caution here: don't let your closing rate build up to the point where you can't control it. This would most likely occur if the target made a tight, level turn, forcing you into a rather steep dive to maintain position. After all your good work in faking him out in the early phases of the maneuver, you sure as hell don't want to go squirting out in front of him and getting hammered now, just because you let your airspeed get too high. If you find yourself closing too rapidly, try to kill off some speed by reducing power, or by S'ing within a 30-degree cone around his tail—but don't swing out too far on the side opposite his turn. If your opponent is alert and notices you swinging a little wide, he could make a hard reversal into you, setting up a modified scissors maneuver that could ruin your advantage.

Going back to the point at which you are floating inverted across the top: if you are rolling counterclockwise and your target starts a level or diving turn to his left, your reaction is a little simpler than countering a turn in the other direction. If he turns against your direction of roll, all you have to do is rapidly increase your rate of roll so that you perform the last half of an aileron roll; at the same time, feed in hard bottom rudder. This will allow you to match his flight path quickly, and will place you above and behind him, diving for the firing position. Once again, be careful to control your overtake speed so it doesn't get too high.

Returning once more to the inverted position, suppose that the target starts a climb in an effort to counter your attack. Your best bet here would be to aileron roll out of the barrel roll, playing your roll rate so that you don't lose the bogey under your nose, and so that you maintain some nose-tail separation to preserve your advantage. Remember: as the other guy climbs, he will be slowing down, and you might end up directly over him, when in fact you need some definite nose-tail clearance to keep your advantage and to give you some maneuvering room as you close in for the kill. Use power, bottom rudder, or fishtailing to slow down and maintain your position behind the target. Try not to get suckered into a steep, nose-down position, because this could carry you well below him, and if you generate too much altitude separation, a quick wingover into a split S on his part will have him eating your socks in no time.

If the target initiates a turn in either direction while he is climbing, apply the procedures described above for turns by the target into, or away from, your direction of roll. In this case, however, your maneuvers will of necessity be a little tighter, with more emphasis on minimizing altitude loss.

Naturally, the timing of your counter to a climb by the target is governed by the first law of basic fighter maneuvers—keep a visual on the target. Wait until his position relative to your bird is such that whatever action you plan to take will not put him in one of your blind spots.

Again going back to the top of your original barrel roll attack (position 7): let's suppose that as you float over the top, you note that your bogey has made no move to counter your attack. Then, as the killer instinct takes over, you realize that this turkey has been completely faked out by your shifty, dazzling display of airmanship, and, having consigned his soul to God, is merely awaiting his fate at the hands of this masterful grim reaper of the skies—or maybe he's just lost you in the sun. In either case, just resume your original rate of roll and continue down the back side of the barrel roll, slide into his 6 o'clock position, and nail him (position 8). Play roll rate, bottom rudder, and power to maintain a good closing rate while staying in his blind area as you close to the firing position.

Although the barrel roll attack may seem like the ultimate maneuver because of the options it offers, there is a counter to it. If the defender counters at the right time, he can even the odds and give himself a chance to plan his next move.

Let's assume that some brash young fledgling who hasn't seen all the victory flags painted on the side of your cockpit spots you at long range and starts to lay a barrel roll attack on you. As I mentioned earlier, the defender may have some problems at this point trying to determine just what the bogey is up to. However, once you see that he is trying to match your heading and is picking up airspeed with a dive, you can bet your long white silk scarf that a barrel roll attack is coming up.

As soon as you realize his intentions, get your power up to max continuous to increase your energy level. It's advisable to use a shallow dive or zero-G maneuver here to gain airspeed more rapidly, especially if your opponent is already in his dive. Keep picking up speed until you see him start his pull-up into the barrel roll. At this point, start your own climb, just as you would for a barrel roll attack— only do your roll in the opposite direction from your opponent's. That is, if he is setting up his maneuver on your right side, his barrel roll will be counterclockwise with respect to the horizon. Therefore, in your countering maneuver, you must roll clockwise with respect to the horizon. This will result in both you and your opponent performing large barrel rolls in opposite directions to each other, and will pretty much even things out for the moment.

Something to remember as you start your pull-up into the counter: if possible, try to climb at a slightly steeper angle than your opponent. Obviously, you will both slow down as you climb; your steeper angle will slow you down a little faster, which will give you a better chance to keep the bogey in your forward hemisphere and maintain a visual.

If both of you stay in your barrel rolls, you can determine how the situation is shaping up as you approach the top of the roll, where your flight paths should cross. If you have succeeded in keeping the other guy ahead of your beam, you'll probably want to hang around and see if he makes a mistake that will allow you to improve your position. If he goes behind your beam as your flight paths cross at the top of the roll, you'll undoubtedly lose sight of him for a few moments, and it might be advisable to start thinking about an escape maneuver to break off the engagement.

Assuming you cross with neither aircraft in a distinct position of advantage, and you each continue the barrel roll, both of you should increase back pressure on the down side of the roll in an effort to work toward the opponent's tail. In this case, a stalemate will still exist, for you will end up at the bottom of the roll in a head-on pass to each other. However, neither of you can afford *not* to load up and pull toward the other's tail, because the one who doesn't tips the balance of a neutral situation in favor of his opponent, who will now be in his rear hemisphere and working toward his six.

Some of the usual mistakes that occur when employing the barrel roll attack are:

(1) Starting the maneuver too late, which allows the defender to generate too much nose-tail separation for you to complete a successful approach to the firing position.

(2) Trying a barrel roll attack when you and the bogey are approaching each other nearly head on. If your angle off his tail is close to 180 degrees, and you are at or near his altitude, you're better off maintaining your heading and diving below his flight path, waiting until he is almost overhead, and using an Immelmann to pull up into his six. Timing on the pull-up must be judged carefully, to insure that you don't roll out too far astern of the bogey; you must also be sure you have enough airspeed to arrive at the top with some maneuvering potential. This tactic offers the advantages of increasing your energy level sufficiently to complete the maneuver, while placing you in the blind area beneath the bogey's nose, and/or against a landscape background, making it difficult for him to spot you or keep a visual on you.

(3) Not going high enough at the top of the roll, which may cause you to lose nose-tail separation.

(4) Going too high at the top of the roll, which will allow an alert defender to gain too much separation by zero-G'ing away.

(5) Starting the roll at too high an angle off and keeping too many Gs on the aircraft during the first half of the roll. This will result in an even higher angle off, and you will overshoot the defender's flight path.

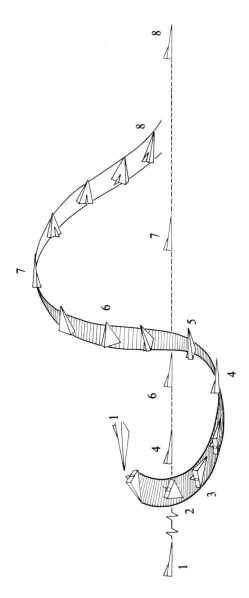

The barrel roll attack

CHAPTER 9
CLOSE FORMATION

The basic purpose of formation flying is to get two or more aircraft from A to B as a controlled, integral unit. The formation acrobatics and formation flybys seen at air shows are more advanced applications of the same basic rules used by flights of two or four.

Like anything new, formation takes a little getting used to. The normal weekend throttle bender doesn't get a chance to fly close to another bird for extended periods, much less to practice the techniques required for flying wing and lead positions. Furthermore, formation flying has its own requirements and discipline that must be added to normal flight routines in order to make it effective, fun, and primarily, safe.

As with the other maneuvers and tactics discussed in this book, in formation flying safety is the *numero uno* consideration. The screwball who doesn't abide by commonsense flying safety rules doesn't belong in the air, much less in close proximity to another aircraft. Safety rules applicable to acrobatics aren't too much different from those that apply to straight and level flight. Formation, however, brings in the added responsibility of being aware of the dangers involved in flying close to another bird, and the precautions necessary to minimize them.

As with other specialized aspects of flying, self-discipline is the primary key to success in formation flying. This means that you and every other member of the flight should be completely familiar with every facet of the job at hand before leaving the briefing room. Know all the basic ground-school elements involved in the proposed mission, especially signals, check-in procedures, and the types of formation to be flown. Air time is for practicing and sharpening your techniques—not for asking about points that should have been covered during briefing.

Once the flight starts to taxi, each member's concentration should be devoted exclusively to the business of formation flying and nothing else. When you're on somebody's wing, your only job is to maintain position and to be alert for signals from the leader. Your job does *not* involve looking around the area for bogies, checking things in the cockpit, helping with navigation, or any other action that requires you to take your eyes off the plane you are flying wing on. Too many mid-airs and countless near misses that are too hairy to reflect on have occurred because a wingman momentarily took his eyes off the lead, expecting things to remain stable—and then the leader started a turn. In turbulent air, with all the birds in the flight bobbling around, concentration on working to maintain your position becomes even more important, and also makes things easier for anyone flying *your* wing. When you add instrument conditions to the turbulent air, the concentration factor can assume critical proportions. Even under the best of conditions, a lapse of attention on anyone's part could have disastrous effects on the entire flight.

Once you get a little practice under your belt, formation flying ceases to be a chore, but it never ceases to be work. A rule of thumb that used to apply when flying gaggles of eight to twelve birds for a flyby was that the guy who returned with a flying suit that wasn't soaked with sweat hadn't really done a good job. Being able to hang in there in spite of rough air, glaring sun in your eyes, and a leader who seems to be as coordinated as a Chinese fire drill is a matter of personal pride for every fighter jock.

Along with the satisfactions of a job well done, there are other, more important reasons for knowing how to fly good formation. Ever lose your airspeed indicator, or get caught on top of a "broken" layer without IFR equipment, or lose your navigation aids in an unfamiliar area and have to be led in? These are just a few of the instances in which knowing a little bit about flying wing can become as important as money in the bank, if there's someone around who can help you out. Then, too, formation flying allows two or more aircraft to operate as one, which can mean a lot of saved time in crowded areas; it lets you in on some of the more skilled and more enjoyable aspects of flying; and, best of all, it fills one of the prerequisites for the exciting area of tactical flying, which will be discussed in Chapter 10.

Briefings

Nobody does this and survives without paying close attention to a number of requirements and formalities. One of the most basic elements of successful formation work is the need for comprehensive, in-depth briefing. It's really the only sensible and safe way to proceed when you're flying formation.

As I said in Chapter 5, briefings should be as long as necessary to cover all the details of the proposed flight, and should leave no questions unanswered in anyone's mind. In addition to the normal briefing items (weather, local procedures, emergency situations, and so forth), the portion of the briefing devoted to formation should, as a minimum, include the topics listed below. These should be amplified as required, and added to as the local situation dictates.

Formation Briefing Guide

(1) Number of aircraft involved, tail numbers if appropriate, and the call sign to be used by the flight. The call sign selected should be short, simple, and distinctive enough so that it is not mistaken for some other word or phrase common to radio terminology. Cute or fancy call signs only tend to confuse the communications process, and have no business in a formation flight.

(2) Times for starting engines, check-in, taxi, and takeoff. Everyone in the flight should write these down to avoid confusion and delays later on. (World War II jocks wrote them on the backs of their hands, but this is a little messy.) If all the birds are parked side by side, these times aren't too important, because hand signals can be used; but if one or more aircraft are located some distance away, these times become essential to a smooth, professional operation. When these times are established, the flight lead should give a time hack to the rest of the flight. Although this sounds somewhat melodramatic, it sure beats cranking up and then sitting in the chocks for ten minutes because some clown's watch is slow. Another point to go over at this time are the radio frequencies that will be used during the mission; again, these should be written down by everyone.

(3) Position numbers. If the mission call sign is Blue Flight, the flight leader is always Blue Lead or Blue 1. The leader's wingman is Blue 2. If two other aircraft are in the flight, they are known as the element; the leader of the element will be Blue 3, and his wingman, Blue 4. Each pilot will keep his original position number once it is assigned, regardless of the position changes that may occur on a practice flight. When position assignments are made, an alternate lead should be designated; he will take over the flight in case the leader aborts or has problems in the air. The alternate lead is normally number three in a flight of four, and should be the next most experienced man, after the lead.

(4) The route to be flown, if it is outside the local area, and the major checkpoints along the way. Every member of the flight should have a copy of the flight plan so that anyone can take over if the lead aborts or loses his radio.

(5) Power settings, airspeeds, and altitudes to be used by the formation. These should be set to make allowances for the slowest aircraft in the flight.

(6) The types of formation to be used during takeoff and climb-out, en route or during the practice phase, and during letdown and approach.

(7) Maneuvers to be performed by the flight, again stressing the planned airspeeds.

(8) Rendezvous points for late takeoffs or lost wingmen.

(9) Hand signals to be used. (These will be discussed in more detail below.)

(10) Bingo fuel.

(11) Alternate mission in case of aborts.

(12) In-flight emergency procedures. Normally, if an air abort occurs in a flight of four, and the afflicted aircraft requires assistance back to the field, the other bird in his element will accompany him. The remaining element will continue with the alternate mission.

Here is a Formation Briefing Guide as used on a mission. For a Formation Flying Briefing Guide and Form you can use, see Appendix D.

Formation Briefing Guide

Weather	Existing	Forecast
Local	500 1000 10↑5	400 800 8H↑3
Working area	800 1200 10→10	800 120⊕ 10→15
Destination	600 15↓5	60⊕ 10 ↓10

Call sign _BLUE FLIGHT_

FLIGHT LINEUP

Position	Tail number	Pilot
1	731	SMITH
2	824	JONES
3	961	DOE
4	533	BROWN
Alternate lead	DOE	

TIME HACK

Start engines ___*0900*___   Taxi ___*0910*___

Check-in ___*0905*___   Takeoff___*0915*___

FREQUENCIES

Ground ___*121.9*___   En route ___*123.8*___   ___*119.65*___ ___*120.8*___

Tower ___*120.7*___   Working ___*122.9*___   Backup___*129.1*___

LINEUP FOR TAKEOFF

Check wind direction

#1 on downwind side

Spacing between aircraft or elements

Line up in center of your half of the runway

Last man on: call in position

Hand signals

TAKEOFF

Formation takeoff: _____ yes ___✕___ no (maximum crosswind component 10 knots)

Power settings

Time interval between aircraft or elements: ___*5*___ seconds

Signals: run-up, brake release, gear/flaps up, power reduction

Aborts

JOIN-UP

Airspeed

Join-up Side

Overshoots:

Remain clear of flight until speed is stabilized

Ease into position when airspeed is under control

No belly-up, blind join-ups—cross under flight and keep
them in view

EN ROUTE

Formation to be used *CLOSE FINGERTIP*

Checkpoints

Frequency changes

Hand and aircraft signals

Level off airspeed *130* ; altitude *5,000*

WORKING AREA

Frequency change

Boundaries of area

Prominent checkpoints and obstructions

Sequence of maneuvers to be performed:

#	Type	Airspeed of lead	Leader
1	CROSSOVERS	120	SMITH
2	LAZY 8's	130	DOE
3	TRAIL	130	SMITH
4	TACTICAL	120	DOE

Rendezvous point for lost wingman or late arrivals _____

OVER THE FORK IN THE RIVER

LEFT orbit; airspeed __110__ altitude _5,000_

Signals to be used

FORMATION PARTICULARS

Reference points: close and tactical

Crossover techniques: close and tactical

Trail: pitchout interval, maneuvers to be performed, distance between aircraft; call lead if thrown out

Rejoins

Stacked and level turns

Minimum altitude

Keep radio chatter to a minimum

Lookout doctrine in tactical

Fuel checks

Bingo fuel __15__

RECOVERY

Formation to be used ___*SPREAD*___

Checkpoints, if different than above

Frequencies

Airspeed ___*120*___ altitude ___*4,000*___

APPROACH AND LANDING

Pre-landing check

Frequencies

Formation to be used; when change to Echelon will occur

Pitchout interval: ___*3*___ seconds

Hand and aircraft signals

Pattern:

Airspeeds
Spacing
Altitude
Don't bunch up
Common base leg

Landing:

Alternate sides—#1 takes downwind side
Stay in center of your half of the runway
Watch for turbulence/prop wash
Passing on runway
Call when aircraft in front of you is clear to turn off
    runway

FORMATION APPROACH

Point of initiating approach

Gear and flap procedures

Airspeed approaching glide path ____90____

Airspeed on final ____70____

Attitude changes at slow airspeeds

Hand signal review

Minimum altitude (drop-off)

Alternate mission ____ACROBATICS____

Hand signal review

Emergency procedure of the day

REMEMBER—SAFETY IS PARAMOUNT

The proper knowledge and use of hand signals is a primary requisite to successful formation flying. Hand signals should be used in lieu of radio calls whenever possible, so that they become second nature to every flight member. Although it is a little more difficult to pull off smoothly, an entire formation flight, including practice maneuvers, can be flown without the use of radios. The primary reason for hand signals is to keep radio chatter down in a crowded area. Hand signals also allow two aircraft to pass a lot of essential information back and forth when one has a radio out; this becomes very important when a flight leader has to make decisions based on every scrap of information he can get from an afflicted aircraft.

Hand signals should be made in a definite, even exaggerated, manner, so they won't be confused with other motions in the cockpit. They should be repeated if necessary. *Never* flash a quick signal and then start to execute the called-for action immediately. It is possible that the wingman wasn't looking at your cockpit when you gave the signal, or he may have misunderstood it. (Wingmen can help out in this area by acknowledging the receipt of all signals with a nod of the head.) Leaders who have birds on each wing should insure that the signal is given on both sides of the cockpit, so that everyone gets the word.

Though almost any agreed-upon motions can be used for hand signals, the ones described below are the most generally accepted, and are in common use.

(1) Start or run up engines: Describe a small circle above the head with an extended index finger.

(2) Channel change: Tap the headset or the ear, and then hold up fingers to indicate the channel number you are changing to. Naturally, this only works if your comm gear has preset channels, or if you designate certain frequencies by single-digit numbers in your briefing. Otherwise, you will have to signal each digit of the frequency individually, remembering to pull your hand down between digits, so that when you want to signal a seven, it doesn't get misread as a five and a two.

(3) Gear up or down: Make an up-and-down motion with a clenched fist, with the thumb pointing upward for "gear up," and downward for "gear down." You should *not* start to put your gear up or down as soon as you receive this signal, because it is only the preparatory signal. The leader should pause for a few moments after giving the gear up or down signal, to allow everyone to get his hand on the switch or crank, and then give the signal of execution. This is a pronounced forward head nod by the leader.

(4) Flaps up or down: Make the preparatory signal by holding the hand horizontal, palm down, and then bending the fingers down, simulating the motion of a flap. Again, the signal of execution will be an exaggerated head nod.

(5) Power advance or retard: Move a clenched fist forward or backward, simulating the movement of a throttle.

(6) Level off: Move the extended hand in a back-and-forth motion, palm down.

(7) Fuel check: Hold up a fist with the thumb extended, touching the lips, to simulate a drinking motion. Wingmen answer by holding up fingers to indicate the number of gallons, or tens of gallons, remaining.

(8) Pitchout, peel off and spacing: Give the same signal as for engine run-up, followed by holding up fingers to indicate the number of seconds of spacing between each aircraft.

(9) Change lead: The leader points at the aircraft he wants to designate as the new leader, and then points out in front of the flight to indicate the new position he should take.

(10) Transmitter/receiver out: Transmitter: pat the lips and then move the hand back and forth in front of the mouth. Receiver: pat the ear and then move the hand back and forth alongside the head.

(11) Aircraft emergency, must land as soon as possible: Hold a clenched fist at the top of the canopy, or at the top of the windshield for high-wing birds.

In addition to hand signals, there are a few signals made with the aircraft itself. When the leader wants to move the flight from close formation to spread, he signals by fishtailing a few times. A rapid wing dip is used to indicate that a wingman or an element should change from one side of the leader to the other. (In rough air, this wing dip has to be more pronounced to make it a distinctive signal.) When the flight is in spread formation or in Trail, the leader signals a rejoin with a slow continuous rocking of his wings. In Trail formation, it is usually necessary for each pilot to repeat the signal to make sure the man behind him gets the word.

Before getting into the techniques of formation flying, I want to describe the various types of formation. The first type is normal, or close, formation. If there are just two birds flying together, they are known as an element. If you add another flight of two, you have a variety of close formation known as "Fingertip," because the positions of the aircraft resemble the tips of the fingers when they are extended. A top and a rear view of the Fingertip formation are shown below.

Fingertip formation

When all the birds are on the same side of the leader, the formation is known as an Echelon. The same views of an Echelon are depicted here:

Echelon

The last variety of close formation, known as "Trail," is misnamed, because it is usually flown with about 500 to 700 feet of separation between aircraft. This is considered the optimum distance—it allows space for performing maneuvers while keeping the aircraft close enough to maintain the discipline and techniques of close formation flying. In a Trail formation, the birds are simply lined up one behind the other, each stacked a little below the one in front of it to avoid prop wash. Of all the formations, Trail is the most fun, because it allows you a little latitude to move around, yet demands a lot of judgment—estimating distances and closing rates from directly astern can be tricky.

Another major type of formation is show formation, which is probably best described as "closer" close formation. Here the same basic formations described above are used, but all the birds are tucked in a little tighter. Usually quite a few more birds are involved in show—probably three or four flights of four. The only reason for flying show is to make it look good for the troops on the ground; therefore, hanging in there real tight is only necessary for the pass over the grandstand. The rest of the time, normal formation should suffice. Because of the greater number of aircraft involved, the lack of maneuverability inherent with a large flight, and the very close positions flown by everyone, show formation should only be attempted by throttle benders who have a considerable amount of wing time under their belts. Flying in a large gaggle such as this is demanding work, and requires that everyone be on his toes at every moment.

There are difficulties associated with show formation that are not found in the other types. You must maintain your briefed position in order to stay out of the prop wash and wake turbulence that is all around you; besides, if you move too far out of position, you will subject the guys behind you to a rough ride because of your wake. And you can't slide out of position a little to check something in the cockpit. Once the pass over the grandstand is started, everyone's attention must be devoted to flying his position properly and smoothly. All fuel checks, switch or instrument settings, and other actions in the cockpit should be taken care of before you start the final run, far enough from the field so that everyone will be settled down in position by the time you hit a point three to five miles from the flyover site.

There is another problem that crops up not only in show formation, but any time you fly quite close to another airplane. As a wingman moves into a very tight position on his leader, the airflow around the wingman's plane starts to affect the leader's. The lead feels as if someone is gently nudging his bird sideways, away from the wingman. This usually occurs when the leader is trying to maintain a definite track over the ground; therefore, he will automatically correct for this apparent drift off course with a move toward the wingman. From this point on, things get fouled up for both birds as they each jockey for position, to all intents and purposes working against each other. Obviously, this causes a lot of bobbling around and makes things tougher for both pilots—to say nothing of the near chaos it creates for anyone trying to fly their respective wings. In large formations, trying to shine your tail by moving in closer than is necessary louses up the entire show, and only points up the fact that you're not ready to play in the big game yet.

There are a number of aircraft arrangements besides Fingertip, Echelon, and Trail that can be used in show formation; some of these are Diamond, Line Abreast, Arrowhead, and V of Vs. They involve problems and techniques associated with the more basic formations; however, they have no practical application except for flybys, so I won't go into them in this book.

Along with close formation, there is another fundamental type that is probably used more often. This is spread formation. The only aircraft arrangement that is suitable or practical for spread is a modified Fingertip. In spread formation, all aircraft remain in the same relative positions as for close formation Fingertip, but the distance between birds is increased to about two to four ship widths. On a typical mission, it's a lot easier on everyone if the flight moves out into spread formation once you're en route and things have settled down. This allows each jock to devote some attention to instruments, maps, switch actions—whatever—and still fly in close enough proximity to the other birds that the flight can be considered a unit. It also permits all members of the flight to practice a little lookout doctrine, and thus help the leader to spot other traffic. Should weather become a factor, or a letdown be started, the flight can be quickly rejoined into close formation. After putting the flight or element into spread, the leader should not let the birds get too loose, because this delays things and complicates the issue if a rejoin or flight maneuvering becomes necessary.

A minor problem associated with spread formation is that the distances between the birds may make hand signals a little indistinct, so radios may have to used. A cardinal rule to be followed in any formation, but especially in spread, concerns the wingman with an emergency. The first corollary of Murphy's Law will apply in nearly every case, and the afflicted aircraft will have a radio failure in addition to its other problems. In close formation, a wingman in this situation should move out a little to insure ample wing tip clearance, and then move slowly and carefully ahead until he attracts the leader's attention. In spread formation, he should rejoin with the nearest aircraft, and then move up on it until his problem is recognized. Naturally, the utmost caution should be exercised when attempting this rejoin, because the bird the wingman is joining with won't expect anyone to be there, and will be maneuvering accordingly. Once the crippled bird gets someone's attention, the pilot should use appropriate hand signals to describe his problem and intentions.

The last major type of formation is tactical, which, as the name implies, is where the action is. Tactical formation is used whenever the flight, or the element, is in an area where it can expect to be bounced; its purpose is to allow maximum maneuverability of the flight, and to provide mutual protection to everyone in it. "Mutual" is the key word here, because flying tactical formation with two or four ships imposes definite responsibilities and duties on every member of the flight. These will be discussed in more detail in the next chapter.

The need for mutual coverage in tactical formation pretty much dictates that the arrangement of the aircraft be either a large, spread-out Fingertip formation, or a variant called the Six Pac.

A detailed description of each basic formation, and the techniques of flying it, will be given below. Though each of the major types of formation—close, spread, and tactical—is discussed separately here, it is common for all three to be flown on the same mission. Close formation is used for takeoff and climb-out, spread during the en route phase, and tactical when you're in the area where you expect a hassle. If you have met the enemy and made them yours, you might even throw in a little show formation when you return to the home drome.

Close Formation

There is a right way and a wrong way to fly close formation. The wrong way is to fly in *any* position except the right one, and not take any corrective action. Everybody falls out of position now and then, but as soon as you realize it's happening, you should take the proper corrective action to get back into the ideal position. This ideal spot is on a line 30 to 45 degrees back from the leader's beam position. The exact angle will be the one that affords the clearest view between cockpits. A clear view is of particular importance if one of the birds has a high wing with struts. But if this isn't a factor and you have your druthers, start out using the 45-degree line, because it's a slightly easier position to fly.

Once you're on the proper line, move the airplane along the line toward the leader until you hit a spot *just before* your wing tip starts to overlap his. You'll know you're there when you start to feel the wash from his wing tip nibbling at yours. Move back out a tad to keep your wing out of his turbulence, and you're in the ideal position.

In most cases (depending on the geometry of the birds), this ideal position will not provide nosetail clearance between you and the leader. Therefore, wingmen normally stack down from the leader, which means that in the ideal position, you will be flying at a slightly lower altitude than the aircraft you are flying wing on. Initially, until you feel comfortable on the wing, you should stack low enough to provide vertical clearance between the two birds, for safety reasons. Then, once you get the hang of it, you can stack down a little less, and you'll be in the normal close formation position. Remember, however, that the normal position *does not* provide adequate vertical clearance; in the normal position, the only clearance you'll want to maintain is wing tip clearance. You can't be too careful about this. If you let your wing tip drift inside your leader's, and you happen to bobble up where your wing is level with his, you'll hit the area of maximum turbulence coming off his wing. If this catches you by surprise, it could force that wing down abruptly, causing an unexpected turn right into number one. Such a gyration will definitely not impress the leader with your prowess in formation.

Once you get over your initial uneasiness about flying close to another airplane, the normal position in close formation should feel comfortable and eventually become routine. This change of attitude is not sudden, but comes about gradually as a result of spending a good deal of time on somebody's wing. The ideal position in close formation is designed with comfort in mind. If you try to shine your tail by closing it up real tight, you create problems for everyone, but especially for yourself. Since flying closer than normal to the lead requires quicker reaction times, you'll find that you're working yourself to death trying to stay with the lead during every bounce and bobble he goes through. On a hot day, with a lot of turbulence, this could make it a long afternoon.

Being too far forward of the 30-degree line or too far aft of the 45-degree line also creates problems. Flying in the former position will not only look bad, but will force you to look out of your cockpit at an angle of almost 90 degrees. This reduces your perspective and makes for a sore neck in a very short time. Flying too far forward is also bad news when the leader starts a turn into you—your corrections will have to be quicker and of greater magnitude than normal, which, again, will generate problems for all concerned.

Hanging too far back behind the 45-degree line also looks bad, and compounds your problem when the leader turns away from you. This position could also cause you to miss hand signals from the lead. As I mentioned earlier, formation flying is work, and you should be working constantly to correct any variance from the ideal position. If you catch these deviations early, only minimal stick and throttle actions are required; however, if you let them develop significantly, you'll be working so hard you'll look like you're trying to kill a snake in the cockpit.

Now that you're at the ideal formation position, you'll need some reference points to help you stay there. These are any two fixed points on the aircraft structure that are aligned when you are in the proper position. The farther apart these points are, the better, because the greater the separation, the easier it will be for you to pick up slight deviations from the correct position. Examples of some reference points that are commonly used are: the wing light and the canopy bow; the leading or trailing edge of the wing tip, and the landing gear; aircraft markings and the exhaust stacks. Any two points on the aircraft that are easy to see at a distance of 50 feet can be used—antennas, pitot masts, decals, seams, and so forth. If you fly formation with a lot of different types of birds, a set of reference points will have to be developed for each. However, before selecting these references, be sure that they exist on both sides of the aricraft. You could have problems when you change sides if one of your points is a pitot head, group of registration numbers, or decal that is unique to one side of the bird.

Flight Lead Requirements

Before I get too much further into the nitty-gritty of formation techniques, I want to say a few words on the requirements for and duties of the guys selected as flight leaders. The flight lead is usually the most experienced jock in the group in total time, and the one who is most familiar with the local area. Another of this guy's qualities can be summed up in three words—he must be SMOOTH, SMOOTH, SMOOTH. People learning to fly formation need a spastic, ham-handed flight lead like Custer needed more Indians. A guy who is smooth on the controls makes all the difference in the world in any type of formation flying, regardless of the experience level of the wingmen. This is doubly true in the learning phase. Leaders should make a conscious effort, each time they move the controls. to move them *slowly and deliberately,* with constant rates of roll in and roll out. Nothing can break up a flight quicker than a leader who is insensitive to the problems of those on his wing.

This consideration for the wingmen is a responsibility that flight leaders have even when the birds are not in close formation—and is no less important when the flight is in spread, tactical, or Trail. During these phases, a good leader will maintain the briefed airspeed or power setting, to give everyone something to play with. You can't expect numbers three and four to hang in there if the lead flies at or near their max cruise or red-line speed, because maintaining position requires a combination of timely maneuvering and a little power advantage.

It is particularly important to avoid the red-line speed of the slowest bird in the formation by a good margin when the flight is in Trail. In this formation, numbers three and four will almost always be a little behind, and will be using the diving portions of the in-trail maneuvers, to catch up. With their attention fixed mainly on the bird ahead, it is very easy to slip through the limit speed.

Another thing leaders should stay away from, particularly in Trail, is unbriefed maneuvers. A good leader knows the capabilities of his wingmen and always avoids maneuvers that are beyond those capabilities. The younger troops in the flight may be able to handle turning climbs and dives, but if you ring in an overhead maneuver on them, they may not be mentally prepared or have the skill level to stick with it, and they could get into trouble.

A leader should remember that the need for smoothness and deliberateness carries with it the problem of reduced maneuverability for the flight as a whole. Things that are relatively simple for a single ship, such as turning initial or maneuvering into a traffic pattern, require no small amount of planning when you've got three other guys with you. In formation, if you roll out of a turn and you're not lined up with the runway the way you'd like, you don't have the option of a jogging correction. All of this means that the leader must be constantly planning how to get from A to B in a manner that is easiest for the flight *as a unit.* If you do make an error in judgment close in to the field, and you roll out on initial lined up to the right or to the left of the runway, it's too late to try a correction turn. If you're close enough to take a shot at it, maintain your heading and make your adjustments *in the pattern.* Otherwise, break out of traffic and reenter.

Other responsibilities that come with the job of leading flights are: making all radio calls outside the flight (the lead should be the only one talking to towers, flight service, or traffic controllers); calling for and copying clearances; navigating; clearing the area for other traffic; and monitoring fuel. On this last item, remember that mission planning for the flight must be based on the bird that carries the least amount of fuel.

Radio Discipline

As I mentioned earlier, the techniques of close formation flying demand a large measure of personal discipline. Everyone must know his job and fly the mission as briefed. Each wingman should keep his attention riveted on the leader so he can catch every turn or maneuver instantly and react accordingly. You should make checks of your instruments or switches only when you absolutely have to, and then only after moving out a little to insure a bit of extra clearance while your eyes are momentarily off the lead.

One of the greatest tests of self-discipline when flying formation involves the use of the radio. For wingmen, the name of the game is speak when spoken to, except, of course, for necessary transmissions: calling out a stranger that the leader can't see or has missed; reporting a problem that has cropped up with your bird, or one that you notice with someone else's, such as a leak or a door that has come open.

The leader does all the talking for the flight, but there are certain times when he will require a check-in from each member of the flight to make sure that everyone is on frequency, or has understood something he has said. This will normally be the case on the initial check-in before or after engine start; whenever there are channel changes; and after the lead gives special instructions for the flight. A wingman will check in or acknowledge calls from the lead with his call sign and flight number only, and on channel changes will check in before and after the change. If the leader calls, "Blue Flight—go channel 2," the wingmen should answer, in sequence, "Blue 2," "Blue 3," "Blue 4." If radio traffic is particularly heavy, these replies can be shortened to "Two," "Three," "Four."

Always answer in order. If number two answers and number three doesn't, number four must wait until the leader asks him specifically to check in. The reason for this is that number three may have had trouble tuning to the new frequency— a common occurrence in close formation. People checking in out of order on a crowded frequency may give the leader wrong information as to who's with him and who isn't. The sign of a bunch of real pros is good radio discipline, accented by quick, crisp check-ins, and no extra chatter except when it's absolutely necessary to clarify a situation. Wingmen, however, should not be too quick on the check-in, because hitting the mike too quickly may mean you block another guy out, and the leader has to call for another check-in—very bad form.

Formation Takeoff

Now down to the meat of the subject—the specific techniques for each phase of a formation flight, from takeoff to final approach. A formation takeoff will be covered here, but I definitely do not recommend that you try it until the wingman has acquired a fair amount of experience in normal formation flying. In actuality, there aren't too many really valid reasons for making a formation takeoff, except for show or for moving a large number of aircraft out of a field quickly—for example, in the case of a severe-weather evacuation.

Although a formation takeoff is a little more difficult and a little more dangerous than a single-ship takeoff, it is something that everyone who flies formation should master. But obviously, a formation takeoff should never be attempted unless the runway is wide enough. This pearl of wisdom means that, as a minimum, the runway should be wider than twice the combined wingspans of the birds making the formation takeoff. After the pre-takeoff checks are completed, the leader should call for permission for a flight of two (or four) to take the active. When cleared, the lead takes the downwind side of the runway, and succeeding flight members take alternate sides, as shown in the diagram below.

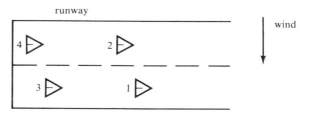

A flight of four in position for a formation takeoff

If a flight of four is involved, the lead element should taxi down the active a little, so that the next element can position itself about 800 to 1,000 feet behind the first. This spacing helps to keep the second element from being rattled around by the prop wash of the lead element during run-up, and also minimizes the effect of pebbles or other debris blown back by numbers one and two. Each pilot should line up in the center of his half of the runway, and the wingman in each element should move up on his leader until he reaches the normal wing position described above. In order to maintain flight integrity, the run-up should not begin until number four is in position. Since the leader can't readily discern when this occurs, the proper procedure is for the last man to call "Four's in" when he has taxied into position.

After giving the cockpit and instruments a last check, the wingman nods to his leader that he is ready to go, and the lead responds with the run-up signal. The pilot leading any formation takeoff should advance the throttle to takeoff power and then retard it a little so that the wingman will have some margin to play with. The leader looks over to get a nod from his wingman, signifying that he is all set; he then places his head back against the headrest, and when he is cleared, gives the signal of execution for brake release—an exaggerated forward head nod. All the lead has to do from this point on is to make a normal, smooth takeoff, making certain that he steers straight down the centerline of his half of the runway.

The wingman should be at full power when brake release occurs. This little extra edge comes in handy to counteract the reaction delay that invariably occurs at brake release. Once the flight is rolling down the runway, the wingman should use throttle and rudder to maintain his position. He should *not* use brakes, because their effect is too drastic in an accelerating condition with the aircraft getting light on the controls—it's like using a meat ax to do a scalpel's job.

If you are the wingman and you start to overrun the lead, ease back on the power just a tad so that you don't start losing ground too rapidly. Reapply the power as soon as you see the relative motion between the two birds stop. If you are really overrunning the lead, you can use this technique in addition to calling, "Lead, push it up." If you're still passing him, it's probably best to carry on with your own takeoff, maintaining the center of your half of the runway. Be sure to advise the lead that you're passing him and will be making your own takeoff.

If the wingman is a little late on the brake release, or is driving a real dog, and the leader starts to pull away, about all the wingman can do is ask the leader for a slight power reduction, saying, "Give me a couple." The leader should then reduce his power *just a little;* but if such a power reduction will lengthen the takeoff roll to the point where too much runway is being used, the leader shouldn't bother with it. In this case it's better to continue with the original power setting and let the wingman join up after the flight is safely airborne. If the wingman does get too far behind to catch up, he should gradually switch from his wing position to flying his own takeoff down the center of his half of the runway.

The seemingly overgenerous requirements for runway widths mentioned above become all too minimal if an abort occurs on the takeoff roll. If directional control is not a problem, the aborting aricraft should call his intentions to the other birds in the flight, and then ease over as close to the edge of the runway as possible. This will allow the other aircraft in the element to continue the takeoff with as much

The correct positioning during a formation takeoff just after breaking ground, as seen from the wingman's position. (Photo by Frank J. O'Brien)

room as possible, a factor that is of particular importance to the wingman who has to convert rapidly from the wing position to a normal takeoff.

During takeoff, aborts are *never* made in pairs. Therefore, if one aircraft in an element has to call it quits while he's on the roll, the other bird should continue the takeoff. A situation in which two pilots try to stop birds that are rolling side by side at high speed is pregnant with possibilities for an accident. A blown tire caused by heavy braking, or going into the overrun, could wrap both birds up very neatly.

Back to the normal takeoff roll: assuming that the wingman is maintaining position, he should raise his tail or lift his nosewheel at the same time as the lead aircraft. When the leader breaks ground, the wingman should start to ease his bird off the deck; but if you're flying wing and your bird isn't ready to fly at this point, don't force it. This is no time to get into a stalled or semi-stalled condition. Take off when your bird is ready, and then move back into position.

When the leader sees that both aircraft are safely airborne, he gives the preparatory signal for gear up, if applicable, followed by the exaggerated head nod for execution. During gear retraction (and especially if it is done manually), the wingman should move out a little, because there will undoubtedly be some bouncing around during the change to a clean configuration.

Although it looks great and is exciting to perform, a formation takeoff should never be made when a good crosswind is blowing, or when the runway is slippery. These conditions really narrow the odds if a mishap does occur.

The most comon and by far the safest method of getting a flight off the ground is to use the in-trail takeoff. This procedure is a must for the first few formation rides, or when weather conditions are not just right for a formation takeoff. A good rule of thumb to follow with respect to weather is to use an in-trail takeoff if the crosswind component exceeds ten knots, or if there is packed snow on the runway, especially if it is patchy.

The lineup on the runway for an in-trail takeoff is the same as that described for a formation takeoff. If adverse conditions are expected, the flight should be briefed for an in-trail departure utilizing a definite time interval between aircraft— usually five seconds. Thus, when number two sees the leader start his roll, he counts five seconds or times them on the clock, and then releases his brakes. Each succeeding pilot does likewise, starting his timing when the bird in front of him starts to move.

Something that wingmen should be aware of during an in-trail takeoff is that any crosswind may cause prop wash or clouds of loose snow to drift over to their side of the runway. If this occurs and things don't look too shiny, hold your position until the problem clears up.

Join-up

After takeoff, the next item to consider in formation flying is the join-up. The same join-up procedures apply to each bird when using an in-trail departure, and to the second element of a four-shipper taking off in formation. Once the leader or the lead element is airborne, number one will delay the turn out of traffic and maintain the runway heading until he is a mile or so from the end of the runway. Then he will start a turn in the proper direction using a *maximum* of 30 degrees of bank. This turn is maintained until the other birds are joined up, or 180 degrees of turn is completed, whichever occurs first. If the latter condition prevails, the lead will roll out on the reciprocal of the runway heading and maintain this course until everybody is on his wing. Once the lead is off the ground and cleaned up (gear and flaps retracted), power is reduced from maximum to the briefed setting for the join-up, and left there until everyone is in position.

If local departure rules so dictate, or the flight is leaping off on a cross-country where fuel is a problem, this 180-degree turn for join-up will have to be modified. If, however, the lead bird does not make at least a 90-degree turn after takeoff, it will take the rest of the flight considerably longer to get into position; in this case, the only thing they will have working for them is the slight speed advantage generated by the leader's power reduction.

As soon as each wingman or succeeding flight breaks ground and has the wheels in the wells, he should immediately start a cutoff turn in the same direction as the leader and keep adjusting this turn to maintain a good cutoff angle on the lead, or on the bird in front of you if he's number three or four, until the join-up is assured. A good rule of thumb for establishing this cutoff angle is to turn so as to place the bird you're joining with in your 10 or 2 o'clock position, and then to keep him there. As long as you're not flying parallel courses, you will eventually arrive on his wing. One thing to remember during a join-up is to keep your power up until you're almost line abreast with the other aircraft; then ease back on the throttle to synchronize airspeeds.

The point at which you start your power reduction is pretty much a judgment call based on your rate of overtake. If you have a good cutoff angle established and a good head of steam built up, you'll really come whistling in there, so plan ahead and start slowing down far enough out that you don't overshoot the lead. Roaring past the lead with the throttle in idle and a hopeless look on your face definitely marks you as one of the new guys. You end up way out in front of the flight in view of God and the whole world, and then your airspeed really starts to unwind, the flight shoots on by, and once again you're out of position. It's much better to make a slower but surer approach to the wing position. A note of caution, in case you do overshoot the lead while you're on more or less parallel courses: you will tend to move the stick in the direction you are looking, which is toward the lead. This could result in a hairy situation if it is not consciously corrected for.

Let's assume you really have the overtake rate hacked and you're now abeam of the lead with your airspeeds matched, and still on the inside of the join-up turn. If your briefed position was on that side of the leader, simply move up into the ideal wing position. If you're supposed to be on the other side of the leader, pause in this position momentarily, and then move to the other side using the crossover techniques that will be discussed in a few more pages. The first few formation rides should be in flights of two, so the wingman can stay on the side he joins up on. This way, the wing will have lots of opportunities to practice crossovers before he has to use these procedures on a four-ship join-up.

There are common errors that occur during join-ups that you should be aware of and try to avoid. The first is establishing an insufficient cutoff angle; this results in a long tail chase, and it takes you forever to catch the leader or the flight. If the lead is still in a turn when you're setting up your cutoff, it might be advisable to increase your angle until he is in your 3 or 9 o'clock position, and to hold this for a short time before easing back to the normal cutoff angle. Doing this gives you an edge on the situation, and if any excess overtake results from this generous cutoff angle, you can kill it off by turning slightly toward the aircraft you are joining with.

A high cutoff angle maintained too long, and/or too high a power setting, can give rise to another problem in join-ups—excessive overtake. As I pointed out above, overshooting the flight during join-up is definitely bad form, and after it happens to you a few times, you'll be able to judge pretty accurately just how much space your bird needs to slow down in a given speed range.

The mark of a jock who has it all together is the ability to bend it around to cut off the leader quickly and facilitate a fast join-up, and then to cool it at just the right moment so that he slides into position without a hitch. A piece of cake! However, if things turn to worms and an overshoot is inevitable, reduce power immediately to save as much face as you can. Don't leave the power off too long, because by the time your overshoot is corrected, your airspeed will be well below that of the rest of the flight, and they'll whiz on by as if you've got an anchor out. During the overshoot, keep an eagle eye on the flight, and as soon as you see that your speeds are synchronized, start coming back in with the power. By the time your engine winds up to the new setting, your relative backward drift with respect to the flight should have you very close to the correct position, where only minor adjustments will be needed to move in on the leader's wing.

One of the hairiest situations that develop during a join-up results when an over-eager wingman tries to make a last-minute correction to salvage a misjudged approach. This occurs particularly when a high cutoff angle is held too long, producing an excessive lateral closing rate. The smoldering stone who is attempting to dazzle everyone with his quick join-up usually doesn't realize his plight until it's too late, and his natural corrective action is a steep bank away from the flight. However, given the delay in reaction time and the immutable laws of inertia, his aircraft will momentarily continue to close on the flight in spite of the steep bank. A high overtake coupled with a late correction will create an extremely dangerous situation—the join-up pilot cannot see the flight because of his belly-up attitude with respect to them, and he could very easily mush into the entire group. This type of maneuver is a definite no-no, and should not be tolerated by anyone in the flight. In most cases the flight lead's attention will be devoted to other things during the join-up, and he may never see this guy in time to lead the other birds in evasive action.

If you find yourself with a high lateral closing rate during a join-up, the correct thing to do is to keep the wings fairly level and dump the nose a little. This will allow you to keep the entire flight in view as you pass beneath them. Then, once you've got things under control, move into your correct position.

Now that we've got everybody joined up, the next job at hand is maintaining the proper position. The first half dozen or so formation rides should be in flights of two, so that the wingman will have the room to move around on the wing until he feels comfortable there. As I said earlier, the wingman should fly a loose position until his skill and confidence improve to the point where he can move into the ideal position.

The secret of maintaining good position lies in small, easy movements of both the throttle and the controls—a light touch on each that could probably be better described as a pressure, rather than a movement. Continuous large power adjustments in either direction and ham-handed handling of the stick only make things tougher on you, and really make it a long day for anyone flying your wing.

In a four-ship echelon, if number two is having a bad day, number three really has his work cut out for him just to stay in the ball park, and by the time the ripple effect reaches number four, he feels like he's on the end of a whip. Line up your reference points and feel out the proper position by noting other things on the lead bird that can and can't be seen from the ideal position. Keep one eye on the leader for hand signals, and, if your bird is so equipped, trim off any excess control pressures to make the whole job easier. Remember: if your attention must be diverted into the cockpit for a check of the instruments or for switch actions, move out a little before glancing away from the leader. Do whatever has to be done as quickly as possible, and then move back into position.

As with other things, some days are better than others for formation flying. A hot summer day with fair-weather cumulus and a lot of updrafts will really make a wingman earn his keep. When the air is turbulent, the best thing for a wingman to do is to fly an average position, and not to try to match the leader's every bobble. Keep a good fore and aft position by using the throttle, and hold your position vertically and laterally to a small, but generalized, envelope. Try to relax and enjoy it. Don't get a death grip on the stick, or stand on the rudder pedals in an attempt to stay in position. This will only fatigue you and make the whole job harder.

Crossovers

Flying on the right or the left side of the leader all day can make for a relatively dull mission, to say nothing of a sore neck. Anyone flying formation should be proficient on both wings, and the procedure and techniques for changing sides should be second nature to all hands.

The signal to change sides is a quick wing dip to the side the leader wants the wingman or the element to move to. If you are flying on the leader's left wing, he will quickly dip his right wing when he wants you to cross. The main idea from here on is not to hurry the crossover—slow and deliberate movements result in a much safer and quicker change.

Retard your power just a tad and allow the aircraft to drop back in a *straight* line from the wing position. During this drop-back, ease down so as to achieve vertical separation between you and the lead, which will allow you to pass below his flight path during the crossover.

After you have moved back far enough to create some nose-tail separation, readjust your power to synchronize speeds again. Your position before starting over should be below, behind, and to one side of the leader. Now move slowly over to a similar position on the other side of the leader by using just a small amount of bank. Don't allow your bird to swing too wide of your new position, because you'll only have to work back to it. Once you're there, all you have to do is add a little power and move up into the ideal wing position on the new side.

A wingman should only change sides at the direction of the leader. Maybe the sun is in your eyes, your neck is bothering you, or you just don't like the side you're on—but don't cross over without the leader's permission, because he may be planning a maneuver that doesn't take your new position into account.

As your formation flying skills increase, the crossover can be smoothed out so that it is executed as one continuous maneuver, with only a slight, imperceptible pause at the corners.

Changing sides in a flight of four is basically the same as doing it in a flight of two. However, the presence of additional aircraft calls for added caution, and a few extra procedures.

As an example, let's consider a four-shipper in Fingertip, with the element (numbers three and four) on the leader's right wing. The signal is given for the element to change sides. Number two continues to fly normal formation, and should concentrate on holding a good, smooth position.

The element lead (number three) will employ essentially the same techniques as would a single ship during a crossover. Number four, in essence, does the same thing, but his job is a little tougher, because all his movements will be in relation to a moving target—number three. As the element lead moves back and down preparatory to crossing, number four does likewise with respect to three. Number three then starts moving across; four delays moving to the opposite side of the element lead until number three has passed behind the leader. The reason for this delay is that it allows number four to keep both number three and the leader in sight at all times. Because of the greater distances he has to travel, number four should anticipate larger throttle movements and slightly greater bank angles to complete his crossover in a timely manner.

If the signal is given to number two to change sides while the flight is in the original Fingertip formation, he will also utilize the same techniques as for a single-ship crossover. But, in this case, the element lead also has some responsibilities. When the signal is given for number two to cross over, and while he is moving to his pre-crossover position, the element must move out to make room for him. So, number three moves out about two ship widths while maintaining the same references on the lead. (For instance, if the original reference line was at a 45-degree angle from the lead, number three just moves farther out along this line.) By now number two should be in his pre-crossover position, but before starting over, he should make sure that the element has left him sufficient room to make the change safely. After two moves up into position on the lead, three simply moves up on number two's wing. Number four's job during all these gyrations is just to fly wing on number three.

The flight is now in a right Echelon formation, and should the lead want number two back on his left wing, the sequence is reversed. In this instance, number two could technically move straight back prior to crossing over and not crowd the element, but it's safer for number three to move out a little and give number two a little room in which to maneuver. Since number two can't turn around to see when the element has moved out, it's helpful for number three to give a courtesy call of "Clear" when he thinks two has enough room to start back.

Turns in Fingertip

Now that we're squared away with flying formation straight and level, and changing sides, what do we do when the leader turns? The primary rule of all turns in two-ship or Fingertip formation is that all aircraft stay in the plane of the leader's wings. Illustrations of turns into and away from the element are shown below, as viewed from behind.

It can be seen from the diagram that during turns, each bird stays in the same position with respect to the leader as he does in level flight. All position references stay the same, and the only extra requirement is adding a little power and easing in just a hint of back pressure on turns away from you, or taking off a little power and dropping down a tad on turns into you. If the leader catches you by surprise with a turn into you, and you're a little late in reacting, it is usually helpful to add a little bottom rudder to facilitate your entry into the turn. This will swing your nose into the arc of the turn a little quicker, and keep you from closing on the lead. Anticipate the power and control pressures needed in turns, and don't let the angled horizon or ground references disorient you. The leader is your whole world, so just concentrate on doing whatever it takes to maintain a normal position in relation to him. Also keep in mind that throttle and control pressures added on the roll in must be taken *out* on the roll out, and vice versa.

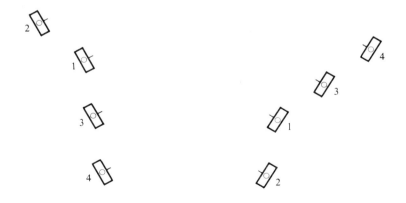

Turns in Fingertip formation

Echelon Formation

Echelon is a variety of close formation that everyone should be familiar with; though its applications are fairly limited, they are nonetheless important. And there are a few techniques concerning this formation that are a little different from those applicable to the other types.

The two main uses of Echelon are to move from close formation to trail formation by means of timed-interval peel-offs, and to bring a flight down the initial approach to a 360-degree overhead traffic pattern. The lead puts the flight into Echelon by having the number-two man, or the element, perform the crossover maneuver I just described.

Once the flight is in Echelon, normal formation position should be flown by all birds. However, numbers three and four can really make the flight look sharp by flying a position that lines up the canopies of all the aircraft. (Naturally, this assumes that number two is in the proper position with respect to lead.) Echelon is where number four really earns his coins, because any movement by the lead or

Lining up the canopies in Echelon formation as seen from the number-three position. (Photo by Frank J. O'Brien)

number two will be amplified quite a bit by the time it reaches his position. If you're number four, a good technique to use, along with lining up the canopies, is to fly an average position and try to ignore the bobbles of the plane you are flying wing on. Look through him and view the flight as a whole.

While the flight is in Echelon, all hand signals must be passed on to the guy flying your wing. If you're in right Echelon, this may require switching hands on the stick to make the signal visible to your wingman.

In Echelon, the leader has a little more to think about than he does in Fingertip. When the birds are returning to the field, he must plan ahead and echelon the flight to the opposite side of the intended pitchout for the traffic pattern. Thus, if he's going to use a 360-degree overhead pattern and the traffic is left-handed or counterclockwise, the flight must be in a right Echelon approaching the field. The crossover into Echelon should be started well before the turn onto initial, so that the maneuver can be completed and everybody settled down before the flight gets over the home drome, where everybody wants to look sharp.

Leaders should *never, never* turn into an Echelon except in an emergency, and then by banking as shallowly as possible. Turns away from the Echelon are made with all birds level, as depicted below.

In Echelon, trying to stay in the plane of the leader's wings, as in other formation turns, would impose a severe "crack the whip" action on number four, and he would be hard pressed to maintain a good position. Since the view from cockpit to cockpit is less than ideal during this type of turn, no hand signals should be given at this time.

1   2   3   4

A turn in Echelon

Trail Formation

In Trail, formation flying starts to be real fun. The main use of Trail formation is to give everyone some "hands-on" practice at staying behind another aircraft during maneuvering flight. It also helps everybody to sharpen his judgment on closing rates and the use of cutoff turns. A little practice Trail in the middle of a formation mission loosens everyone up, and provides an enjoyable diversion from regular formation flying.

Before trying Trail formation, the leader should insure that the flight is in the designated acrobatics or formation area, because a good in-trail workout will cover a lot of space—both horizontally and vertically. Furthermore, the flight should be in an area where other pilots expect the types of maneuvers it will be performing.

The entry into Trail is accomplished from Echelon formation. The leader gives the peel-off signal, and then holds up fingers to indicate the peel-off interval in seconds. This interval is normally three seconds between aircraft. The lead pauses long enough for the signal to be passed to the last man, and then peels off by executing a steep turn away from the flight into a moderate dive. The bank angle is held until a turn of 135 to 180 degrees is completed.

After the leader peels off, the rest of the flight continues in straight and level flight, while number two counts to himself, "A thousand and one—a thousand and two—a thousand and three," and then peels off to follow the lead. The proper cadence during this count is important to establish the correct spacing between birds—it should be neither hurried nor drawn out, and should be as close an approximation of three seconds as possible. The count for each bird starts as soon as the wing of the bird in front of it starts up into the peel-off. Each succeeding aircraft in the flight follows this procedure.

Once the leader is established on his new heading, he should set the power as briefed for Trail, and leave it there for the rest of this phase of the mission. He is then free to maneuver at will, utilizing turning dives and climbs, but making sure he avoids by a good margin the upper and lower airspeed limits of the most restricted bird in the flight. High-G turns should be avoided so that numbers three and four won't exceed their G limits trying to hang in there. The lead should not try any overhead maneuvers, such as loops or cloverleafs, unless everyone in the flight is very proficient in formation flying and has a bird cleared for these maneuvers.

Even though you are not really close to another aircraft and working to stay in an ideal position, trail formation demands just as much concentration as any other type—perhaps more. None of the usual positional references are available during Trail because of the distances involved; depth perception and the relative size of the bird in your windshield are the major clues to correct position.

As you finish your peel-off from the flight, roll to the same heading as the bird in front of you and get slightly below his flight path to avoid wake turbulence. Adjust the power to obtain the proper interval (500 to 700 feet) behind the aircraft ahead, and, if your position is good, follow through the maneuvers by maintaining the same bank angle as the bird you are following. This technique is called "matching the wings."

If you do get out of position, utilize the turns that the leader will be making in both the horizontal and the vertical to get back into place. To work the horizontal component of the leader's turns to your benefit, do *not* match wings with the bird in front of you. If you are behind, increase your bank angle to establish a cutoff angle that helps you close the gap. If you're too close to the guy in front of you, bank by a lesser amount in the turns to achieve some lateral separation, and then S back into the proper position. Don't swing too far out of line, because the leader may suddenly tighten his turn, leaving you out in left field.

Turns in the vertical, such as entries and exits from climbs and dives, can also be worked to your advantage—start your pull-up or pullout a little early, or increase your G loading. A good corrective action to use if your find yourself pretty far back is to maneuver constantly so that you're pulling lead on the aircraft in front of you. However, in a climb or dive, don't pull so much lead that you lose the guy ahead below your nose.

The other alternative to staying in position in Trail is the use of power. Learn to anticipate power changes in climbs and dives, because you will probably tend to fall behind at the start of a dive, and to overtake the bird in front of you during a climb entry. Be prepared to make the required power changes at these points; otherwise, you won't be able to maintain a proper position. During Trail, it's a good idea for all birds to keep an eye on the tach during these climbs and dives, and to adjust the power to avoid an overspeed.

Flying Trail is a very good test of whether you are skillful enough to maintain your position without power changes, by means of cutoffs and S'ing. Using these techniques is excellent practice for basic fighter maneuvers, during which no extra power will be available, and you will have to gain and maintain a position of advantage by maneuver alone.

The number-four position in trail formation has some advantages and disadvantages. Whereas the leader's maneuvers are amplified quite a bit by the time they get back to number four, he can see all the other aircraft in the flight and can plan his moves a little as the leader starts each maneuver. By viewing the whole picture, and reacting to the leader as well as to number three, a good number-four man can stay in Trail formation even if number three gets thrown out. If this does happen, number four should exercise extreme caution and try to keep an eye on both number three and the rest of the flight. If you're number four, don't try to close it up and fly in number three's old position, because he will most likely be trying to get back into the action and won't be expecting you to be in the way. Besides, if you get into his position, your attention will be fixed on the flight, and the potential for a midair will be high.

If *anyone* gets thrown out of the formation during the maneuvers, or loses sight of the aircraft in front of him, or is trying to hang in there but is hopelessly out of position, it's best for him to call the leader and 'fess up to his plight. When this happens, the leader should signal for a rejoin (the signal to be passed on back by succeeding aircraft), and try the Trail sequence again. If the one who is out of it doesn't have a visual on the flight, it may be necessary to rejoin over a prominent landmark. Make sure the culprit learns something from all this by making him buy the first round after debriefing.

If a pilot gets a little disoriented during the Trail phase and doesn't have a visual on the flight, the leader or anyone else who has an eyeball on the lost bird should give him clock-code directions to the flight—for example, "Number four, the flight is in your 2 o'clock high position."

After the Trail phase of a formation mission, or after any sequence of events that splits the flight up, a rejoin is necessary. The leader facilitates the rejoin by starting a turn in either direction and slowing down a trifle. He should be sure to let the other birds know what airspeed he'll be holding, in order to prevent overshoots.

If the flight is really strung out, it may be necessary to hold the turn for 360 degrees or more to get all the birds joined up. If a turn cannot be made for fuel or emergency reasons, the leader should establish a vector for home plate and keep the airspeed at a slow cruise to expedite the rejoin.

Unless briefed otherwise, all birds will join up in Fingertip, using the standard procedures described in the join-in procedure, and each bird will return to his original position in the flight. Birds arriving early, out of sequence—for example, number four before number three—will hold clear of the flight so the latecomer can move into his proper position. Each wingman should use dives and/or cutoffs to get back into formation as soon as possible. A quick rejoin is the mark of a professional. (Look at the Air Force Thunderbirds after the crossover following their bomb-burst maneuver—this is the worst possible situation, yet they are rejoined within a few minutes.)

After the join-up, the lead should ask for a fuel check from everyone so that he can be aware of any potential problems and plan accordingly.

Spread Formation

Once you've got the techniques of close formation down pat, the next area to work on is spread, also called route, formation. Spread is used on cross-country formation flights and while going to and from the working area if any distances are involved. It gives the flight more flexibility and allows for more complete surveillance of the area around the flight.

The leader signals for spread by fishtailing, or yawing, his aircraft back and forth for a few seconds. In spread, the wingmen will maintain their positions with respect to their reference points, but they will move farther out along their reference lines. The move from close to spread is not a sudden one, utilizing a lot of bank, but is a slow, easy, sliding movement along the reference lines until there are two to four ship widths between aircraft. The end result is an expanded Fingertip formation. The normal Fingertip is visualized using the hand with the fingers together—spread the fingers and you have spread formation.

In this configuration, the leader is still responsible for everything that concerns the flight, but each member should keep his eyes peeled for strangers, and call them to the leader's attention. The leader signals for a rejoin by rocking his wings; the birds join up by simply sliding back up the reference lines into close formation.

Confidence Maneuvers

As you can well imagine, after the novelty wears off, flying formation in a straight and level attitude all day can get a little boring. Take heart, all you tigers, for the powers that be have devised something called "confidence maneuvers" to keep things from getting too dull. These maneuvers are nothing more than a constant series of turning climbs and dives in both directions—the equivalent of a series of lazy eights. This constantly changing, three-dimensional exercise involves climbs, dives, turns *into and away from wingmen,* and continual power changes.

Confidence maneuvers should be tried in a flight of two at first, and then, as the experience level grows, in a flight of four.

As the skill of the flight builds up, the leader steepens the climbs and dives, and increases the bank angles in the turns. After a little practice, the flight should be able to follow the leader through a normal lazy eight, including the near-vertical bank at the top of the climbing portion of the maneuver.

Another thing the leader can do to build up the confidence of the flight is to try turns of about 45 degrees of bank while pulling two or three Gs. If any of the birds have retractable gear, another worthwhile maneuver to practice is cycling the gear in close formation. If you're flying lead, slow the formation down to a speed that would be held for a straight-in approach; then cycle the gear a few times. This will get everybody used to the different flight characteristics in the dirty configuration, and the problems of changing attitudes during cycling. It also allows the flight to practice holding their positions during gear cycling, and to learn what corrections they must anticipate. It's probably best to try this at high altitude a few times before doing it at an actual approach altitude near the ground.

A procedure that should be included in every formation mission is letting one of the wingmen lead the flight for a while. This is a valuable experience that gives everyone a chance to learn and to appreciate the problems of leading a flight, including getting hammered for not being smooth enough, or for always flying so that the wingmen are looking into the sun.

Letdown and Pattern Entry

The next phase of formation flying has to do with getting back down from the wild blue onto the deck. Before starting any descent, the flight lead should call for a descent check while the flight still has the opportunity to loosen up and do whatever is required—set up defrosters, carburetor heat, fuel tank selection, mixture, pitot heat—any necessary switch action.

Don't neglect the defrosters if you'll be letting down into an area where the ground temperature and humidity are high. You could get caught in a situation where the canopy fogs over, making it very tough to keep an eye on the bird you're flying wing on. A corollary of Murphy's Law says that this fogging over will probably occur when you're turning initial and want things to look the sharpest.

During the descent, the lead should switch the flight to tower frequency while they are still far enough out from the field to plan an approach to any runway, in case there's been a change in the wind. If you're the leader, the key here is to think ahead. Echelon the flight to the side opposite the traffic pattern while you're still on the 45-degree entry leg to initial. Thus, if the overhead traffic pattern will be to the left, the wingmen should be echeloned on the leader's right wing. Remember to allow sufficient time for the flight to cross over and settle down before the turn onto initial.

Before I go into the techniques of flying the traffic pattern, I should mention why a 360-degree overhead is used. There are no earthshaking reasons for this, but it keeps the flight together until you're over the runway, and almost guarantees a place to set down if an engine quits in the pattern. Probably the best reason is that no self-respecting fighter pilot would consider any other way of getting into a field during VFR conditions. When the weather is good, entries onto the downwind, long, dragged-in en route approaches, or straight-in descents to landing, are strictly for the multi-engine drivers.

If local procedures prohibit the use of an overhead pattern, the flight should be broken up somewhat when you are close to the entry leg for the downwind, so that each pilot will have time to set up his own pattern entry. If a 360-degree overhead is not normally used at your field, the leader should call the tower and request this type of pattern before the flight turns initial.

Entering the traffic pattern and landing is not all formation flying per se, but the basic formation techniques concerning timing and spacing will apply until you turn off the runway after landing. *This* is the time to look good—when you're over the field with your fellow pilots watching and critiquing. You better believe that anyone who is out of position will certainly hear all about it when he gets on the ground.

The Overhead Traffic Pattern

The initial leg of the overhead traffic pattern starts at pattern altitude about two to three miles from the end of the runway, on a line that is an extension of the runway centerline. As the flight progresses down the initial, the leader lines up with the center of the runway and gives the pitchout signal, followed by the signal for the interval—normally three to five seconds. If a crosswind is known to exist, the lead should adjust his initial approach to compensate for this, so as to arrive over the end of the runway on the centerline. For example, if the wind is from the left, the leader should line up with the left edge of the runway, or even more to the left if the wind is fairly strong. If the crosswind is really hairy, it's probably better to make individual approaches, because too many problems can develop in the pattern and on the landing rollout in this situation.

As the flight passes over the approach end of the runway, the leader rolls smartly into a steep turn in the direction of traffic, using 60 to 90 degrees of bank and pulling a few Gs, while the rest of the flight continues straight and level. This is known as the break. As soon as the leader starts his break, number two starts counting the interval seconds, just as described for the peel-off into Trail formation. At the proper count, he starts his own break, and subsequent flight members follow the same procedure.

By the time the leader completes 180 degrees of turn, he should be slowed down enough to lower the gear, if so equipped. If the break turn didn't slow the aircraft down to about the normal airspeed for downwind, the lead should make a power reduction at this time. When he is abeam of the end of the runway, the lead checks for a safe gear indication, and then starts the normal descending turn to base and final.

All the remaining members of the flight should adjust their rollout from the break onto downwind to place themselves directly behind the leader and at his altitude. If the lead deviates from the pattern altitude, everyone else should deviate, too—within reason, of course. Uniform spacing and altitude are a must if the traffic pattern is to look good from the ground, and good spacing is determined mainly by proper counting for the break interval. Something else that helps to keep the spacing good is having all members of the flight turn base leg at the same spot. Once this point is set, whether properly or improperly, it is pretty much a given for all succeeding birds, if they wish to avoid bunching up on final or on the runway.

Back to our fearless leader on final! Number one's final should line up with the center of the traffic-pattern side of the runway. That is, when landing from a left-handed traffic pattern, the leader should plan on using the left half of the runway. The rest of the flight take alternate sides in turn: number two, the right; number three, the left; and number four, the right. This procedure allows for safer passing in case of a brake failure or a hot landing.

Each bird stays on his side of the runway until the turnoff point to the taxiway is reached. If this turnoff is on number two's side of the runway, he should call the leader as soon as he has his aircraft under control, and let number one know that he is clear to turn off the active. This call should be short and simple—for example, "Number one, you're clear." Each succeeding member of the flight should do the same.

If you don't hear a call from the guy behind you, *don't* turn into his lane without making a visual check behind you. He may have had simultaneous brake and radio failure and be whistling down the runway right on your tail. If you do land hot and long, and it looks as if you'll have to pass the guy in front of you despite its being very bad form, you should be sure to call the affected airplane and let him know what's going on—for example, "Number two, I'll be passing on your left." Upon hearing this, the airplane being passed should ease over toward the edge of the runway as far as practical, to give the aircraft with problems as much room as possible. If the runway is slippery, or is of insufficient width to allow two birds on it comfortably side by side, all aircraft should take greater spacing on the break (at least five seconds), and land in the middle.

There are a few caveats to flying the overhead pattern that can really keep things looking sharp. The first is: don't bunch up in the pattern—it not only looks bad, it causes lots of problems on final approach and the landing roll because of prop wash and general safety considerations. If the guy in front of you takes the base leg too deep, about all you can do is follow suit. Don't try to correct things by turning early, because this will put you too close to him on final, and you may be forced to go around. This is the unpardonable sin of formation flying—everyone works hard and keeps it tucked in while approaching the field, and dresses up the pattern so it looks great, and then in front of God and the whole airfield, some clown blows flight integrity by having to go around because he tried to cut a corner. A stunt like that is usually worth a couple of rounds after the debriefing—courtesy of the offender.

The second caution is: don't drag out the pattern until it is so big that number four has to file a revised landing time with the tower. Although it doesn't look too shiny, a large pattern with a long, dragged-in final *is* preferable to bunching up and forcing a go-around—but only slightly so. Both are errors that can easily be corrected if the lead selects a sensible base leg, keeping everyone's capabilities in mind, and if each bird turns at the same spot.

Something to be on the lookout for, even in a well-spaced pattern, is prop wash. You will be landing closer behind another aircraft than you normally do; you should expect turbulence and be prepared for it on final. If you really hit a gasser of a bump, and it throws you far enough out that a good landing is doubtful, swallow your pride and initiate a go-around then and there, rather than trying to salvage a losing proposition.

Finally, no one in the flight should relax once the lead bird peels off in his break. A lazy pitchout, or break, on your part will louse up the pattern for everyone. Don't forget that your job isn't done until you're in the chocks.

Formation Approach

A formation approach is one of those things that you may never have to use in a real situation; however, it is also one of those things that, should an emergency arise, you won't have time to practice. You'll have to have it down cold the first time.

A formation approach is normally used for leading in a bird whose airspeed is out, or for bringing in someone who is lost or unfamiliar with the area. It is essentially a straight-in approach flown by two birds in close formation, utilizing VASI, GCA, ILS—or just eyeballing it. As the name tells us, it is a formation approach, not a formation landing; only the crippled bird or the lost guy will land on the first pass.

If the situation is one involving a lost or disoriented pilot, he usually can be cut loose after being led to a point where he has a visual on the field. On the other hand, an airspeed-out emergency requires more precision, and must be flown almost to the touchdown point. In this case, the afflicted bird gets on the leader's wing and lets him know what the problem is. Since it looks like it's going to be that kind of a day, the leader can expect that the emergency bird will have radio failure, and that hand signals are the name of the game. To signal a formation approach, use both hands to depict two birds going down final in close formation.

When he joins up, the pilot in the ailing bird should try to fly a comfortable, normal formation position. Let's say this guy is you. If you have your druthers, pick the side that you fly better, and where you are more relaxed. The leader must then determine your final approach speed by radio or through hand signals. If you have to use signals, the leader might move his hand back and forth at a downward angle, with the index finger extended, to get across the idea of a final approach and the pitot boom for airspeed. You answer by holding up a finger for every ten knots you want to hold on final. For airspeeds over 100 knots, hold up all ten fingers and then repeat the signal for the additional airspeed required. If the leader can't fly as slow as you want, he should use the minimum safe speed for his gross weight and, if radio is available, let you know what the speed on final will be. The approach will still go as described below.

You, as the driver of the afflicted craft, should set up the cockpit for landing before getting on the wing, unless you are still quite some distance from the field. As a minimum, everything should be done before you reach a point five to seven miles from the runway. If you have retractable gear, *don't* let the airspeed emergency make you forget to put the wheels down! This is especially important if the lead aircraft has fixed gear, because he won't think of yours as a part of the normal landing procedure. If you do have retractable gear, it's probably better to get it down and checked before settling down to close formation flying. But if you've got a long distance to go, wait until you're within ten miles of the field to put it down.

The leader should notify the tower of the emergency situation and tell the tower just what he intends to do. He should plan the approach so as to be lined up with the runway at pattern altitude at least three to five miles out. If both birds have retractable gear, the wheels go down on the leader's signal before starting the descent. The whole idea is to get both aircraft in the landing configuration and trimmed up for the approach before starting down final.

Back to you in your sick airplane. Just concentrate on holding a good wing position, and let the leader take care of lining things up and getting tower clearance. As the flight slows down to final approach airspeed, your controls will become less effective and less sensitive. You should expect to make larger stick and rudder movements to get the desired control response. (On a real bumpy day, or with a spastic leader, slow flying in formation can work a wingman to a frazzle in no time at all.)

Proceeding down the final approach, you will start to see trees, buildings, and other ground references rushing by. Since your gaze is focused intently on the lead aircraft, or should be, and you are not used to flying formation so close to the ground, these visuals picked up peripherally will seem to be magnified. This may give you the impression that you are descending too fast. The closer you get to the ground, the more pronounced this becomes, especially if there are trees on either side of the approach to the runway. Although this phenomenon is disconcerting, trust that the leader is doing his job properly and hang in there. Without airspeed, you definitely don't want to fall off the wing before you get to the runway.

When the flight is about half a mile from the end of the runway, the lead aircraft should ease over a little to line up with the edge of the runway that is on the opposite side from the wingman. In other words, if the emergency aircraft is flying on the left wing, the lead should line up with the right edge of the runway. This move will put the wingman close to the centerline of the runway, and will make his transition off the wing to landing his bird a lot easier.

Assuming that the flight is flying at the wingman's desired approach speed at the time of this lateral move, the leader should also adjust his rate of descent so that he is aiming for a touchdown point at least 1,000 feet down the runway. Naturally, the lead can't do this if there is insufficient runway length remaining to allow a safe, controlled rollout. But this precaution can really pay off when the flight is close to the runway threshold and the wingman gets antsy and drops off the wing a tad early. If this happens, it's a good idea to have some concrete under him, in case in his anxiety he stalls the bird and hits short.

Lead's change in rate of descent is better accomplished by a power change than by a change of pitch attitude. Making a power change should keep the wingman from overcorrecting and starting to bobble up and down trying to maintain position. The correct technique for this adjustment is to fly your airspeed and keep it constant. Then, by adding just a hair of power, you will move the touchdown point farther down the runway; conversely, squeezing off just a little throttle will move it closer to the threshold.

During this type of approach, a wingman will probably swear by all that is holy that the leader is flying the approach too slow and he's going to fall out of the sky at any moment. If radios are working, a considerate leader will call out the airspeed he's holding once or twice on final to reassure the wingman that he's as safe as in God's pocket. This airspeed call should be mandatory at the drop-off point, to give the wingman one last reference as he wrestles his bird to the ground.

As you might guess, this drop-off point is the most critical point in the entire approach. The leader should bring the emergency aircraft down to about ten feet above the runway, and then wave good-bye—literally and figuratively. The wave is the signal that the wingman should now take over and complete his own landing, while the leader executes a go-around and reenters traffic. Since any approach from this point on is done entirely with visual references, all the wingman has to do is ease her down and plunk it onto the runway.

If the runway you're going to use is relatively short, still plan on aiming for a touchdown point about 1,000 feet down from the approach end. The consequences of dropping off the wing early and touching down in the unprepared overrun are far more serious than running off the far end of the runway, because at the far end you'll be going at a much slower speed, and will have more control over direction. If the surface beyond the runway is really rough, and would tear up your bird, you can always ground loop it just before you run out of concrete. Another last-ditch solution would be to really stand on the binders, and possibly luck out with only a couple of blown tires. The only problem with this last course of action is that with blown tires you lose nearly all your directional control.

Formation Problems

As you will discover on your first mission, the sun is probably the biggest problem you'll have. All wingmen know deep in their hearts that flight leaders stay awake nights thinking up ways to put their wingmen directly downsun from the lead aircraft. About the only way you can deal with the sun is try to live with it; it is unavoidable, and, in most cases, the situation is only temporary. Always wear aviator-type sunglasses while flying formation, and if you wear a helmet with a sun visor, that's even better. If the sun becomes a problem when you're in show formation near the home drome, about the only advice I can give is, "Squint!" However, don't let the sun cause an accident—if it's too much, move out a little until the flight turns. When you're flying practice formation, a technique that may give some respite, especially if the sun is low in the sky, is to move your bird up or down a little so as to get in the lead's shadow. But this maneuver might be a little tricky if you have other guys flying your wing.

Keep your hand on the throttle at all times, unless you're making a switch action elsewhere in the cockpit. You've got to be prepared for anything, and except for long, straight, cross-country legs, all formation flying is typified by small, but constant, throttle movements.

A mike button on the throttle or stick grip is almost a necessity in formation, because holding good position is so demanding that you really can't take your hand off the go handle in order to grab a mike for each radio call.

Know the location of all equipment and switches by feel, and which way the switches should be moved to get the desired action. If you have any doubts about selecting the proper switch, move out, make the switch action, and move back in. Do this only as a last-ditch measure, because there may be times when you won't have the option. If switches are grouped together, identify the critical ones by using tape to give them odd shapes, lengths, or bumps so you can pick them out by feel alone. (It's also good practice to try this switch-picking exercise with gloves on.)

A final problem in formation flying is one where the ability to fly a good close position really pays dividends, and that is weather formation. Let's say your instrument flying techniques are a little rusty, and you find yourself trapped on top of an overcast. It's a lot safer to penetrate an overcast on the wing of someone who is instrument qualified than to try to fake it by yourself—especially if your bird is not really equipped for muckering around in the klag. If you get caught in this situation, make sure that all your heating/anti-icing equipment is turned on before you get on somebody's wing and enter the clouds. Watch the leader closely for hand signals, especially in the clouds. As you approach the cloud deck, move into a tight, close formation position, just a little aft of what would be show formation position.

For those whose instrument experience is limited, absolute calmness and attention to the job at hand is required, despite the urgency of the situation. Try to ignore the clouds rushing past between you and the leader; expect turbulence, periods of reduced visibility due to precipitation, and dark areas in the clouds. Just concentrate on holding a good position until you break out underneath. And *don't* relax and drop off the wing as soon as you think you're through the cloud deck, because there still might be another layer below you, and you don't want to get caught out of position.

Once in the weather, a leader should make a concerted effort to be ultra-smooth on the controls, and use easy rates of roll into and out of any turns. If the wingman falls off the wing in the weather, he should immediately notify the leader of his predicament, and the leader, in turn, should start trying to get assistance from any ground agency available to help sort things out. While he is letting the leader know about his problem, the wingman should at once slow down a little and start a turn of at least 15 degrees away from the lead aircraft. The idea behind these actions is to create some separation between the two birds.

Above all, *don't* try to rejoin the leader by pressing on and hoping you'll catch a glimpse of him. In all likelihood, the only glimpse you'll get of him will be just before the collision.

If the flight was in a turn away from the wingman when he falls off, the leader continues the turn, and the wingman rolls to a wings-level attitude in order to create separation. If the turn was into the wingman, his only recourse is to slow down and try to maintain the turn for a moment or two so that some separation is established. Falling off the wing in the weather is a pretty hairy situation, and all actions are, to a large extent, predicated on the wingman's instrument proficiency. There are no pat answers; each situation must be judged on its own merits, and reacted to accordingly.

There are times when the leader can help out in these predicaments, especially during turns into the wingman. As soon as he learns that the wingman has dropped off, he should ease off some of his bank and increase his airspeed by about ten knots—again to help create separation. In a wings-level situation, this airspeed increase may be the only course of action available to the lead to open up the distance between the two birds.

If there are occasional breaks in the overcast through which the ground can be seen, and a high enough ceiling exists underneath, an alternative to weather formation can be used to get the flight down safely. Holes in an overcast are usually too small to allow a flight of four to go through in Fingertip—at least not without some pretty wild maneuvering, and excessive bank and dive angles. The answer here is to put the flight into a close Trail formation, with about three ship lengths between birds. This gives everyone a lot more maneuvering potential and permits the flight to slip beneath the overcast while maintaining VFR conditions.

A very good example of what can happen when wingmen try to do nonessential tasks occurred one Saturday morning during a mass flyby of 16 F-86Ds. The Dog, as this version of the Sabre was known, was one of the first fighters to have a full flying tail—it did not use elevators per se, but had a horizontal stabilizer that was made in one piece, so the entire unit pivoted to produce the desired elevator action. As you might guess, this feature, plus the hydraulically operated control system, made the 86D very, very sensitive in pitch control. Formation flying in the Dog definitely took some getting used to.

The 16 ships were arranged in Diamond formation, with a flight of four in close Fingertip at each point of the diamond. The entire gaggle was on a long, straight-in approach, to fly down the center of the runway, and was in a gentle descent, aiming to hit pattern altitude about five miles from the field.

I was flying number-two position in Blue Flight, and we were on the lead flight's left side—that is, on the left point of the diamond. Remembering the exhortations of our flight leads during the briefing—that we definitely wanted this flyby to look good because our sister squadron would be watching—everyone was tucked in real tight, and things were shaping up pretty well as we approached the field. About a half mile out we received final tower clearance for the flyby, and, as a matter of course, the tower gave the latest altimeter setting.

Because we were in show formation, I was a little farther forward than usual and concentrating on my flight leader's wing and cockpit, and suddenly, out of the corner of my eye, I caught a glimpse of movement on my leader's bird in the area of the speed brakes, which were located on the aft third of the fuselage. I couldn't believe that he was extending his speed brakes right over the reviewing stand, and especially with no call, but that's exactly what was happening. I immediately threw my brakes out and yanked the power to idle in an attempt to stay with the lead, as did the other two wingmen in our flight.

Needless to say, we were too late, and Blue lead dropped back behind the rest of us as if he had an anchor out. While the three of us were bouncing all over the sky in vain attempts to get back on the lead's wing, he suddenly realized what had happened, closed his speed brakes, and firewalled the throttle. By the time the three of us had slowed down enough to get back on the lead's wing, his engine had accelerated to full power, and he went past us as if he'd been shot out of a gun.

Again we tried to get back on his wing by jamming the throttles full forward, but again it was too late, because the electronic fuel control on the F-86D only allowed the engine to accelerate at a given rate, which was too slow to solve our problem. All of this happened just about over the field, and the wild gyrations of Blue Flight also disrupted the flight below and behind us; they scrambled all over the place trying to avoid a midair with the apparent madmen in Blue Flight.

You could almost hear the peals of derisive laughter from the pilots in our sister squadron as they watched this bedlam unfold over the field. A lot of humble pie was eaten that day.

Naturally, our squadron commander was livid at the debriefing, particularly after he heard the reason for the incident. It seems that when Blue lead heard the new altimeter setting given with the final clearance from the tower, he reached up to set his altimeter instead of tending to the business of flying formation. As he brought his hand back down to the throttle, the cuff of his glove caught on the speed brake switch, which was mounted on the top of the throttle, and that was all she wrote. The only one who needed the altimeter setting was the squadron commander who was leading the flyby, and Blue lead, who was technically a wingman, simply forgot that his only job that morning was to fly good formation on Red Flight. If such an incident had occurred in the weather, the consequences could have been far more disastrous than laughable.

The folly of bunching up in the pattern was dramatically brought home to me at the conclusion of a massed flyby for some visiting firemen in 1965. The flyby itself had gone well, and the squadron had now broken up into individual flights of four, which were entering initial for an overhead pattern at about two-minute intervals. Naturally, with the dignitaries still on the field, we wanted the pattern and landing to look as sharp as the flyby.

I was flying an F-106 in the number-three slot, and by the time our group was in position to pitch out, the pattern had been considerably enlarged by the preceding flights. Rolling out on downwind, I could see that the base leg was much too far from the field, and that if we extended it any more it would look more like a pattern for bombers than for fighters. The bird in front of me turned on the deep base leg, but I felt that if I shaved my turn just a little, we could start tightening up the pattern to the point where it would look more respectable.

When I rolled out on final I was too close to number two, but felt that I could slow down a little more to establish the desired separation. However, number two was flying his approach at the absolute minimum speed for our gross weight, and even though I was as slow as I dared to be, I was still much too close for the proper spacing at touchdown. The correct procedure at that point would have been to initiate a go-around, but the old Chinese proverb kept running through my mind: "Fighter pilot never go around—lose face if go around—bust tail first, but never go around."

In low-speed conditions the delta-winged F-106 doesn't stall like aircraft with conventional wings, but instead develops a high sink rate. In my attempts to slow the bird down I had gotten into a moderate sink rate, which brought me closer to the jet wash and exhaust plume from number two, who was at a slightly lower altitude. At about 1,000 feet from the runway threshold, and about 50 feet in the air, I hit the turbulence, and immediately my 28,000-pound bird flipped over into a 135-degree bank as if it was a feather. Finding myself nearly inverted in a nose-down attitude and only 50 feet in the air, all I could think was, "My God, I'm going to hit on my side."

I guess the only thing that saved my bacon was the marvelous low-speed control response of the 106. I lit the afterburner and applied full right aileron and rudder. The bird responded like a champ and rolled smoothly to the upright position. I suspect that quite a bit of the infield was dusted off on my go-around, until the airspeed built up enough that I could start a climb. Probably the only good thing that came out of the incident—aside from my indelible resolve not to bunch up in the pattern again—was the exciting footage it provided for the squadron photographer, who was filming the whole show from the side of the runway.

CHAPTER 10
TACTICAL FORMATION

While close formation is a great way to get a lot of airplanes from A to B, it is definitely not the arrangement to be in if you're out looking for a hassle. Under these conditions, tactical formation is a must for either flights of two or flights of four. The basic purpose of tactical is to enable the flight to be deployed as a flexible, maneuverable, offensive unit. The freedom of maneuver afforded by tactical allows the flight to engage an opponent as a coordinated, integral unit. This type of formation also enhances the defensive posture of the flight by increasing mutual coverage, thereby decreasing vulnerability to being bounced. If a bounce should occur, the increased maneuvering potential of tactical allows the flight as a whole to counter effectively, or for the element under attack to break while the other lends support.

Fingertip Tactical

There are two basic types of tactical formation that have proved effective over the years. Both have their good and bad points. The first of these is Fingertip, in which the arrangement of the aircraft is the same as for close formation—the only difference is the greater distance between birds. In tactical, the distance between the two aircraft in an element is determined by the turning radius of the aircraft concerned. A compromise figure that can be used for most of today's birds is about 200 feet. The distance between the element lead and the flight lead should be twice that much. As in close formation, all aircraft should stack down slightly from the lead. About the only positional reference available during tactical is the 30- to 45-degree reference line, extended to the new distances.

The normal fine points of reference for maintaining position in close formation—aircraft structures or markings—will not be available in tactical because of

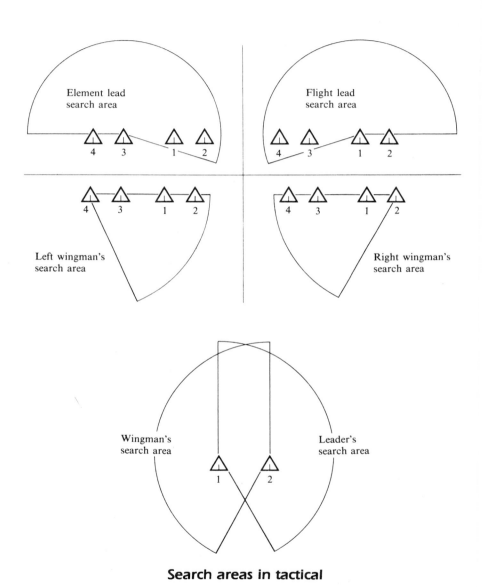

Search areas in tactical

A restored P-40N in the desert pink camouflage used by the Ninth Air Force in Africa. Although it rarely outperformed the opposition, this sturdy fighter was the first to be mass-produced, and was available when it was most sorely needed. (Photo by Keith Caulton)

F8F Bearcat restoration. Designed to replace the
Hellcat, the F8F was lighter and faster, had a better
rate of climb, and was more maneuverable. However,
the war ended before any Bearcats could be put into
service. (Photo by Joe Naphas)

A restored P-47D—as of 1943, the largest and heaviest
single-engine fighter ever built. The "Jug" was an
extremely rugged plane that could absorb a terrific
amount of punishment. It was armed with eight .50-
caliber machine guns and had a top speed of 429 mph.
(Photo by Keith Caulton)

A restored 1909 Blériot at Old Rhinebeck Aerodrome in New York. The large elevators and broad warping surface of the wing make this aircraft extremely touchy on the controls.
(Photo by Frank J. O'Brien)

The guy wires and wing warping controls of the 1909 Blériot. The cylindrical copper object between the gear is the fuel tank. (Photo by Frank J. O'Brien)

A restored F4U Corsair. Despite the Zero's vaunted maneuverability, the Corsair was the better aircraft in a turning fight above 200 knots. At 175 knots, it could stay with a Zero for about 180 degrees of turn by using full flaps. (Photo by Joe Naphas)

A restored F4U Corsair. In comparison tests against a captured Zero, the Corsair was faster at all altitudes up to 30,000 feet by an average of 64 mph. The rate of climb of the F4U and the Zero were equal up to 10,000 feet, above which the Corsair was definitely superior. (Photo by Keith Coulton)

A seven-tenths scale Stuka built by Louis Langhurst of
Carriere, Mississippi. The project required 8,000 hours
over a nine-year period. This bird cruises at 120 mph
with a 220-hp Lycoming. (Photo by Louis Langhurst)

A restored P-51D painted with D-Day invasion stripes for easy recognition. World War II pilots flying this model were among the first to utilize G suits in a dogfight. (Photo by Keith Caulton)

A Fokker DR-1 replica built by Cole Palen from factory plans and drawings. The project required about 2,000 hours of work. Palen utilized the same construction methods and techniques as the builders of the original. (Photo by Frank J. O'Brien)

A close-up of the rotary engine and fragile structure of a Royal Aircraft Factory FE-8 at Old Rhinebeck Aerodrome, New York. (Photo by Frank J. O'Brien)

FM-2 restoration. The Wildcat was the mainstay of the fleet air arm during the first half of the war in the Pacific, and is mainly remembered for its part in the defense of Wake and Midway islands.
(Photo by Joe Naphas)

F6F restoration. The Hellcat turned the tide of battle in
the Pacific, and was credited with 4,947 of the 6,477
enemy aircraft Navy pilots claimed they had shot down.
(Photo by Joe Naphas)

Spitfire restoration. Two major factors in the Spitfire's
superb maneuverability were a roll rate of 140 degrees
per second, and about 34 percent less wing loading
than that of the BF-109.
(Photo by Tim Foster)

the distances involved. However, these are pretty much superfluous, because in tactical wingmen fly in an area rather than an exact position. The reason for this is that they must be free to maneuver their aircraft in small S turns, or to drop a wing now and then, in order to fulfill their surveillance duties.

Scanning the airspace surrounding the flight for any and all targets is known as the lookout doctrine. If a flight is to operate effectively and not be surprised by an opponent, the lookout doctrine should be adhered to *like* a doctrine by each member of the flight. Here the rallying call for the Three Musketeers applies—"All for one, and one for all"—for a lapse in visual coverage by any one member of the flight could put the whole group in jeopardy. The lookout doctrine does not apply only to situations in which you are expecting a hassle; it applies any time the flight is spread out and other traffic may present a maneuvering problem. "Keep your head on a swivel" is an old adage that really applies when you're flying tactical formation. There are, however, specific areas of primary visual responsibility assigned to each member of the flight, and these are depicted below.

It should be noted that although each flight member is assigned a specific surveillance area that he should keep an eyeball on, all traffic should be called to the leader by the first guy who spots it, regardless of the area. Four aircraft in tactical formation take up a good bit of airspace, and a stranger passing through the area might pick up one or two of the flight and never see the rest. Everyone should keep the eyeballs peeled for transients and call them to the attention of the leader. When making this call, identify the stranger's position by clock code from the *lead* aircraft—that is, as the leader would see it from his position. This is particularly important if the stranger is picked up by a wingman maneuvering during a turn. The leader must know exactly where to look so that he can quickly decide whether he must maneuver the flight to avoid the stranger.

Once an engagement is started, all tactical formations normally break into two elements of two aircraft each—the idea is that the elements will provide support for each other. In the wild melee of a dogfight, this mutual support may be more theoretical than actual, unless everything works out just the way it does in the classic textbook example, and there's about a one-in-a-million chance that it will. Each element should plan and work toward this ideal, but don't purposely get into a situation where you need the other element to bail you out. They may be busy saving their own bacon just when you need them most.

Within the element, it is the leader who does all the fighting. The wingman's job is to keep an eye peeled to the rear of the element, and to let the leader know if anyone is trying to sneak up on him from behind. Once the "Tally Ho!" is called and the element lead starts maneuvering, the wingman moves into a position known as "fighting wing." This "position" is really the area inside a 60-degree cone extending out about 200 feet from the element lead's tail. The wingman is free to maneuver anywhere within this cone in order to stay in the optimum position. Normally he will need all this space and more to stay behind the leader once he gets into the hard-maneuvering phase of an engagement. The name of the game in fighting wing is to stay *away* from the dead-astern position on the leader. Although it is easier to maneuver with him when you are in this position, you can give the element no coverage in the rear hemisphere if you stay in the lead's six.

Flying the fighting wing position is admittedly great practice, and the ability to hang in there during a hard-turning engagement really separates the men from the boys. However, hanging in there demands so much of the wingman's attention that he may not have any time or opportunity to look over his shoulder to spot bogies attacking from *his* rear. The unpredictability of the leader's moves as he reacts to the target's maneuvers demand the undivided attention of the wingman if he is to avoid falling off the wing and becoming easy pickings for an alert adversary.

Fingertip tactical, or the Fluid Four as it is sometimes called, does have the advantages of good maneuverability and good visual coverage of all flight positions; however, the basic arrangement of the aircraft, and the drawbacks of the fighting wing concept, do set up less than optimum conditions in a lot of cases. The first problem crops up when some, or all, of the birds have poor rearward visibility due to aircraft structure or small windows. Inability to get an eyeball in the flight's deep 6 o'clock position allows the bad guys to get too close in before they are detected, and thus limits the countermoves the leader can make. If number four falls a little behind under these conditions, as he is likely to do, he can be picked off before anyone even knows the flight's been bounced. Another problem with Fingertip tactical is that all the birds are in more or less the same horizontal plane. This makes it easy for the opposition to keep the entire flight in view as they maneuver for the attack, and even if the bad guys are spotted, they can see any defensive maneuvers developing and counter them effectively.

The Six Pac

The problems associated with Fingertip tactical are solved by a rearrangement of the aircraft into what is known as the Six Pac. The modern version of this tactical formation came into being in 1968 during a training exercise involving the F-106 Delta Dart. These aircraft were flying simulated air-to-air combat missions against F-104 Starfighters, and as long as the "Sixes" stayed in Fingertip tactical, the "High Fasties" ate them alive. Even the best talkers among the Six drivers had to eat humble pie when confronted by the Starfighters' gun-camera film showing with what embarrassing ease the Sixes had been picked off. In order to save face, and to keep from going broke from always buying the beer, the Six pilots had to come up with a definite change of tactics. Thus was born the Six Pac, named after the birds who brought it back into vogue—for, in reality, this formation was not strictly a new invention.

The same general arrangement was first developed by Oswald Boelcke, the great German tactician of World War I. The basic line-abreast concept of Boelcke's *Schwarm* is retained in the modern Six Pack; however, the two elements are separated vertically by about 3,000 to 4,000 feet. A horizontal and vertical depiction of the Six Pac is shown below.

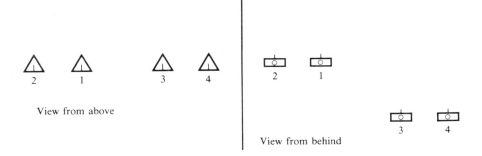

View from above

View from behind

Six Pac formation

Positioning the element below the lead as shown in the drawing is not a hard-and-fast rule. Since the most important feature of the formation is maintaining the altitude differential between the elements, numbers three and four also can be placed at a higher altitude than the lead. The sun is the determining factor in the placement of the element, and the rule is: the upsun birds stay low. In the drawing above, the sun would be on the right side of the flight; here, the element can fly its position without losing the lead in the sun. If the flight turns so that the sun becomes a factor, and the element decides to move to the high position, it should do so only after advising the leader of its intentions, because if the flight should be bounced, the element's position will affect the leader's choice of tactics.

The areas of primary visual coverage used when flying the Six Pac are the same as for Fingertip, but now numbers two and four can give a little more warning of an attack from the rear.

When the bogies are spotted and the flight must split into elements, things pretty much revert to the procedures used in Fingertip. The element lead does the fighting, and the wingman tries to cover the lead's tail. If the wingmen are fairly experienced at flying the fighting wing position, they can swing a little wider on the lead than the 60-degree cone described above. This looser position will give a wingman the opportunity to look around while keeping him close enough to the leader to give support should the need arise. However, flying this wider position is a lot harder than flying normal fighting wing, because the wingman must travel such great distances to maintain a position where he can keep an eye to the rear, and be able to lend a hand when the leader calls for it.

The worst thing that can happen to a wingman flying the Six Pac is to have the element lead start a hard turn into him, with little or no warning. About all a wingman can do here is dump his nose and use a lot of bottom rudder to keep the leader in sight while jockeying for a chance to swing back out where he belongs. A hard-turning engagement will really test the mettle of the wingman, but if he can manage to stay in a good position, he will make the leader's job a lot easier, because his presence out to one side or the other will limit the defensive options of the aircraft the element is chasing.

The greatest problem in any engagement is initially locating your opponent, and keeping an eyeball on him while you maneuver for the attack. With this in mind, let's assume that number four is the first to spot the bogey, and calls him out via the clock code to the leader. If the lead doesn't pick him up immediately, he should tell number four, "You've got the bounce." Four then turns to initiate the attack and number three automatically becomes his wingman. The lead element will maneuver with three and four until number one gets a visual on the target, and then will take whatever action is necessary to support the element making the attack. If the latter has things pretty well in hand, one and two can watch from the high ground to insure that no other bogies surprise the element at work below.

While this situation demonstrates the high degree of flexibility that the Six Pac offers, a man other than the lead should initiate the bounce only when each jock in the flight is experienced enough to assume the lead, and to think for a flight of four, tactics-wise. If this high experience level is not present throughout the flight, number four in our example should tell the leader where to turn to set up the attack, and keep calling the bogey's position until the leader has a visual and can take over the maneuvering.

Flying tactical formation is a lot tougher in actuality than it appears to be from the diagrams and discussion presented here. The primary reason for this is that positions are maintained almost strictly by maneuver, rather than by use of power. Not too much throttle will be available to the wingmen, because tactical formation is normally flown in an area where you are expecting an engagement, and all birds should be flying at max cruise so as to have some maneuvering potential available when the bad guys are sighted. Also, judgment becomes a key factor in maneuvering to keep a good position. Knowing just how much cutoff angle to take, or how steep a dive or a climb should be, can mean the difference between staying in position and being hopelessly behind during every turn. Although the positions in tactical formation are very flexible, they should be flown with only limited variance from the ideal. The allowable area can probably best be visualized as a football-shaped piece of airspace around the ideal spot.

Since a wingman must be prepared for sudden hard maneuvering by the leader, he should not roam much above a position level with the lead. If the lead started a quick high-G turn in the wingman's direction, he would be hard pressed to get out of his way, much less maintain good position.

Turns

The most difficult part of flying tactical formation occurs during turns. For every 90 degrees of turn the flight makes, everyone but the leader makes one crossover behind the bird he is flying wing on. The flight paths that each aircraft should describe are shown in the following diagrams for a 90-degree and a 180-degree turn, and are the same for Fingertip and the Six Pac. An important thing to remember during turns is that flight integrity *must be maintained* in order to preserve the formation's advantage of mutual coverage and support. Laggards who are constantly behind can't be covered by the rest of the flight and are easily picked off, which in turn makes the others more vulnerable.

The techniques for turns will be described for the number-two position and will be fairly generalized, because once the turn starts, the where and the when of each control action depends on the individual situation. In time, and after a little practice, these judgment factors will become instinctive, and that's when flying tactical becomes a lot of fun.

During the initial practice sessions for tactical formation, leaders will usually make all turns from cardinal headings, because it's easier for them. While you're in this learning phase, it may be helpful to glance at your directional gyro, if you have one, a couple of times during the turn. By doing so, you can correlate your position with the amount of turn that has been accomplished, and the amount left to go, and play things accordingly.

Let's first consider a 90-degree turn into the wingman. Although your first impulse will be to ease off a little throttle to stay roughly in position, *don't* reduce power. You'll need all the airspeed you can muster after the crossover, and if any excess speed should develop, it can always be killed off with a slight climb once the turn is completed and you're in position.

Establish a bank angle somewhat less than the leader's, and play your position and turn rate so as to cross behind and below the leader about halfway through the turn. In other words, you should be passing behind the leader about the time he has completed 45 degrees of his turn. Don't pause in this position behind the leader, because this is the point at which you are most vulnerable to attack due to the lack of rearward visual coverage. After crossing the lead's flight path, increase your bank angle slightly so as to stay with the lead and not end up too far out on the other side. If it looks as if you'll be behind after the crossover, it may be necessary to dive slightly at this time to pick up the airpseed you'll need to regain the proper position.

Don't depend on power to salvage a misjudged position after a turn, because there probably won't be enough throttle left to make much of a difference. Learn to utilize a slight dive as a matter of course on all turns to generate the airspeed necessary to get back into position. If you happen to pick up too much speed in your dive and it becomes apparent that you will complete the turn ahead of the leader, *don't* kill it off by a large power reduction to stay in position. Remember:

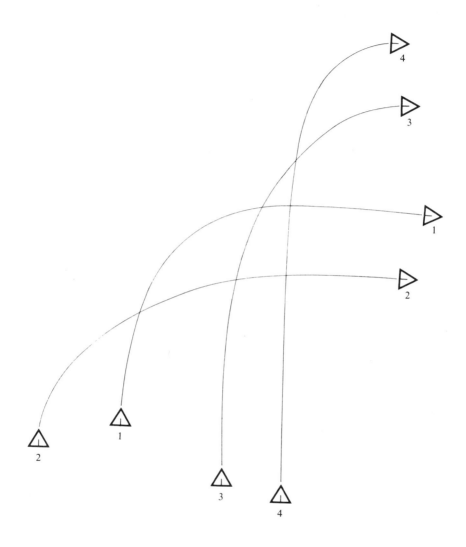

Typical 90-degree turn in tactical formation

tactical position is not a fixed point, so just climb a little, or S-turn until you're back where you should be.

A note of caution on climbing too high in this situation: don't let yourself get too far above the lead, because flight leaders are a perverse lot and often cannot resist the temptation to teach you a lesson for misjudging your turn. The leader will do this by waiting until you are quite a way above him, and then starting a quick turn into you. If this is done properly, the lead can be almost under number two before he realizes what is happening and figures out what he can do about it. About this time he loses sight of the lead beneath him, and then it's anybody's guess as to what number one's intentions are. An added twist the leader can use here to really drive home his point is to stop his turn below and behind the wingman. Old number two's original can of worms just overflowed—he's working like mad to correct for the surprise turn without losing too much face, but he has to wait for the lead to reappear on his other side so he can figure out what he needs to do. When the lead doesn't show up, you can almost see the light bulb go on in the wingman's cockpit as he realizes he's been had. (This ploy works even better when you're practicing 180-degree turns, and things are normally a little more confused.)

Ninety-degree turns away from the wingman are the more difficult of the two, because the wingman is a little behind right from the start of the turn. In this situation, he more or less has to play catch-up throughout the entire turn. Therefore, when you detect that the lead is starting a turn away from you, immediately establish a bank angle a little greater than his; it would also be helpful to add a little rudder into the turn, because this will start the nose around right away. Let the nose drop a little and start a slight dive to pick up the airspeed that will help you regain your position on the other side; however, don't go so deep that you destroy flight integrity. As before, plan to cross behind the lead at the 45-degree point, but in this case, it doesn't hurt to be just a little bit early. Don't take this too literally, because crossing *too* much before the 45-degree point forces you into flying a loose wing position on the lead as he continues his turn. On the other hand, getting caught in too close may force you to increase your bank to the point where your wing is blanking out the lead, and you won't be able to accurately judge the remainder of your turn. This higher bank angle will also cost you in the airspeed department; you'll have to add more back stick to stay in relatively good position.

After you cross, keep your bank angle a little greater than the lead's, so you sort of slide out to your new position without losing too much airspeed. As before, if you have a little excess airspeed as you approach the proper position, kill it off with a slight climb or an S turn. A corollary of Murphy's Law states that if you overshoot your position in a turn, it is guaranteed that the leader will immediately turn in your direction, just to see if you can hack it.

If a flight of four is involved in a tactical turn, the problem is compounded for numbers three and four because of the greater lateral distances they must travel. Number three's actions during the turn with respect to the lead are the same as number two's—that is, one crossover per 90 degrees of turn—but his timing and judgment must be a little more precise. He must react immediately when the leader starts his turn, and he has to play his bank angle and dive to the utmost to avoid falling behind the flight. In all probability, his dive to pick up airspeed will have to be a little more prolonged than number two's because of the distance he has to go.

Things can really get fouled up when the leader executes two 90-degree turns away from the element in succession, without much of a pause between them. In this case, a slow reaction and/or improper judgment during the turn will really put the element out in left field.

There are a couple of things to be cautious of during a four-ship tactical turn. The first of these is the relative crossing levels of the three birds maneuvering behind the lead, and the obvious possibilities for a midair. In order to keep from stretching the flight out too much in the vertical, number two should pass behind the lead just low enough to avoid his prop wash. This allows him to keep a visual on the lead, and he doesn't force number three down too far. Three and four should cross just below the flight paths of two and three, respectively, thus allowing each pilot to keep an eye on all the birds in front of him. Before starting any dives to pick up airspeed, each jock should insure that the area below him is clear, and that he won't be forcing those behind him too far out of the picture.

The other thing to avoid during a tactical turn is having all three aircraft crossing behind the leader at the same time. Obviously, the entire flight would be momentarily lined up in Trail at the 45-degree point. Under these circumstances, a pair of enemy birds could wax a whole flight in short order—maybe they were even just waiting for the lapse in visual coverage that usually occurs at this point in a turn. Don't be so intent on the mechanics of the turn that you forget to keep your head on a swivel, because, to be effective, a flight must be able to spot a threat in *any* position, and stay loose enough to counter it properly by maneuvering as a unit.

When you're practicing turns as a flight of four, remember that the rule about whether the element stacks high or low on the leader still applies. If you're upsun from the lead element at the completion of the turn, stack down so that those responsible for covering the area behind you won't be looking directly into the sun.

Now that we've got the 90-degree turn down pat, let's try 180 degrees. Looking at the 180-degree turn abstractly, all the procedures and techniques are exactly the same as for 90-degree turns, but they are performed twice. In practice, however, things can get pretty well hammered up during a 180-degree turn. Except during the initial phase of tactical practice, a leader will not announce that he is going to make a 90-degree or a 180-degree turn. Therefore, if you're approaching your new position after the first 90 degrees of turn and the leader isn't rolling out, immediately start working toward the second crossover. Even if you know it's going to be a 180-degree turn, shoot for the proper position after the first crossover, and don't let the whole thing degenerate into flying loose trail on the lead until the last 45 degrees of turn and dashing into position at the last minute. In a situation such

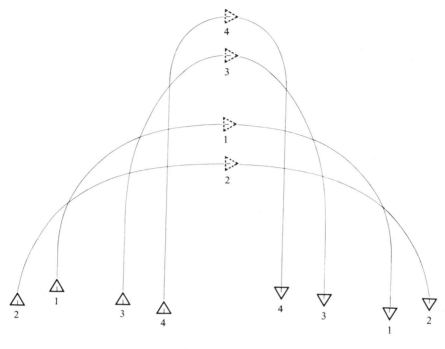

Typical 180-degree turn in
tactical formation

Typical 180-degree turn in tactical formation

as this, nobody is covering anybody, and the entire flight is a bunch of sitting ducks.

The rules for crossing levels still apply during 180-degree turns. However, since the possibility for getting faked out of position is a little greater in 180-degree turns, it's a good idea to keep an eye on the other birds in the flight as you approach the crossover point. Everybody might be a little off altitude because of diving to pick up airspeed, so don't stand on principle where crossing levels are concerned—just make sure your intended path is clear.

One cardinal rule that wingmen follow is: never try to anticipate the leader's moves. Assuming that he will make a 90-degree or a 180-degree turn, and then acting on that assumption, can really put you in a horribly embarrassing position. If the leader starts a turn, and you jump to the conclusion that it will be 90 degrees or 180 degrees, and you go whipping across the flight with the intent of dazzling everybody with your fancy footwork, you might suddenly realize that nobody else is moving, and now you're what seems like a zillion miles out of position. If the leader stops his turn after 30 degrees, everyone should stay in place, but if he continues much past 45 degrees, a crossover is appropriate. This doesn't mean you should hold your position until he commits himself one way or the other; you should start turning as soon as he does, but if he stops short, slide right back out into position. Maybe there was a reason for the short turn—for example, to put the flight in a little better position to meet an impending threat; or maybe the lead was just turning a little to get the sun out of his eyes, or into yours.

Ninety- and 180-degree turns in the Six Pac require the same basic techniques used in Fingertip. However, a nearly line-abreast formation requires a very rapid and positive reaction by wingmen during turns, since they have no nose-tail clearance at the beginning of a turn. A fast reaction is particularly important when the turn is into your position. A moderately steep turn by the lead can quickly force the wingman on the inside of the turn out in front of the flight. To prevent this, and to keep the leader in sight, you should dump your nose in a hurry while banking in the same direction as the lead. Once a safe altitude difference is established, level off and finish the turn as you would in Fingertip. Don't let too much nose-tail clearance develop, so you won't have to go too far to regain your line-abreast position after the crossover.

In the Six Pac, wingmen will be passing beneath and *perhaps* very slightly behind their leads at the crossover point. Again, since safety is the first consideration, wingmen should adjust their flight paths to maintain a visual on their leads. On entry into turns when the element is below the lead, number three should dive only enough to generate sufficient airspeed to regain position after the crossover. A long dive here could strain flight integrity, and may interfere with keeping an eyeball on the lead. If numbers three and four are above the lead element, they should not get down too close to the lead's altitude, because this would destroy the positional advantage that the Six Pac altitude differential offers.

When number three crosses over above the lead element during the turn, he will momentarily lose sight of the flight leader. Therefore, he must rely on number four to let him know if he's getting too close to the other element while they are in his blind spot—another example of the cooperation and coordination that tactical formation requires.

Don't let this short description of four-ship tactical deceive you into thinking it's a piece of cake. There isn't that much to describing the mechanics of what should be done. However, flying it properly is tough and frustrating until you get the hang of it. Nearly all fighter pilots consider it a matter of professional pride to be able to fly good tactical formation, no matter how little power the leader gives them to play with.

The procedures described here are merely guides for getting from A to B in tactical formation. Nothing will take the place of practice, and nothing is written in stone except the rules of safety and common sense. Position and mutual coverage are still the bywords. If either is lost, the flight ceases to be a fighting unit and becomes just four aircraft relatively close to each other and going roughly in the same direction.

If it is apparent that the element will be above the lead and upsun after a turn, wait until the turn is completed before changing altitude. This is a lot less hairy than complicating matters by diving through the other element while everyone is turning.

CHAPTER 11

THE DO-IT-YOURSELF FIGHTER: RESTORATIONS AND REPLICAS

The thrill of flying a real, full-size fighter ranks, in my estimation, among the most exciting experiences there are. The power, the speed, and the maneuverability are all there, and, in combination, they provide a pilot with the supreme test of his mettle. Putting one of these birds through its paces demands a high degree of skill, yet the exhilaration in such a flight is well worth the effort. Probably the only thing that could add to this experience would be owning the fighter you fly, and many individuals achieve this ambitious yet rewarding goal by restoring old fighters used in either world war to flyable condition. The restoration of any aircraft is a formidable project; however, bringing a fighter back to life is even more formidable, given the complexities of military aircraft technology. The process is a severe test of patience and demands no small amount of skill in the various types of aircraft construction and engine overhaul, along with a considerable investment in time and money.

As the finding of a rabbit is the first step in making rabbit stew, so the first step in restoration is to find a suitable bird to restore. In most cases, fighters don't wander too far from their primary mission in the autumn of their years. Surplus fighters can be purchased from the government and picked up at either the base of deactivation, or from the aircraft boneyards in Arizona. Used fighters may also be purchased from the air forces of small and less developed countries that are in the process of modernizing their fleets. In the past, upgrading has made P-51s and F4U Corsairs relatively easy to come by; other types are fairly scarce, with the Japanese Zero being perhaps the rarest. There is only one restored Zero known to be flying today.

Old warbirds can also be located in private industry, where they were converted for use in specialized projects such as drones, or radar evaluation targets. Naturally, old hangars, garages, and barns sometimes yield one of these birds—usually a decrepit hulk with considerable corrosion, the fabric in tatters, and innumerable parts missing or damaged beyond repair.

This is the most sobering side of aircraft restoration. It is difficult to visualize the decaying framework, covered with hardened oil and dirt, as something that could ever fly again. Nevertheless, it is at this point that the potential owner must make some tough aeronautical and economic decisions about whether the bird can be restored without remanufacturing all of its major components. Maybe it would be better to plan on starting from scratch and building a replica of the airplane, rather than attempting to restore one that is beyond hope. Unless he is looking for a very long-term project, the average restorer will buy the bird only if at least 75 percent of it is in good shape, and only needs cleaning and painting.

On the other hand, a rebuilder may want a particular type or model so bad he can taste it. In this case, he may be willing to purchase a hulk on which nothing but the nameplate is usable, and start his restoration project from there. If the nameplate is genuine, such a dedicated enthusiast may consider all the rest of the parts as a bonus. Along with the general condition of the bird, and/or how badly you want it, consider the number of parts and pieces that are included in the deal, because these can be used as trading materials later on. Swapping components with other rebuilders throughout the world is one of the primary methods of obtaining parts that are becoming scarcer each day.

If it's a go for restoration, the next big step is getting the bird back to the shop. In most cases, preparing the bird for transport involves removal of the wings and possibly other structures, and a vital step in the restoration process begins immediately. The removal of all components and assemblies should be thoroughly documented with photographs, sketches, and notes detailing how each part was installed and the sequence in which it was removed, relative to other parts. Each piece has to be identified and numbered, and then carefully packed away for future reference.

Although all this may seem like a lot of idealistic, nit-picking detail, the rewards of meticulous care and attention to such items will be reaped manyfold during reassembly. When it's time to reinstall a gizmo three years downstream, a lot of time and effort can be saved if you know just where, how, and when it came off. The same care has to be given even to those parts whose present condition makes it obvious that they will have to be replaced. The reason for this is that your pictures, sketches, and notes may be the only guides available when you determine that, with no replacement part available, the part must be remade entirely. This identification and labeling process also extends to the boxes of spare parts and items that come with the aircraft as part of the purchase agreement.

Once an aircraft has been disassembled to the point where it is transportable, it must be loaded on a trailer and properly secured so that additional damage will not occur during the move. This is particularly true of World War I fighters, whose wooden frames have to be carefully padded and supported to prevent breakage along the way.

The real work starts after the bird has been moved into the shop. The first task is to strip the frame of everything that can be removed—all cables, plumbing, wiring, pulleys, hinges, bolts, and so forth. In some instances, this may even involve such extensive teardown as removing all the rivets from the frame of the bird. This is usually required when incompatible metals were used on the original—for example, magnesium rivets in an aluminum skin—and the resulting corrosion must be arrested and steps taken to prevent its recurrence. Of course, all painted surfaces have to be cleaned down to the bare metal so that a detailed inspection of the entire frame can be made, inside and out, for any damage or corrosion that may have been hidden by layers of paint, the nests of previous occupants, or parts just removed. Of particular importance here would be the stress components of the aircraft, which should be Zygloed or magnafluxed and then corrosion-proofed before reinstalling. (X-raying is another inspection technique that might be used at this point.)

During this phase of the restoration process, it is essential that an intelligent and methodical approach be taken to solving the problems that start to crop up by the dozens. This is where sketching, note-taking, photographing, identifying, and labeling really swing into high gear. And here again, nothing is thrown away, no matter what shape it's in, because it may be invaluable later on to show just how the new part should be bent, shaped, or drilled.

If everything checks out okay after you've got the frame stripped, the entire surface of the frame is epoxy primed inside and out to prevent further corrosion.

During the disassembly and removal process, you will be determining the condition of each part and whether it can be reused or not. As the list of needed replacement parts grows, the restoration process temporarily becomes more of an art than a science. The task is now one of determining where each part can be found. Is it in usable condition, and is the owner willing to sell or trade? This is a fairly tough job, given that old fighters and their components are scattered literally all over the globe. Keeping tuned to the grapevine in the world of used aircraft parts is one of the major keys to success in the restoration business. It is not uncommon for one rebuilder to purchase many large assemblies just to come up with one usable component.

An organization that can be of immense help in your search for parts is the Warbirds Division of the Experimental Aircraft Association. This group acts as a centralized information exchange to assist its members in locating required parts. (It also helps them to solve the innumerable other problems that arise during any restoration.) The Warbirds' monthly newsletter also keeps everyone informed about what's going on in the world of restored military aircraft, publishing (among other things) flight safety information pertinent to these birds, and the latest word on various restoration projects that are underway.

If a suitable replacement just cannot be found for a given part, the only alternative is to have it remanufactured. To do this properly, you need a set of original plans and specifications. Since most of the companies that made World War II fighters are still in existence in one form or another, these drawings can usually be obtained. For example, if a Spitfire is under restoration, the RAF Museum in London maintains a file of 30,000 drawings for this bird. The Smithsonian and its National Air and Space Museum are also good sources for old aircraft blueprints and drawings.

However, in restoring planes of World War I vintage, finding plans is considerably more difficult, and you often draw a blank. About all that can be done in this case is to fall back on your sketches and photos and the remains of the old parts. Here the rebuilding process becomes a series of cut-and-fit attempts until the new piece is just right. Some help in this endeavor can be had from the blueprint-like plans and drawings found in old model airplane publications, such as those drawn by William Wylam in *Model Airplane News* many years ago.

In the interests of doing the teardown and reassembly procedure only once, nearly all restoration projects include the replacement of control cables; hydraulic, fuel, oil, and air lines; and all electrical wiring. This is where the saving and labeling of all the old plumbing starts to pay dividends—the originals can be used as models for the multiple bends and angles needed in the new pieces.

As reassembly progresses, all the notes and sketches made when the airframe was stripped, possibly years ago, become worth their weight in gold. During the rebuilding process, some of the strictly military components—armor plating, guns, ammunition boxes and feed belts, and the bulky electronics gear common to the World War II era may be omitted for weight and/or space considerations. If some of these items—for example, cockpit armor—form a part of the aircraft structure, they are sometimes replaced with a lighter material.

The engine, like the airframe, is usually a mini-restoration project in itself. One consolation here is that engines are usually a little easier to come by than airframes. However, even when you can find power plants that were pickled and crated by the military years ago, they usually require a complete teardown and inspection before use. For the older engine whose stock of spare parts has long since been exhausted, any needed replacements must be custom-made, and factory blueprints are just about a must for this type of work.

During all phases of the restoration, everything must be inspected by a licensed Airframe and Powerplant mechanic, and after the job is done, a new weight and balance has to be computed for the aircraft, to insure that the inevitable additions and deletions have not adversely affected the CG. After the last bit of paint has been applied, and all the inspections have been complied with, the born-again fighter is probably in better shape than it was on active duty.

As I said earlier, restoring a fighter (or any aircraft, for that matter) is a very time-consuming project that can take years and years to complete, and is rightly labeled one of the absolute tests of man's patience. According to some restorers, it takes X number of years to do 95 percent of the job, and the same number of years to do the last 5 percent, with searching out and reconditioning parts being the biggest problem. For the average World War II fighter restoration, a ball park figure for the major work involved is two to eight years; during this time, about 10,000 man-hours of labor will be required. Given the time and the facilities needed to undertake such a venture, and the price of all aviation materials these days, it is easy to see that the costs of putting an old fighter back in the air are staggering. Most restorers are a little reluctant to discuss the costs involved in their projects, probably because of the tears that such thoughts bring to their eyes. However, here's one indication of what the restoration process entails fiscally: in one project, just the required new Dzus fasteners amounted to $700. A very generalized estimate for restoring a fighter that was in pretty good shape to start with is $125,000, and that doesn't include the cost of obtaining the basic airframe. Starting with a framework that was in worse shape could run these costs to around $350,000. And if the project is started with little more than the nameplate, the only approach to the costs involved must be the philosophical view taken by one of the country's top restorers: "The desire comes first, the money comes later." It is probably better to look on such expenses as an investment, which in a way they really are, for the value of warbirds has been steadily climbing over the years. Recent issues of trade publications have listed restored fighters with an asking price in excess of a quarter of a million dollars.

With all of this in mind, a question that invariably crops up is, "What motivates people to invest so much time and treasure in a project whose only guarantee is lots of headaches and heartburn?"

The personal pride and sense of accomplishment that result from producing one of these masterworks of the restorer's art is reward enough in itself. When asked what most rebuilders do with airplanes they have restored, one expert replied, "They stroke them." And, if credence is to be given to the theories of transactional analysis, these airplanes, in return, stroke their owners. The rest of the answer to the question "Why?" is the fulfillment of the desire to fly the "big iron" of yesteryear; having your name painted on the side of the cockpit is just the icing on the cake.

Individuals who have the expertise and the resources to undertake the restoration of a fighter are not too plentiful. It is estimated that there are only about a dozen people in the United States considered to be top-echelon restorers of fighter aircraft.

An organization that has made a significant and continuing contribution to the field of military aircraft restoration is the Confederate Air Force. The CAF is dedicated to preserving the aura that the aircraft of World War II created. They do this by collecting and restoring aircraft from all nations involved in the war, and displaying them in an air show extravaganza that re-creates some of the more significant aerial battles of the Second War. Among these are the Battle of Britain, D-Day, Pearl Harbor, and the Battle of Midway. In these vivid portrayals of just about how it really was—even to the original cast, airplane-wise—can be found P-51 Mustangs, a P-40, Messerschmitt Bf-109s, a P-38 Lightning, and a Spitfire Mark IX, to name just a few. The CAF stable is not limited to fighters, but also includes bombers of all sizes, from an A-20 Havoc to a B-29 Superfortress, and a lot in between, including the B-17 and the B-24.

The group was formed in 1957 by five World War II veterans who pooled their resources to buy a P-51. Over the years the membership has grown to over 2,800, and the fleet now consists of 60 birds of 40 different types. In this air force, every man is a colonel, no matter what his job. Headquarters is at Rebel Field in Harlingen, Texas, which is a former Air Force gunnery base. There are also 14 CAF wings in cities throughout the United States, and members hail from 35 states and 18 countries.

Some of the unusual or relatively rare restorations flown by the CAF are: the only Curtiss SB2C Helldiver that is still flying today; one of the three flyable Douglas SBD Dauntlesses; and an F-82 Twin Mustang. The restoration work on nearly all of the birds seen in the CAF air show is done in their own shops. However, for the big yearly event, many members fly their own restored fighters to Harlingen so they can play an active part in the gaggle. Of course, all the members would love to have a chance to fly one of the CAF's fighters, but because of their rarity, only five of the most experienced crews are assigned to each ship, and even then, flying time is strictly limited to air shows and proficiency checks.

Owning and restoring a World War II fighter is obviously the best route to go—first class all the way. However, for the average tiger, such an undertaking is pretty much out of the question. The combination of skills, facilities, and wherewithal required fairly well limits the number of people in the restoration business. For those with even a little bit of fighter pilot's blood in their veins, the next best way to get a dream bird in the air is to build a replica. Home-built versions of the original bird can be made in any size to fit the builder's shop space and pocketbook. Practical considerations, such as minimum cockpit size, as well as the aerodynamics involved, usually limit the smallest replicas to one-half scale; at the other end of the spectrum is the full-size copy of the real bird.

In order to maintain good flying characteristics, you usually cannot build the empennage of a less-than-full-size replica exactly to scale, but the differences here are too small to be noticeable, and the classic lines of the bird are retained.

One of the big advantages over restoring the real McCoy that replica building offers is the variety of materials and construction techniques available to the homebuilder. The traditional Sitka spruce framework covered with aircraft plywood and/or fabric, and the welded tubular steel frame with a fabric or aluminum skin, are still chosen by most do-it-yourselfers. But about five years ago, a new technique utilizing fiberglassed Styrofoam for primary aircraft structures was introduced. This has since proven to be quite successful, because the material is relatively easy to work with and provides a high strength-to-weight ratio.

Another advantage for the homebuilder is the latitude with which he can approach the various problems of replica building. If he wishes, he can use a combination of construction techniques on his aircraft, getting the best of each world: a steel tube frame for the fuselage, a wooden spar and ribs for the wings, plywood covering, and fiberglass for the compound curves of fillets, cowlings, and gear doors. Another combination he might use is a basic wooden box frame with Styrofoam to achieve the shape of the airplane, followed by fiberglassing to provide extra strength. One builder of a P-51 replica covered a tubular steel frame with fiberglass shells molded to the correct shapes.

The selection of an engine is another area in which the homebuilder comes out ahead, because in any given horsepower range, he normally has a variety of commercial models to choose from. If these don't suit his fancy, or cannot be accommodated in the space limitations of his replica, certain automobile engines can be converted for aircraft use.

The costs of building a replica are only a fraction of those involved in a restoration, and are mainly a function of the materials used, the tools that become necessary to fabricate the parts, and the level of sophistication the builder desires in the finished product. (Such niceties as full IFR instrumentation and retractable gear, plus necessary navigation equipment can put a severe strain on the old pocketbook, and also complicate the building process.) In the area of costs, the replica builder has another slight advantage over the restorer: his investment can be made incrementally, whereas the restorer must lay out a sizable piece of change just to get something to work on. However, the two processes do have one thing in common—both seem to generate a long series of problems to be solved as the work progresses.

Since the average homebuilder is usually not as well equipped as the restorer, some of his problems can assume monumental proportions. Here is where the local chapter of the Experimental Aircraft Association, headquartered in Hales Corners, Wisconsin, can really be a godsend. The members of this group become "partners" with the builder by finding answers to his problems, providing good advice on how to avoid the pitfalls they've all heard about or experienced, and acting as a valuable source of information on locating parts and materials. In most cases, the chapter will have one or two qualified A&P mechanics among its members to field the tougher, more technical questions, particularly on compliance with the regulations governing home-built aircraft. The headquarters of the EAA has a staff of experts who can also be called on; in addition, it provides a valuable service by acting as a centralized point for the exchange of information and ideas.

There is no great abundance of plans on the market for building replicas of fighters—plans are probably available for fewer than a dozen different aircraft. Most replica builders who have a yen for a particular aircraft of a particular scale must resort to reducing full-size drawings to the dimensions they want. This method adds an enormous amount of work to a task that by itself is no small undertaking, but when the end result looks like the Stuka in the color section of this book, it is well worth the effort.

Although most replica fighters are built smaller than the originals because of available shop space, engine limitations, and overall costs, some full-size versions do exist. For the most part, these birds are World War I fighters whose general size and method of construction lend themselves more readily to home building techniques.

In the world of flying wires, wooden struts, and canvas wings, the replica builder par excellence is Cole Palen of Old Rhinebeck Aerodrome, New York. Antique aircraft buffs who visit this little air patch made over from an abandoned farm will think they've died an' gone to heaven. Assembled here are 51 replicas and restorations of aircraft whose heyday was the World War I era; of these, 29 are flyable.

The basic fuselage structure of a half-scale home-built Corsair—a Sitka spruce framework covered with 1/16-inch birch plywood.

The fin and stabilizer structures are complete—only a root and a tip rib are required to act as sanding guides when the foam is shaped.

The same Corsair with polyurethane foam sections applied and sanded to shape.

Completed half-scale Corsair that was built in four years by Fred Bauer of Winona, Minnesota. Powered by an O-235 Lycoming, it indicates 142 mph at 2500 rpm with an external tank installed. (Photo © by Marc Siem.)

The term "flyable" is used here with some provisos—many of the birds at Old Rhinebeck are just barely airworthy, due to a combination of their vintage, general design, handling characteristics, and power plants. For example, the Blériot only flies about 20 or 30 feet above the ground for the length of the grass strip. It then lands, and after being turned around repeats the trip. After a close inspection of this bird's narrow-tread gear, fragile construction, small rotary engine, and wing warping controls (which it has instead of ailerons), it is easy to understand a cautious approach even to bringing this valuable antique out of the hangar.

A good many of Cole Palen's airplanes are full-size replicas, built in the same manner and from the same plans as the originals. These reproductions are faithful down to the lack of such modern conveniences as brakes and most basic instruments, and all use the same kinds of engines as their predecessors. In a good many of the planes of that period, this was a rotary engine, and Old Rhinebeck is probably the only place in the world where three aircraft powered by rotary engines can be seen in the air at the same time—in formation. Given that there is no throttle on a rotary, this last feat becomes that much more impressive. The absence of wheel brakes requires the use of wing walkers to push and pull the birds through turns while taxiing, and also to literally catch the wing tips on the landing rollout to help stop the airplanes. When you add up all the quirks inherent in flying these old birds, you can see that it represents quite a challenge just to get one up and down, especially in windy conditions, to say nothing of putting on an air show.

Air show performances at Old Rhinebeck display the old-time fighters to the best of their advantage; there are dogfights complete with chattering guns, bombing and strafing runs, and lots of explosions, fires, and smoke. Complementing the air show is a melodrama on the ground involving tank battles, antiaircraft guns, uniformed troops, damsels in distress, and, of course, the evil Black Baron. These weekly excursions into history have made Cole Palen a preserver of attractive memories of World War I, just as the Confederate Air Force rekindles memories of the Second War.

In addition to displaying their handiwork at air shows and fly-ins, restorers and replica builders occasionally have a chance to break into show business. Consider the dilemma of a producer with a great wartime script on his hands, but no authentic airplanes with which to stage the aerial action. Without replicas or restored aircraft, the television series featuring the Black Sheep Squadron, and such movies as *The Battle of Britain, 633 Squadron,* and *Tora! Tora! Tora!* would not have been possible. (In some of these productions, and in the air show put on by the Confederate Air Force, AT-6s modified to resemble Zeros are substituted for the real thing. Restored Zeros, as I said earlier, are practically nonexistent.)

Probably the best place to see the largest number of restored fighters and replicas of every size is at the Experimental Aircraft Association's annual bash in Oshkosh, Wisconsin. To this largest of all air shows come the best of the restorer's and homebuilder's art, to be judged by the experts and vie for the title of Grand National Champion Warbird. It is an event well worth the time of any tiger, young or old.

Conclusion

This book covers nearly all the basic fighter maneuvers you need to master if you're going to get in there and mix it up with another bird. (There are a few others, but they are just modifications of those covered here, or adaptations of basic acrobatic maneuvers to the combat situation.) Unless you have a photographic memory, you will probably have to go over each maneuver again and again on the ground, and a few times in the air, before all the pieces fall into place. Discuss the maneuvers with other jocks, using models to help you see just how you perform each one. Be fully aware of the strengths and weaknesses of each one of these gyrations so that you don't apply them mechanically. Herein lies the secret of a successful fighter pilot: stay loose and stay flexible.

You will rarely get a chance to execute any of these maneuvers in their entirety. Pick and choose that portion of a maneuver that meets the needs of the moment, and always be ready to switch to another tactic the instant the situation dictates it.

An air-to-air engagement is an extremely fluid situation; at times, every move you make will be a judgment call based on how things are going at that instant. The sequence of events may even preclude a chance to use any of the maneuvers discussed in this book. This is the time to be adaptable.

Since you'll be reacting to a moving, thinking target, you must be prepared to take whatever action is necessary to get into his 6 o'clock position and hammer him. These actions include canned maneuvers and others that are not so canned. An unorthodox maneuver that is unexpected by your opponent can turn the tables in a hurry. Conversely, if you have the advantage and the other guy tries something wild in an effort to shake you, don't be suckered into following him through it too closely. You can even momentarily give up a good firing position, ease back a little to maintain your positional advantage, and let him thrash about. Use just enough Gs and turn to keep him out in front, and after he's finished his act, move back in for the kill. The idea here is to let him expend his energy while you are conserving yours.

Although an oddball gyration may prove effective in a given set of circumstances, remember that the basic fighter maneuvers described in this book have been tested over the years and proved to be the best ways of getting on someone's tail and staying there. They are not, as I've just said, the complete answer to every situation you will find in a simulated air-to-air engagement. They are the basics— the foundations on which advanced air combat tactics, designed for multiple attackers working against multiple defenders, are based. However, once you have a working knowledge of the basics under your belt, you will probably find that you can give a good account of yourself in almost any one-on-one situation.

There are a lot of do's and don'ts in this book, and these, together with what may seem like a lot of other chicken recommendations, might give the impression that the whole fighter game is more trouble than it's worth. Don't let your first reading discourage you. There *is* a lot of work involved, but the procedures discussed here are the distillate of a lot of work by a lot of knowledgeable people over a lot of years. Every recommendation has a time-tested reason behind it, and practically every attempt to short-cut recommended procedures results in a lot of needless effort to reinvent the wheel. Innovation certainly has its place, but only after a firm grounding in the basics. This firm grounding is all that differentiates a guy who innovates from one who engages in dangerous folly. As I mentioned before, a lot of enjoyment can be had from learning how to tangle with another aircraft, but the fun in basic fighter maneuvers lies in doing it safely. All the effort spent on briefings, safety checks, preflights, checklists, and so forth will not be wasted, and, in reality, attention to these details in this type of environment is a measure of each man's professionalism. Anyone whose approach to this type of flying is less than professional soon marks himself as a mere fledgling. Unfortunately, his mark in many cases may be a permanent one—a hole in the ground.

Good luck, good hunting, and check your six.

Go get 'em, tigers!

APPENDICES

Appendix A

Glossary of Terms

Angle off the nose (or tail): the angle from the nose (or tail) of your aircraft to another aircraft, usually measured in the plane of your wings. Thus, an aircraft in your 10 o'clock position would have an angle off your nose of 60 degrees (see Clock code.) Can also refer to your angle off from another aircraft, such as the ideal firing position being about a 15-degree angle off your opponent's tail.

Ballistic curve: an arcing flight path followed by an aircraft being flown under zero G conditions.

Bandit: a known hostile aircraft.

Bingo fuel: the amount of fuel that will allow you to make a normal recovery at your home base, plus the amount necessary to divert to an alternate base if necessary. When anyone in the flight reaches bingo fuel, all aircraft should re-form and head for home.

Bogey: an unidentified aircraft that is probably hostile.

To bounce: to attack another aircraft, element or flight, usually taking it by surprise.

Clearing the area: visually inspecting all quadrants around your aircraft before starting a maneuver, to insure that they are free of any traffic that would conflict with the intended maneuver.

Clock code: a frame of reference used to locate traffic in the area of a given aircraft, with the nose of the aircraft being 12 o'clock and the tail being 6 o'clock. "High" and "low" are also used with clock code directions to further pinpoint a position. For example, "bogey at 2 o'clock high" would mean that this aircraft is approximately 60 degrees to the right of the nose of your aircraft, and above your present altitude. When using clock code directions, be sure to state whether they are relative to your bird, or to the one you are talking to—e.g. "Strangers in *your* 3 o'clock low."

Ding: an aircraft accident or incident.

E6B: a hand-held navigation computer with a circular slide rule on one side and a translucent compass rose on the other; used for solving heading and ground speed problems involving wind direction and velocity.

Eating his socks: maintaining a close position of advantage despite the defensive maneuvering of an opponent.

Element: a pair of aircraft acting as a unit under the direction of the element leader; also, the number three and four aircraft in a flight of four.

Engagement: a real or mock air-to-air combat situation—a dogfight, or a hassle.

Flight: four aircraft acting as a unit under the direction of the flight leader.

G: a unit used to express the force of gravity—e.g., a force of two Gs will cause an object to double its weight while the force is being applied, due to the doubled gravitational pull on the object.

G loading: the number of Gs you put on your aircraft during maneuver.

G suit: a tight-fitting garment worn around the abdomen and legs, containing bladders that are automatically inflated with air when the airplane is pulling Gs. The amount of air pressure delivered to the suit is proportional to the G loading on the aircraft. The purpose of the suit is to prevent the pilot from blacking out by squeezing his abdomen and legs in an effort to prevent blood from pooling in his lower extremeties. The suit is uncomfortable, but is effective up to six or seven Gs.

Gaggle: a formation of many aircraft, usually made up of four or more flights of four aircraft each.

GCI: Ground Controlled Intercept; a ground radar station capable of controlling a fighter on a mission to intercept a hostile raid.

GIB: the Guy in black; the crew member in the back seat of some fighters who operates the radar, weapons delivery system, and navigation gear.

Grunt: a ground soldier, as opposed to someone who flies; anyone who doesn't fly.

High cruise position: the throttle setting recommended by the engine manufacturer for maximum continuous power—usually climb power or slightly below.

Initial: the approach leg to the overhead pattern, flown along the extended runway centerline from a point three to five miles from the end of the runway. This point is called the "initial point," and is normally where the tower is called to let them know you are entering traffic.

To jink: to make rapid, random movements of an aircraft, usually at high speed and high G loadings, to avoid being shot down by another aircraft or by ground fire. In the former case, it is also referred to as a "last-ditch maneuver" to shake an opponent off your tail.

To lock on: to fix the transmitted radar beam of a radar set on a desired target with respect to both range and azimuth. With these two parameters known, the computer section of the radar set will continuously track the target and supply steering or guidance information to the operator of the set.

Lufbery: a circular tail chase involving two or more aircraft, in which the speeds of all aircraft are just about equal. This similarity of speed prevents the attacker from closing, and the defender from escaping, unless some modification or counter to the Lufbery is made. The usual situation is two aircraft on opposite sides of the circle, each flying at maximum speed and pulling maximum available Gs.

Mach: the relationship of the speed of an aircraft to the speed of sound at that altitude; e.g., if you are indicating .8 M, you are flying at 80 percent of the speed of sound at that altitude.

Maximum intercept line: the farthest distance from a base that an incoming raid can be intercepted and the fighters recovered safely (though not necessarily at their home base).

Overhead approach: a racetrack-shaped traffic pattern beginning with a pitchout, or level 180-degree turn from the initial to the downwind leg. This turn helps to slow the aircraft down from traffic pattern entry speed to gear-lowering speed. A level downwind leg is flown parallel to the runway while the gear and flaps are lowered. If judged properly, the turn from downwind to final is a continuous descending turn to rollout lined up with the runway centerline. The distance from the end of the runway where this rollout occurs will vary with the type of aircraft and the landing configuration. If a crosswind blows the aircraft toward the pattern side of the runway, a pause may be made halfway through this turn in order to remain on the base leg for a few moments until the proper wind correction is made. To correct for a crosswind *from* the pattern side of the runway, one angles the downwind slightly *away* from the runway, rather than trying to tighten up the turn to final.

Pipper: a dot of light at the center of the image projected on the windshield by a gunsight—used as the primary aiming reference for air-to-air or air-to-ground weapons delivery.

Pitchout: a level turn utilizing 60 to 90 degrees of bank and moderate Gs, made in the traffic pattern to turn the 180 degrees from the initial approach over the runway to the downwind leg.

Position of advantage: a position achieved by an attacking aircraft so that he is stabilized behind an opponent, at or inside firing range (normally 500 to 800 feet). The attacker should be able to stay in this position a sufficient length of time to keep the pipper on the target long enough to effect a kill (three to five seconds).

SAMs: Surface-to-Air missiles.

Scramble: the act of getting a fighter airborne in the least possible amount of time, normally a maximum of five minutes.

Six: the most commonly used clock code term. Six always refers to the area behind an aircraft. Examples: "Check your six," meaning keep an eye peeled behind you, or check the area immediately to the rear of your bird; "I'm in his six and closing," meaning you are behind an opponent and have an overtake rate established; and "He's in your deep six," meaning another aircraft is behind and below the aircraft you are calling.

Speed brakes: drag-producing doors or panels on jet aircraft, actuated by hydraulic pressure, that are opened in flight to slow the aircraft down quickly.

Stranger: an unidentified friendly aircraft.

Tracking solution: the stabilized position behind an opponent, within firing distance, at which you are able to pull the proper lead to insure hits on the target; also, a position of advantage; the answer to the geometric sighting problem provided by the gyroscopic gunsight.

Vector: the heading given to the interceptor by the radar controller at the GCI sit.

Visiting firemen: dignitaries from higher headquarters on a tour of your installation.

Waxed his tail: won an engagement.

Wing loading: the weight of the aircraft divided by the wing area, usually expressed in pounds per square foot.

APPENDIX B
Acrobatics Briefing Guide and Form

This briefing form is designed primarily for dual instruction in acrobatics. Little is to be gained in the early phases of training from two-ship missions, where the instructor observes the student's maneuvers from a distance.

This form can also be used as a checklist for a pilot who is preparing for a solo acrobatics mission.

WEATHER	EXISTING	FORECAST
Local	_____	_____
Working area	_____	_____
Destination	_____	_____

CALL SIGN _____

Time Hack

FREQUENCIES

Ground _____ En route _____ _____ _____

Tower _____ Working _____

Route to working area _____

MANEUVERS TO BE PERFORMED

#	Type	Entry altitude	Entry airspeed	Gs	Exit altitude	Exit airspeed
1	————	————	————	——	————	————
2	————	————	————	——	————	————
3	————	————	————	——	————	————
4	————	————	————	——	————	————

Minimum altitude for all maneuvers ————————————

ACROBATICS BRIEFING GUIDE

(1) Preflight; stow all loose items.

(2) If dual instruction is available, instructor demonstrates each maneuver; student may follow through, *very lightly,* on controls.

(3) Student practices maneuver until proficient.

(4) Review the techniques and requirements for each maneuver:

> Clearing the area.
> Lining up with reference lines/points.
> Power settings.
> Entry airspeed and altitude.
> Initial references of maneuver.
> Desired G loading.
> Expected airspeed increase/decrease.
> Intermediate references of maneuver.
> Minimum allowable airspeed.
> Desired intermediate altitude.
> Final references for maneuver.
> Desired altitude and airspeed at completion.
> Effect of torque on maneuver.

(5) Common errors found in each maneuver, and corrections to minimize the effects of these errors.

(6) Recognition of normal and accelerated stalls.

(7) Momentary engine stoppages while inverted or in zero-G conditions.

(8) Spin recovery procedures for your aircraft.

(9) Review vertical recovery procedures if overhead maneuvers are planned:

> Apply full power.
> Release excessive back pressure.
> Roll to nearest horizon.
> Use rudders to help get the nose down through the horizon.
> Allow the aircraft to assume a moderate to steep dive to regain airspeed.
> Recover only when airspeed is well above stalling speed.

(10) Check fuel quantity occasionally.

(11) Watch for rpm overspeeds.

(12) Observe airspace boundaries.

(13) Discontinue mission if aircraft is over-G'd.

(14) Determine route to destination.

(15) Note approach and landing particulars.

REMEMBER—SAFETY IS PARAMOUNT

APPENDIX C

BASIC FIGHTER MANEUVERS BRIEFING GUIDE AND FORM

WEATHER	EXISTING	FORECAST
Local	_____	_____
Working area	_____	_____
Destination	_____	_____

Call sign _____

FLIGHT LINEUP

Position	Tail number	Pilot
1	_____	_____
2	_____	_____
3	_____	_____
4	_____	_____

Alternate lead _____

TIME HACK

Start engines _____   Taxi _____

Check-in _____   Takeoff _____

FREQUENCIES

Ground _____ En route _____   _____ _____

Tower _____ Working _____   Backup _____

TAKEOFF

Check wind conditions

Runway lineup

Formation takeoff: _____ yes _____ no (maximum crosswind component 10 knots)

Takeoff interval: _____ seconds

Aborts

JOIN-UP

Side(s)

Airspeed _____

EN ROUTE

Formation to be used _____

Frequency changes _____

airspeed _____; altitude _____

WORKING AREA

Frequency change _____

Boundaries of area _____

Minimum altitude for this mission ("floor" of area)   _____

Prominent checkpoints and obstructions   _____

Sequence of maneuvers to be performed:

Type	Altitude	Airspeed	Attacker/De-fender
1 _____	_____	_____	_____/_____
2 _____	_____	_____	_____/_____
3 _____	_____	_____	_____/_____
4 _____	_____	_____	_____/_____

REVIEW OF TECHNIQUES FOR EACH MANEUVER

Airspeeds

Initial setup: relative positions and altitudes

Call rolling in

Actions by the attacker and defender

Basic Fighter Maneuvers Briefing Guide

(1) Key reference points for the attacker and defender throughout the maneuver.

(2) Corrections to achieve the desired position.

(3) Watch G loading and minimum airspeeds.

(4) Disengage when tracking solution is achieved.

(5) Common errors found in each maneuver.

(6) Watch for rpm overspeeds.

(7) Fuel check after each sequence.

(8) Disengage criteria:

>Exceeding airspace boundaries.
>Going below minimum altitude.
>One aircraft achieves a position of advantage.
>Maneuver has been demonstrated and/or practiced.
>Radio out in any aircraft.
>One aircraft reaches bingo fuel.
>Problems with an aircraft or a pilot.
>Attacker loses sight of defender except for brief instants.
>Other aircraft transiting area.

(9) Safety considerations:

>Thorough preflight; stow loose gear.
>Observe ceiling and visibility minimums.
>Adequate "floor" established for maneuver area.
>Leading aircraft has responsibility for maintaining separation during pull-ups into the sun.
>Don't press the attack beyond minimum range.
>Spatial disorientation over water areas.
>Know how to recognize and correct for adverse yaw.
>Maintain good radio discipline.

Rendezvous point for lost wingman or late arrivals _____

_____

_____ orbit; airspeed _____; altitude _____

RECOVERY

>Formation to be used   _____

>Frequencies _____

>Airspeed _____; altitude _____

APPROACH AND LANDING

Frequencies _____

Type of approach: _____ formation _____ single-ship
[check one]

Formation to be used _____

Pattern _____

Alternate mission _____

Emergency procedure of the day _____

Bingo fuel _____

REMEMBER—SAFETY IS PARAMOUNT

Formation Flying Briefing Guide and Form

Weather   **Existing**   **Forecast**

   Local   _____   _____

   Working area   _____   _____

   Destination   _____   _____

Call sign _____

FLIGHT LINEUP

Position	Tail number	Pilot
1	_____	_____
2	_____	_____
3	_____	_____
4	_____	_____

       Alternate lead _____

TIME HACK

Start engines _____   Taxi _____

Check-in _____   Takeoff_____

FREQUENCIES

Ground _____   En route _____   _____ _____

Tower _____   Working _____   Backup _____

LINEUP FOR TAKEOFF

Check wind direction

#1 on downwind side

Spacing between aircraft or elements

Line up in center of your half of the runway

Last man on: call in position

Hand signals

TAKEOFF

Formation takeoff: _____ yes _____ no (maximum crosswind component 10 knots)

Power settings

Time interval between aircraft or elements: _____ seconds

Hand signals: run-up, brake release, gear/flaps up, power reduction

Aborts

JOIN-UP

Airspeed
Join-up Side
Overshoots:
    Remain clear of flight until speed is stabilized
    Ease into position when airspeed is under control
    No belly-up, blind join-ups—cross under flight and keep
        them in view.

EN ROUTE

Formation to be used _____
Checkpoints
Frequency changes
Hand and aircraft signals
Level off airspeed _____; altitude _____

WORKING AREA

Frequency change
Boundaries of area
Prominent checkpoints and obstructions
Sequence of maneuvers to be performed:

#	Type	Airspeed of lead	Leader
1	_____	_____	_____
2	_____	_____	_____
3	_____	_____	_____
4	_____	_____	_____

Rendezvous point for lost wingman or late arrivals _____
_____
_____ orbit; airspeed _____; altitude _____
Signals to be used

FORMATION PARTICULARS

Reference points: close and tactical
Crossover techniques: close and tactical
Trail: pitchout interval, maneuvers to be performed, distance
    between aircraft; call lead if thrown out
Rejoins
Stacked and level turns
Minimum altitude
Keep radio chatter to a minimum
Lookout doctrine in tactical
Fuel checks

Bingo fuel _____

RECOVERY

Formation to be used _____
Checkpoints, if different than above
Frequencies
Airspeed _____ altitude _____

APPROACH AND LANDING

Pre-landing check
Frequencies
Formation to be used; when change to Echelon will occur
Pitchout interval: _____ seconds
Hand and aircraft signals
Pattern:

Airspeeds
Spacing
Altitude
Don't bunch up
Common base leg
LANDING:

Alternate sides—#1 takes downwind side
Stay in center of your half of the runway
Watch for turbulence/prop wash
Passing on runway
Call when aircraft in front of you is clear to turn off
runway

FORMATION APPROACH

Point of initiating approach
Gear and flap procedures
Airspeed approaching glide path _____
Airspeed on final _____
Attitude changes at slow airspeeds
Hand signal rview
Minimum altitude (drop-off)

Alternate mission   _____

Hand signal review

Emergency procedure of the day

REMEMBER—SAFETY IS PARAMOUNT

Flight Data Card

[front]

Call sign _____ Bingo fuel _____
St. eng. _____ Ck.-in _____ Taxi _____
T.O. _____
Radio: Grnd _____ Twr _____ Working _____
         En route _____ _____ _____
Backup _____

LINEUP (Designate alternate lead by asterik)

Position	Tail number	Pilot
1	_____	_____
2	_____	_____
3	_____	_____
4	_____	_____

Takeoff interval _____ seconds   Join-up airspeed _____

Alternate mission _____

NOTES:

[back]

SEQUENCE OF MANEUVERS

#	Type	Lead/Wing or Attacker/Defender	Airspeed of Lead/Att./Def.
1	_____	_____/_____	_____/_____/_____
2	_____	_____/_____	_____/_____/_____
3	_____	_____/_____	_____/_____/_____
4	_____	_____/_____	_____/_____/_____

PARAMETERS

#	Entry airspeed	Entry altitude	Gs	Exit airspeed	Exit altitude	Other
1	_____	_____	____	_____	_____	_____
2	_____	_____	____	_____	_____	_____
3	_____	_____	____	_____	_____	_____
4	_____	_____	____	_____	_____	_____

Minimum altitude _____

Rendezvous point _____
_____ orbit; altitude _____; airspeed _____
Bingo fuel _____ Score _____

NOTES:

Appendix F
Key Points to Remember

Know your mission, your airplane, and yourself.

Maintain a good commonsense approach to each phase of training.

Brief every mission thoroughly.

Make a good preflight.

Use parachutes on all acrobatics and basic fighter maneuvers missions.

Use an instructor whenever possible, especially in acrobatics.

Clear the area before every maneuver.

Meet minimum entry speeds for all maneuvers.

Learn and practice the maneuvers that are easiest first—then proceed to the more difficult ones.

Keep your head on a swivel, both in the air and on the ground.

Know your aircraft's emergency procedures perfectly.

Know the sound and feel of a normal and high-speed stall in your airplane.

Know the spin recovery procedures for your aircraft.

Know how to execute a vertical recovery before practicing overhead acrobatics.

Know how to recognize and correct for adverse yaw.

Know your bird's Split S characteristics.

Plan well ahead if you are leading a formation.

Try to be extra-smooth on the controls when leading a flight.

Know the hand signals used in formation.

Keep alert for, and acknowledge, all signals in formation.

Work constantly to achieve and maintain the ideal formation position.

Insure adequate clearance before starting crossovers.

Know switch locations and proper directions to move switches by feel alone.

Maintain a good lookout doctrine.

Keep a visual on all aircraft in front of you during turns in tactical formation.

Keep the windshield and canopy clear.

Use the clock code when calling out strangers.

Know the egress procedures for your aircraft, and practice them occasionally on the ground.

Refocus your eyes to infinity after checking something in the cockpit.

Keep your energy level as high as possible before and during an engagement.

Think offensively during an engagement.

Stay loose and flexible.

Remember that the name of the game is "fly it safely."

Don't exceed the G limits or placarded airspeed for your aircraft.

Don't attempt maneuvers prohibited for your aircraft.

Don't go below the minimum altitude established for the mission.

Don't attempt to fly a mission if there are restrictions to visibility in the working area.

Don't lose sight of the boget once the initial contact has been made.

Don't bounce aircraft that are not a part of the briefed mission.

Don't press an attack inside minimum range.

Don't continue maneuvering once a "disengage" has been called.

Don't continue the mission below bingo fuel.

Don't talk unnecessarily on the radio.

Don't fly with a known or suspected malfunction.

Don't leave the briefing room with questions unanswered.

Don't attempt any maneuvers that were not briefed for that mission.

Don't practice acrobatics or basic fighter maneuvers over water if it's at all avoidable—the lack of positive ground references can cause spatial disorientation.

Don't fly acrobatics, formation, or basic fighter maneuvers in other than the designated area. If no such area exists, use a minimum-traffic area.

Don't forget to plan ahead when leading a flight.

Don't check in out of turn.

Don't attempt to join-up with excessive overtake or rate of closure.

Don't take your eyes off the airplane you are flying formation on, except for the **briefest** of instants to make necessary cockpit checks.

Don't try to impress everyone by flying too close to your leader.

Don't change sides in formation without a signal from the leader.

Don't anticipate a leader's moves and react prematurely.

Don't ever turn into an Echelon.

Don't bunch up in the traffic pattern, especially on final.

Don't forget that the name of the game is "fly it safely."

Production Aircraft Certified for Acrobatic Flight

LIMITED ACROBATICS (NO INVERTED OR SNAP MANEUVERS)

Cessna 150, 152 Aerobat
Beechcraft Bonanza 33*
Beechcraft Musketeer 23*

UNLIMITED ACROBATICS

Great Lakes 2T-1A2*
Pitts S1S
Pitts S2A
Bellanca Citabria*
Bellanca Decathlon*

*Not in current production

Many homebuilt designs may also be flown in acrobatic flight; however, their airworthiness for these maneuvers is indicated only by the G limits specified by the designer. Therefore, even basic acrobatic maneuvers should not be attempted until a careful testing of the flight characteristics of the particular aircraft has been accomplished.

Selected Bibliography

Childers, James Saxon. *War Eagles.* New York: D. Appleton-Century Co., 1943.

Editors of *American Heritage. The American Heritage History of Flight.* New York: American Heritage Publishing Co., 1962.

Frizzell, Colonel Donaldson D. and Bowers, Colonel Ray L., editors. *Air War: Vietnam.* New York: Arno Press, 1978.

Funderburk, Thomas R. *The Fighters.* New York: Grosset & Dunlap, 1965.

Futrell, Robert F. *The USAF in Korea.* New York: Duell, Sloan and Pearce, 1961.

Galland, Adolf. *The First and the Last.* New York: Henry Holt & Co., 1954.

Green, William. *Famous Fighters of the Second World War.* New York: Hanover House, 1957.

Grinnell-Milne, Duncan. *Wind in the Wires.* New York: Doubleday & Co., 1968.

Gurney, Gene. *Five Down and Glory.* New York: G. P. Putnam's Sons, 1958.

Hess, William. *Fighting Mustang.* New York: Doubleday & Co., 1970.

Jabara, Captain James. *We Fly MiG Alley.* Washington, D.C.: *Air Force* Magazine, June 1951.

Jablonski, Edward. *Airwar: Wings of Fire.* New York: Doubleday & Co., 1971.

Johnson, J. E. *Full Circle.* New York: Ballantine Books, 1964.

Littauer, Raphael, and Uphoff, Norman, eds. *The Air War in Indochina.* Boston: Beacon Press, 1972.

Makanna, Philip. *Ghosts: A Time Remembered.* New York: Holt, Rinehart & Winston, 1979.

Norman, Aaron. *The Great Air War.* New York: Macmillan Co., 1968.

Oughton, Frederick. *The Aces.* New York: G. P. Putnam's Sons, 1960.

Phelan, Joseph A. *Heroes and Aeroplanes of the Great War 1914–1918.* New York: Grosset & Dunlap, 1966.

Reynolds, Quentin. *They Fought for the Sky.* New York: Rinehart & Co., 1957.

Sakai, Saburo. *Samurai.* New York: E. P. Dutton & Co., 1957.

Sorenson, Chris, and the editors of *Flying* Magazine. *Antique Airplanes.* New York: Charles Scribner's Sons, 1979.

Stewart, James T. *Airpower: The Decisive Force in Korea.* Princeton, N. J.: D. Van Nostrand Co., 1957.

Sunderman, James F. *World War II in the Air.* New York: Franklin Watts, 1963.

Tillman, Barrett. *Corsair.* Annapolis, Md.: Naval Institute Press, 1979.

Toliver, Colonel Raymond F., and Constable, Trevor J. *Fighter Aces.* New York: Macmillan Co., 1965.

Ulanoff, Stanley M. *Fighter Pilot.* New York: Doubleday & Co., 1962.

U.S. Department of the Air Force, Aerospace Defense Command. *Basic Aerial Combat Tactics.* Washington, D. C.: U.S. Department of the Air Force, 1972.

U.S. Department of the Air Force, Air Training Command. *Advanced Flying, Jet.* Washington, D.C.: U.S. Government Printing Office, 1977.

Wagner, Ray. *The North American Sabre.* New York: Doubleday & Co., 1963.

Whitehouse, Arch. *The Years of the Sky Kings.* New York: Doubleday & Co., 1959.

Windrow, Martin C., ed. *Aircraft in Profile.* Vol. II. New York: Doubleday & Co., 1965.

Index